ENEMY SALVOES

Selected Literary Criticism

ENEMY SALVOES

Selected Literary Criticism

by

WYNDHAM LEWIS

Edited with Sectional Introductions and Notes by

C. J. FOX

General Introduction by

C. H. SISSON

BARNES & NOBLE

BOOKS

10 East 53d St., New York 10022

(a division of Harper & Row Publishers, Inc.)

Barnes & Noble Books
Harper & Row, Publishers, Inc.
10 East 53rd Street
New York

ISBN 0-06-494258-9

First published in the U.S.A. 1976
© 1976 Anne Wyndham Lewis

Printed and bound in Great Britain

MCMLXXVI

Contents

CONTENTS

General Introduction

by

C. H. SISSON

The twentieth century is not short of writing called 'critical'. The production of it has become an industry, supported by the existence of so many libraries with a disposition to buy even unreadable books which can be described as serious, even though their seriousness may not go very deep. It is easier to recognize a 'serious' book than a good one. There is also the favouring circumstance of the vogue of examinations in our society, for the most part sustained by examinees who are without passionate interest in the nominal subject of their study, particularly, perhaps, when that subject is one of the branches of literature. With all this array of 'critical' material the work of Wyndham Lewis has nothing to do. He hardly even noticed it; he certainly did not bother to be its enemy. For this final insult he has been rigorously excluded from the academic canon of criticism in our time. It is only now, perhaps, when the persistent interest in his work is beginning to have its inevitable effects, that the no less persistent attempt to ignore Lewis's contribution to criticism will have finally to be abandoned.

The neglect of Lewis's critical writing is in a sense largely his own fault, in so far as a man may be said to be responsible for his own qualities and quirks. A chronic independence of mind is unpardonable in any age; in our own it has certainly been safer to praise independence than to exemplify it. No-one was ever less a respecter of persons than Lewis was. The reading public at large is always more aware of reputations than of merits; a critic who combines a clear eye for merits with a knowledge of the mechanics of literary reputation is sure to be in trouble. These objective considerations apart, there are aspects of Lewis's personality, as it presents itself in his prose fiction and his verse as well as in his critical writing, which many people find repugnant while others, it need

7

hardly be said, relish the performance as providing an essential ingredient in the comedy of our time. To arrive at an assessment of Lewis's contribution to criticism one has to accept the heartless knock-about comedy, whether one likes it or not, as part of a method and admit that the critical question is, what it achieves. There is some help and some hindrance in it, as is indeed the case with the more ingratiating critical personality of T. S. Eliot, *the* critic of the first half of our century, whose influence has seeped into every nook and cranny of the literary departments of universities, and beyond. A point which must be made about Lewis's method of slapping down the great is that it leaves their greatness intact. The satire is directed against what he sees as the weak or frivolous aspects of their performance. Lewis does not through envy, wrong-headedness or even mere boisterousness seek to diminish what is of value. He clears away the rubbish so that we can see precisely that. *Men Without Art*, which treats Henry James with a roughness which would hardly have given unmixed pleasure at Rye, ends by exhibiting the opening page of *The Ivory Tower* as an example of a piece of work actually *written*, in contrast to the opening page of *Point Counter Point*, by Aldous Huxley, who at that time (1934) still counted as one of the intellectual luminaries of the century. The bastinado thus ends with something like the evidential criticism of Pound's *ABC of Reading*, in which the argument is really in the display of specimens.

In Lewis as in Pound one can point—though rarely—to purely literary judgments which it is hard to sustain. What are we to make of the assertion, in an article on Arnold in *The Times Literary Supplement* in 1954 (p. 179) that 'no greater poetry was ever written than the concluding song of Callicles in "Empedocles on Etna" '? There is much in Arnold which deserves pondering and he was a more than merely noticeable poet, one of the very few of his period who count. It is a small fault to give excessive praise to work which is both praiseworthy and neglected. Lewis has in fact not the gift, which Pound and Eliot at their best both had, of putting his finger on valuable literary work with the sureness which guarantees that what he says on such matters, even in an aside, will offer new light to the reader. No writer can give such tips within more than a limited range and indeed Eliot, looking back on his own performance, says (in *To Criticise the Critic*): 'I feel that I have spoken with authority . . . only about those authors—poets and a very few

8

prose writers—who have influenced me.'[1] So far as the evidence goes, Lewis came to ruminate on Arnold only when he was past the stage at which he was still taking his directions. Eliot goes on to say: 'on poets who have not influenced me I still deserve serious consideration; and . . . on authors whose work I dislike my views may—to say the least—be highly disputable'.[2] One must not ask of any critic more than he can give, and what he can give will, if he is also a creative writer, be related to his own creative performance. It is so with Lewis. His technical performance as a writer is of course very great and puts him easily among the first half-dozen of his contemporaries in the English language. Yet what he did in literature is so saturated with his personality, in a sense so peculiar, even quirkish, that he is a dangerous literary master. He started with his eye on the external object. His was a painter's eye, he was never averse to pointing out, and although the early stories show a clarity of observation so great as to amount to an originality of method which would have been sufficient to establish the claims of a lesser writer, there is a sense in which Lewis must be regarded as not having trained himself so rigorously, or so fully, for his work as a writer as he did for his work as a painter. It is not that he did not do far more than most writers, or that he does not rank with the two or three greatest of his contemporaries, but that the centre of his technical interest was elsewhere. The centre was in the visual arts, but Lewis early had the gift or burden of an extraordinary capacity for handling words and the end of the struggle was the production of what might well have been two life works, one on canvas or the drawing-block and one in literature. The literary work did not—because such work cannot—emanate chiefly from what is seized by the eye, though there are times, in the work of this 'personal-appearance artist', when that organ seems over-sized in relation to some others not less important. Moreover, much of the work which is loosely—or in a strictly non-academic sense—philosophical or at any rate theoretical, bears on it the mark of the painter and arises from a need to explore and defend the situation of the artist. A double burden is felt also in the work of the draughtsman and the painter, which is self-evidently that of a painter troubled by the possession of an intellect. It is perhaps no wonder that it has taken so long for this many-sided and one might say unmanageable man to achieve the width of recognition which came more readily to contemporaries of less varied achievement. If the whole man is anywhere marshalled it is perhaps in *The Human Age*, a literary masterpiece the later volumes of which are the work of his later years and take him back, so to speak, to all his roots.

The crucial *literary* influence on Lewis's formation was one which lay poles apart from the precisions which must have formed him as a draughtsman. It was not in the world of 'the dry hardness which you get in the classics' and which T. E. Hulme made it his business to recommend,[3] that Lewis found 'the intellectual *coup de foudre*' which, as he says, 'revolutionized my technique of approach to experience'. It was indeed in something outside Hulme's classical canons altogether. Hulme insisted on 'the limits inside which you know man to be fastened'.[4] Lewis recounts (p. 78) how, in his early days in Paris, he came up against 'a solid mass of books . . . the creative literature of Russia', which he read in French translations. The whole of this chapter from *Rude Assignment* is of the highest importance for the understanding of Lewis's work. One gathers, from the manner in which he told the story when he looked back in 1947, that when the lightning originally struck him so many matters were engaging him that he was far from understanding the importance of the event and of course, as he says, the influences of the Russians were not the last or the only ones. But in a curious and unprecedented way this shapeless wind from the steppes blew into his mind and agitated the precise shapes seized by his painter's eye. The influence of the Russian novelists was much abroad in the period immediately proceding the first war. Katherine Mansfield is full of it, or full as so small and delicate a vessel could be. The influence on the powerful mind of Lewis was of quite a different order. A chasm of nihilism was opened and he never recovered, so to speak, from what he saw in that glimpse. It is interesting that, in recalling those times, Lewis should remember also the Russian students who then thronged Paris, who 'conversed with no-one— they were contemptuous of Western levity, stern and self-absorbed'. (p. 79). One of the elements which has been found least forgivable in Lewis is his profound earnestness in the midst of the wildest comedy—something as remote as could be from the humorous and comfortable Anglo-Saxon world he was born into, the legitimate succession to which continued throughout his life-time to corrode the minds of most of the best-placed intellectuals and *littérateurs* in these islands. But if he was against 'typical modern English things' he did not mean 'English in the Elizabethan or cavalier sense . . .—just Hanoverian English—how shall we explain or describe it?'[5] It is difficult to explain, and nobody much cares to be told that he is not what he thinks he is. Yet that is the nature of satire, and it was Lewis's contention that 'by stretching a point, no more, we can without exaggeration write *satire* for *art*'.[6]

2

There are fashions in what is meant by criticism, and the overwhelming victory of one conception results in other kinds being for a period misunderstood and undervalued. Such fashions have their heroic phases. The undergraduate coming after F. R. Leavis might be surprised to learn that there was a time when universities did not make much of Eliot, or even confused him with Edith Sitwell. Yet *The Sacred Wood* sold only a few hundred copies in the first seven years after its publication in 1920; a modern publisher might well have pulped it before it reached its public. The victory of this book has been as complete as such things ever are. Wave after wave of academic battalions have followed in the wake of Eliot's circumspect reconnoitring. Yet what was valuable in Eliot's performance could certainly not be repeated by a massed movement. The most dispiriting of his remarks, after dismissing various classes of unsatisfactory critic, is that 'for the rest, there are merely various degrees of intelligence'.[7] Eliot swept whole schools of critics out of his way. He had 'once committed himself to the statement that "The poetic critic is criticizing poetry in order to create poetry" '[8]—a motive not very different from Lewis's, who engaged in battles in order to clear the ground for the artist. It was not Eliot's fault if thought later congealed around his work. It congeals around that of every innovator. The imperfections he sought out and annihilated have been replaced by others at least as damaging, and this time claiming the authority not of the critics he swept from the scene but his own. No doubt his own impersonality and discrimination were imperfect; he has said so himself. 'They show all the weaknesses inseparable from the age and country of their origin', as Leslie Stephen said of Richardson's characters.[9] The famous essay on *Tradition and the Individual Talent*, which has been widely influential and is embalmed in other places besides the 'anthological text-books for American college students'[10] to which Eliot noted ruefully that it had found its way, perhaps owes something to Marxist habits of mind, with their continual re-gestation of the past to suit the needs of the present, as well as to the theological notion of the development of doctrine. There is no way of avoiding what is in the air, whether it is healthy or not. Eliot certainly came no nearer to escaping such ambiances entirely than Lewis did. He himself proved how fallacious is the protection he sought in tradition. Lewis was dogmatically aware of his nakedness.

The relative obscurity of Lewis's critical writing—for probably not one person has read *Men Without Art* for every hundred who have read *The Sacred Wood*—is due partly to the fact that the immense success of Eliot's apologetics has turned people's minds away from other methods of criticism. The question of what criticism can do comes back one way or another to Matthew Arnold's endeavour—which embodies its own fallacies—'to see the object as in itself it really is'.[11] One can understand why Lewis came back in his later years to the reading of Arnold. 'To try and approach truth on one side after another, not to strive or cry, nor to persist in pressing forward, on any one side, with violence and self-will', as we read in the preface to *Essays in Criticism,* '—it is only thus, it seems to me, that mortals may hope to gain any vision of the mysterious Goddess, whom we shall never see except in outline, but only thus even in outline'.[12] Some would probably say that there was 'violence and self-will' in Lewis's methods, but that can only be after a careless and unsympathetic reading of his work. There is sometimes blustering, filibustering, heartless comedy and outrageous satire, but all these are, in Lewis, merely so many methods of trying to approach truth 'on one side after another'. No condemnation is absolute, no hatchet-blow attempts more than to remove more than a false limb or to swipe off a wig. The play is rough but the temper of the player is a remarkably good one; he is even benign. It is the very open-ness of Lewis's mind which has got him into trouble with politicizing and other gang opponents of various kinds. If we have to 'approach truth on one side after another', will that not necessarily mean approaching it, sometimes, from the side which all decent people at the moment abhor to see? It is a terrible thing to treat the conventions of the moment lightheartedly, almost as bad as so

12

treating the successes, where it is not indeed the same thing. It is yesterday's prejudice that it pays best to belabour, and whole literary industries are based on this sluggishness of the human mind. The prejudices of Victorian morality, even now, are fair game, but the dogmatics of Marxist-liberal enlightenment, which by defi-nition can hardly embody the whole truth, are defended ferociously by the phalanxes of the well-meaning young, middle-aged and even the old, with a zeal and quasi-unanimity which Mrs. Grundy can never have commanded even at the height of her vogue. Lewis was, incorrigibly, averse to these mass fixations and if he is to be con-demned by moralists and politicians it must be for the liberalism and independence of his outlook, the diversity of the approaches he attempted. The objectives of his criticism were quite different from those of Eliot or of Pound although, like them, he is of course a creative performer whose criticism serves primarily the producer and only secondarily the mere consumer of art. Whereas Pound, and Eliot in his early stages, aimed at a criticism which drew attention to the qualities of the literature as such—in so far as there is such a thing distinguishable from the material that is poured into it—Lewis is concerned much more with the impediments to art, as he saw them, the fashionable drifts which set the artist's vision askew. It is this which draws him repeatedly to the frontiers of politics. In his essay on *The Perfect Critic* Eliot cleared the ground for his own role by saying that 'historical' and 'philosophical' critics of litera-ture 'had better be called historians and philosophers quite simply'.[13] One might say that Lewis was a 'political-theorist' critic and con-sider whether he should not on the same grounds be considered a political theorist *tout court*, but since Eliot himself long ago aban-doned the impossible notion of critical purity which he once pro-posed perhaps that is a refinement which can be ignored. In any case, the political theorist is an important ingredient in Lewis's make-up though—since there has been much misunderstanding on this point—it is necessary to insist that his political theory is tenta-tive rather than dogmatic and concerned with the well-being not of society as a whole but with that of the artist who has to work in whatever sort of society there happens to be, much as Machiavelli was concerned with the success of the ruler and not over-scrupulous about the fate of the governed. If the politics of what suits the artist is a somewhat specialist subject, as is the politics of what suits the governor, both are relevant parts of the larger subject of political philosophy and have their bearing on what is necessary for the well-being of the ordinary man and woman in the street and elsewhere. And anyone who wants to consider the further implications of Lewis's critical writings should certainly get hold of *The Art of Being Ruled*, where Lewis's rooting around among the remains of Bernard Shaw, Bertrand Russell, Nietzsche, Sorel, Proudhon and others and among the phenomena of millionaire society and of socialism is merely a preliminary to an attempt to state a position 'beyond action and reaction' from which the artist can operate in a society which dominates 'speculation and invention in a way it has never done before'. This concern is evident throughout Lewis's critical writing, a large part of which is given to identifying and seeking to eliminate from the work of serious writers the forces which tend to sweep them away to be mere servants of the *Zeitgeist* rather than artists standing on their own feet and using their own eyes. This is a matter highly relevant to the judgment of literature as literature and indeed one criticism of this proceeding might be that it is, no less than Eliot's earlier revolutionary attack on criticism as practised, a search for an impossible purity. It is certainly powerful and resourceful enough for one to suggest that *Men Without Art* ought to be at least as much read by students of twentieth-century literature as Hazlitt's *Spirit of the Age* by students of the Romantic period. That is indeed the minimal claim one might make for the book.

3

In his *Letters* Edwin Muir made the point that although in his attack on Whitehead in *Time and the Western Man* Lewis had the pretension of standing for *reason* against *emotion* as represented by his opponent, when one looks into their respective works it is in Whitehead that one finds page after page of logically articulated sentences while in Lewis there is evidence of a mind deflected hither and thither by the author's feelings. This charge cannot be altogether set aside.[14] Whitehead had all the equipment of an academic philosopher while Lewis's discursive writing everywhere bears traces of the inadequacy of his formal training in this field. Lewis had attended lectures by Bergson at the Collège de France and ingested a good deal of that writer as of a number of other French and

14

German as well as English theorists. His *aperçus* are often brilliant and he approaches his subjects with a freshness which he might have lost had he been ground through a series of orthodox academic courses in the way that Eliot, for example, was. Yet it would be taking a very partisan view to assert that Lewis lost nothing by not having this training. With the multiplicity of his activities and interests, which are without parallel in any of his great contemporaries in English literature, it is no wonder if there was too little to restrain him from finding in his authors only the points that interested him. He ran to earth in the most unexpected places what he saw as the common tendencies of the age, tendencies which, to most of his contemporaries, were invisible or barely visible simply because they were too widespread to be noticeable. It spoiled the game of the emptier among those whose work he criticized to have these tendencies drawn into the light of day while his more considerable subjects, more genial perhaps in both senses of the term, could see with satisfaction how much was left intact by the criticism. If Edwin Muir's remark has a certain superficial justification in the manner of Lewis's approach, the touch of the variety artist about so much of what he wrote, it does not go anywhere near the root of the matter or recognize the merits—which include a comparative impartiality—of Lewis's own methods. Though the flippant manner of some of Lewis's criticism may be objectionable to the academic philosopher, as it was to Muir, it is the depth of his perception which is disconcerting. For this painter-writer who has been so much advertised, and so much advertised himself, as being concerned with surfaces, was notable above all as a critic for the lightness with which he brushed aside the pretensions of the surface and revealed the implications of a particular line of thought or mode of literary expression. The offence which Lewis has repeatedly given to the liberal-socialist orthodoxy of our day is not due to any hostility to a socialist organization of the economy, if that is the best that can be managed in our time, or to a liberalism which really demands that individuals should have such freedom as they can have to move around in the spaces of their own minds, but to the imprisoning and unquestioned dogmatisms which so often underlie a plausibly-woven surface of discourse. There has been an almost limitless amount of discourse, in our own day, which really amounts to an apologetic for the chaotic interior of things. What made Lewis's criticism uncanny and aroused so much hostility was the fact that, as a great artist, he was naturally not less but more aware than many of his opponents of the unplumbed depths of things and for that reason was the more determined that the little hard-won gains of civilization in making a tiny order here and there on the surface should not be filched entirely away, leaving the whole historical task to be done again or perhaps for a considerable future not done at all. It is of course only those whose view of the world includes in its perspective the possibility of a catastrophic outcome of the present stage of our history that such criticism can have its full appeal. 'Beyond a certain well-defined line—in the arts as in everything else—' Lewis says in *The Demon of Progress in the Arts*, 'beyond that limit there is *nothing*. Nothing, zero, is what logically you reach past a line, of some kind, laid down by nature, everywhere'.[15]

Lewis's critical writings are scattered around in a number of volumes. C. J. Fox, whose services to the study of Lewis's works have included the collection, editing and introducing (with Walter Michel) of his art criticism—*Wyndham Lewis on Art*—and (with Robert T. Chapman) of *Unlucky for Pringle: Unpublished and Other Stories,* has not only scoured the long array of volumes for matter representative of Lewis's literary criticism but has dug up from periodicals articles in the same field which have long lain unnoticed. The very first extract, from *The Enemy* No. 1, shows clearly in what light the whole is to be read. It is 'more the period', Lewis says, 'its infections, and the actions of those infections on the tissues of [the] work, than the brilliant individual energy they may possess, at which criticism is directed'. It is moreover promised that 'it is in their *work*—in what they publicly have set down, all that posterity will know of them, and that by which they ultimately must rank—that various people will find themselves arraigned . . . the social envelope, or the drapery of boost [is] removed'. (p. 29) These are impeccable principles. The light of the latter is perhaps a little dimmed by the incursion of the satirist who, in *Apes of God* and elsewhere, has left delineations of certain of his victims of which posterity is likely to be at least as much aware as of the victims' own work. But there is no doubt that it is the work which is central for Lewis, and the personal pretensions which surround artistic invention and non-invention in the social scene are of importance to him only as they obscure the nature of the work. As to the search for

16

infections, that defines the essential purpose of all Lewis's critical writings. It defines the nature and limitations of his criticism, in which we should, generally speaking, look not for the kind of assessment which it was Eliot's objective to arrive at but rather a disengagement of the work which matters from the less durable elements adhering to it. This difference must be clearly understood if Lewis's criticism is to take its proper place in the literary studies of the period. As to what is left when the less durable elements are removed, that is a form of the unaswerable and often answered question as to what exactly constitutes a work of art. Lewis does give here and there in his critical writing indications of the kind of answer he would favour, and it cannot be said that any of the answers which have been devised in the long history of criticism and aesthetics have done more than give such an indication, even when they have been formulated in a manner which gave them a momentary success as supposedly comprehensive definitions. Anyhow Lewis is at the opposite pole from those who have promulgated definitions of the kind which see art as empty. That a work of art 'is *about* something is an axiom for me,' Lewis says in the introduction to *Men Without Art*, 'and *art-for-art's-sake* I do not even trouble to confute'.[16]

Lewis was, ineluctably, an artist who thought; a man of a certain intellectual prowess even. So he finds a thinker in Shakespeare, and if *The Lion and the Fox* does not take us very close to the text, or anywhere near the secrets of Shakespeare's technical mastery, it does cast an interesting light on the mind behind the plays—or rather on one or two aspects of it only, for with Shakespeare who could hope to do more? There are in C. J. Fox's selection also extracts from Lewis's criticism of the novelists—Cervantes and the Russians, James, Gertrude Stein, D. H. Lawrence, Joyce and Virginia Woolf; as to the poets, we can read him on his younger contemporaries such as Auden and Spender as well as on Pound.

In a final section we are presented with some of the matter indicating Lewis's stance on the matter of *Writers and Politics*, and the reader should remember that it is a peculiar form of artist's politics that he is here called upon to consider, not the kind which sets people at one another's throats at the hustings or behind various instruments of violence. Lewis is a man of peace, wanting to get on with his work, and it is worth recalling that in the editorial of *The*

Enemy No. 1 he said (pp. 29–30): 'I had thought . . . of taking *No Politics* as the device of this enterprise. But then I thought that that would appear misleading, since in the attempt to exorcize politics from art, I have had to have so much commerce with them.'

NOTES

1   T. S. Eliot, *To Criticise the Critic*. London: Faber & Faber, 1965, p. 26.
2   Ibid.
3   T. E. Hulme, *Speculations*. London: Routledge & Kegan Paul Ltd., 1949, pp. 126–7.
4   Ibid., p. 120.
5   Wyndham Lewis, *Men Without Art*. London: Cassell & Co. Ltd., 1934, p. 230.
6   Ibid., p. 289.
7   Eliot, *The Sacred Wood*. London: Methuen & Co. Ltd., 2nd edition, 1928, p. 16.
8   Ibid., p. 15.
9   Sir Leslie Stephen, *Hours in a Library*. London: Smith, Elder, 1909, Vol. I, p. 66.
10 *To Criticise the Critic*, p. 17.
11 Matthew Arnold, *Selected Prose*. Harmondsworth, Middlesex: Penguin Books, 1970, p. 130.
12 Ibid., p. 126.
13 *The Sacred Wood*, p. 16.
14 *The Selected Letters of Edwin Muir*. London: The Hogarth Press, 1974, p. 62.
15 Lewis, *The Demon of Progress in the Arts*. London: Methuen, 1954, p. 32.
16 *Men Without Art*, p. 8.

Preface

Enemy Salvoes is a selection of Wyndham Lewis's literary criticism, designed to assemble the widest possible range of his writings in this field. In line with this intention and for reasons of space, excerpts from his longer essays have had to be limited in length—though with no sacrifice of the highlights—and the extensive quotations commonly used by Lewis omitted in many cases. This, unfortunately, detracts to some extent from the impact here of what C. H. Sisson calls the 'evidential' method of criticism as found in Lewis. But still further point is thereby added to the cause this selection is meant to promote—the republication in full of key Lewis books long out of print.

In the texts that follow, omissions involving one or more sentences or paragraphs are indicated by the symbol [. . . .]. When only a few words have been omitted in mid-sentence, the symbol used is [. . .]. Lewis's unusual style of capitalization and punctuation is preserved, being most obvious in his earlier writings.

This book could not have been prepared without the permission and kind co-operation of Mrs. Anne Wyndham Lewis, who has copyright to all the material by the late Wyndham Lewis used here. Acknowledgements are also due to the ever-efficient Cornell University Library for use of writings from its vast Lewis archives, notably a typescript of 'The Machine Poets'; Hutchinson Publishing Group Ltd., publishers of *Rude Assignment* from which 'The Puritans of the Steppes' and several quotations were taken; the Editor of *The Times Literary Supplement*, where Lewis's essay on Matthew Arnold first appeared; Mr. Alan Munton of Clare Hall, Cambridge, for his invaluable help, and the staff of The London Library for their great courtesy.

C.J.F.

I

Critical Principles

1

The Solitary Outlaw

(From *The Enemy* magazine, 1927)

This editorial[1] is Lewis's most elaborate affirmation of his chosen role as outsider and unrelenting critic of the *Zeitgeist*. It introduced the first of three numbers of *The Enemy* magazine, which Lewis published and edited from 1927 to 1929. In its short life, *The Enemy* featured contributions by T. S. Eliot, Roy Campbell and others but consisted largely of writings by Lewis himself, later integrated into three of his books—*Time and Western Man*, *The Diabolical Principle and the Dithyrambic Spectator* and *Paleface*. The venture, financially burdensome, was Lewis's last in the 'little magazine' field. But it resoundingly demonstrated Lewis's powerful and salutary penchant for unorthodoxy. As he wrote in *Rude Assignment* (1950): 'My mind likes penetrating the depths, where it is dark and cold, or disporting itself upon the sparkling surface, where it is warm and gay.—I do not wish to belong to a *school* of fish: that is I think the only complication.'[2]

By name this paper is an enemy, though over against what particular individuals or groups it occupies that position is not revealed in the general title, nor whether a solitary antagonist or an aggressive communion is concealed within its covers. The second point may be cleared up at once: there is no 'movement' gathered here (thank heaven!), merely a person; a solitary outlaw and not a gang. What has driven him into the bush, or out under the greenwood tree, is the usual thing. Not to build a labyrinth in the gatehouse of my paper, then, the nearest big revolutionary settlement lies some distance behind me. I have moved outside. I found it impossible to come to terms with the canons observed in it. Outside I am freer.

The advantages incident to this removal are many. First, being in solitary schism, with no obligations at the moment towards party or individual colleague, I can resume my opinion of the society I have just left, and its characteristics which else might remain without serious unpartisan criticism. My observations will contain no social impurities whatever; there will be nobody with whom I shall be dining tomorrow night (of those who come within the scope of my criticism) whose susceptibilities, or whose wife's, I have to consider. If the public is not aware of the advantages it derives from such circumstances as these, it is time it awoke to its true interest. Why does it not exact of its chosen servants some such social or unsociable, guarantee?—on the principle of the treatment of the Chinese painters of the great period, who, when their talent became noticeable, were at once exiled to a beautiful wilderness, more suitable than the city to the confinement, or rather the delicate metaplasis, expected of them.

The remarks of Plutarch on the subject of 'enemies' provide a general clue to the baptism of this enterprise. From the start its name secures for it, at least, this virtue; that it does not arrive under the misleading colours of friendship or of a universal benevolence. Only its reverse side, as it were, is its compatissant, its avowed one that of a hostile criticism, which it guarantees to maintain vigilantly directed towards those antagonists assigned it by circumstances.

There is a further benefit ensured by the title. So named it publicly repudiates any of those treacherous or unreal claims to 'impartiality', the scientific-impersonal, or all that suggestion of detached omniscience, absence of *parti-pris*, which is such a feature of our time (in which every activity, even the least amenable to exact method, apes positive science) that it is become, indeed, the stock-in-trade of any fairly knowing critic—as though to be a 'critic' at all were not to be an 'enemy'; or as though it were possible, or would even occur to anybody, in any time, to *criticize*, if he did not wish to *change*.

If incidentally the first of the age, the very glasses of revolutionary fashion, are subjected to criticism, it will be noticed, I think, that it is more the period, its infections, and the action of those infections within the tissues of their work, than the brilliant individual energy they may possess, at which criticism is directed. For it would be to argue yourself of a curious density if you did not see that such a period as the present is of more danger to genius, or to any personal energy, than ever genius, or personal energy, can be to it; so that no individual today is our enemy, but rather our time that of each of us severally, in our capacity of individual—in some cases of energy. No abstract 'time' or epoch has ever taken it into its abstract head to deconcretize, as this one has, its children. In its progressive prescission of all that is individual, its rage to extinguish the independent life of persons, this abstraction has assumed, for us, a physiognomy, along with its purpose, not possessed by other mere 'times', mere 'epochs', coloured and characterized by the individuals within them. Our period is like a person, in short, just as we are less and less like one; the secret of its being is technically expressed in terms of 'mass-psychology'. But that name describes the trick of it, without touching on its origins or significance.

Anybody relying upon this time to any peculiar extent will, I am certain, be bitterly deceived. It will not in the sequel be found to waste much sentiment upon them; nor will it, itself, I imagine, be much cherished by posterity. As soon as it has served its purpose, or begins to pass, the weaknesses, contracted at its instance, will find out its friends; the more obsequious they have been, the worse off they then will be.

It is not from any idle desire to baulk the beaten track that I have taken this unorthodox step. I am single-handed, as I have said. But in severing my connection with that spurious doctrine of fashionable 'revolt', no longer anything but a parody of the real article, I am by no means alone. I was not, for example, the first to notice that peculiar, debilitated, *unanimity*, typical of the present period. It is not very easy to miss, it is true. Benda, notably, in his review of post-war french society, draws attention to this. He says :

> Our documents for determining the aesthetic tendencies of present-day French society are, . . . above all, the works of those authors that must give, we can assume, seeing their success, the greatest satisfaction to the public taste, and must most accurately represent it. One is sorry to have to remark that those authors are not only of second rank, and that that law enunciated in other times by a critic (Faguet), according to which *good writers, far from incarnating the prejudices of a time, are, on the contrary, opposed to them*, no longer holds in our day.[3]

That is an extremely valuable observation. All other times have bred criticism, and its wholesome revolts and corrections, in their midst. Bad as sometimes they have been, by this toleration they have shown that they possessed some humility, or in other cases that they were great enough to allow censure. The names we remember in european literature are those of men who satirized and attacked, rather than petted or fawned upon, their contemporaries. Only *this* time exacts an uncritical hypnotic sleep of all within it. This, as elsewhere I am showing, is the sleep of the machine or, humanly, of the mass. This assumption of a unique pattern, of a universal standard or norm, is in its origin an effect, not of political innovation, but of the technique of science and industry. 'Thou shalt have no other Times but me!' our Time appears to fulminate; for, as I have said, we have become so conscious of this obsessing 'Time', that we tend to personalize it. But it is in reality less of a personal-Time than any other, far more of an abstraction. For it is simply a machine.

By the Time, however, I mean something more superficial than may at first be supposed: I mean rather what passes itself off as the Time, and exists as the chronological figure-head of an only conventionally discrete and homogeneous something that is 'us', and not the creative impulses at work beneath the distorted surface of our world. It is essentially our crust or shell that is today highly mechanized, uniform and stiff, although extremely distorted. A 'Time' is in any case always a congeries of the most insignificant people within it. It is the habit of the fashionable majority at the surface to take the credit for things they have never done, and are incapable of even conceiving. It is they who pass themselves off as a mysterious Force, from which, in fact, they slavishly receive all that they possess. Today they are less in touch than usual with that Force: there seems to be a growing hiatus. The majority are more critically separated from the directive source than is the case in a less complex society. That is no doubt the main reason why they so grossly misrepresent it; why they tend to deteriorate, and why they have no longer, as it seems, the energy to differ, and are apt to approximate to one stale, violent, pattern.

Before passing on, I will stop at the question of the specifically *critical* nature of this paper.

'Criticism'—in the sense of written and printed independent comment—is generally in the hands of supposedly non-partisan professionals. It is in connection with the influence or significance of public 'criticism' that an unfortunate illusion occurs. It is not real-

26

ized that we of the literary or art world, and our patrons, are in the nature of a large family, in the same way that the politicians are, and that what transpires in print is of very contingent importance, as a general rule. So public superstition invests the written word with a gravity and weight (to which, unfortunately, it can lay no claim) denied, as it supposes, to the private, spoken, criticism.

This superstition is generally encouraged, often by professional critics. People perfectly aware of its emptiness will affirm that in writing about his 'Fellow-artists' (this means, of course, *members of the family*) an artist is guilty of a breach of etiquette or good faith.

This would be a praiseworthy sentiment, perhaps, if the world were not what we know it to be. It would be very well if all families, large or small, were happy and united, if justice reigned within these closed systems, and if the most valuable member, from the standpoint of a detached observer, or of 'the public', or even in the interests of the family itself, were certain, without hindrance or oppression, within these rather stuffy circles-within-circles, to have his way or get his due, and to be issued to the world outside as representative of that sodality. Such, however, is not often the case.

The pathetic belief in the opinion handed out to it, therefore, can only rank as a groundless delusion of the public, in the sense, and to the degree, that I have indicated. Anyone who has been privileged to penetrate, at any time, the particular family-circle of which I am speaking, is aware that an artist, writer or musician, as any other kind of individual whose personality is a factor in his success, does his competitors all the harm he can socially and in private, and has a well-founded contempt for what may happen in public. He knows that the decisions of the family-circle will alone secure him an income; that it is there, above all, that his rival can be circumvented and that without any impertinent questions (such as the mere merit of the respective work) coming into it. He knows that the decision will rest solely on the matter of who flatters Mamma most, or who it is gives himself the fewest airs in the opinion of the family, who is most obedient, most vulgarly accommodating, who laughs loudest at the family jokes.

Most 'artists' are the family average, of course; much of such people's time is spent in a social round (which would be extremely wasteful if there were anything there to waste) in order to hold their own, commercially—that is socially (as Diana Bourbon so truly

27

says)—in this far-flung system of intrigue. This is all the more the case today, when, with the intensive popularization of the patriarchal, communal family-spirit, the individual is more and more absorbed into, and crushed by, these various social-cum-trade organizations. Even artists of some calibre drop many valuable hours in this traffic. But many 'artists' do nothing at all today, quite literally; they find it more lucrative. Business first! Then the more art— (what is, all said and done, the rationale, in the first instance, of that usually parasitic animal we call 'an artist')—comes into contempt (and in that direction it is impossible for it to go further than it has already), the more its practitioner has to redouble his social activities.

Everyone who has had opportunities of observing these forms of life (secluded from the general gaze) knows, then, that the battles of art, science, or philosophy are not won where they ostensibly occur, nor in the pages of the press, nor in open encounters. (In the end that may be the case, but we are talking about the lifetime of the artist.) The 'critical' shafts that accumulate upon our San Sebastians, like the pelt of arrows upon the body of the painted saint, come from the ambushes of the social world. They are not publicly despatched by evident gladiators. If, however, they happen to be so despatched, it is in the talk-shop of the tea-party and salon that they are manufactured. The dirt with which we are covered from head to foot, if we are famous artists, comes from the social gutter, the 'ruelle' of the high-Bohemia, via the Press, perhaps. 'Some dirt sticks longer than other dirt; but no dirt is immortal,' Cardinal Newman said; but it gathers, as it gathered upon him, from the social sewers and faucets, the salon, the café. Under these circumstances, what more innocent and honourable than a printed article?

The only alternative to that distasteful burden of the dinner and tea-party, if you care to look at it only in that way, would be found in occasional sallies, such as Whistler indulged in; and actually anybody who tends to transfer these encounters from the private world to the public world, in pursuit of whatever object, will be, in that respect, a benefactor. For the progressive encroachment and overwhelming of the traditional public life by the private life, of the general by the personal; the greater and greater importance of what happens in private, the less of meaning that can be claimed by anything that may be known to the public, is the sign of the vast decay of our liberties in every direction.

The object of our interest here is very strictly things, not people. These remarks seemed necessary only in view of the fact that the ideas discussed are held by people after all; the works under review have names attached to them. So when we are attacking things, we are sure to be accused of attacking persons. *If* we were attacking them, however, which we are not, at least the onslaught would be open and unequivocal; and by any rule of averages and as the times go, it would be certain that the number of words we expended against them in public would be immeasurably outnumbered by those flung against us in private; and the impersonality of a public utterance cannot weigh as much, floated on mere ink, as the word winged upon even the foulest human breath.

So if now here for once (whatever else may or may not come to pass) it is in their *work*—in what they publicly have set down, all that posterity will know of them, and that by which they ultimately must rank—that various people will find themselves arraigned; if there is something disconcerting in this directness, and a sensation of nakedness suddenly overtakes some person, here or there—the social envelope, or the drapery of boost, removed—that cannot be charged to me. We get directness, if anything, from the source of all good gifts, whether it is imposed on us by circumstances or is ours by nature, not its opposite. If it had ever been uttered, what a strange belief would there have found expression—in that saying that 'cunning is the weapon which heaven has given to the Saints wherewith to withstand the brute male force of the wicked world which marries and is given in marriage.' For a Saint would have his work cut out to excel in cunning the 'brutal world', whose characteristic quality that is along with brutality; and it would be a worldly Saint, indeed, who had the idea of competing in that masquerade.

There are a few more objections, perhaps, that I should cast over before proceeding, such as arise if a practising artist (not a critic or layman) writes about art, or if a writer writes directly about writing, so unusual is the practice, so outraged are those suddenly revealed by this unorthodox firsthand bullseye.

I had thought, for instance, of taking *No Politics* as the device of this enterprise. But then I thought that that would appear misleading, since in the attempt to exorcize politics from art, I have had to have so much commerce with them.

Politics must be for us, in artistic creation or criticism, what *morals* was for the best of the nineteenth century critics : a bugbear, if you like. Politics, even, are very closely related to morals and the legal mind, so different to the mind of the artist; and you can scarcely achieve an effective purgation of the one, without including, and still further disintegrating and thrusting deeper into the dustbin of recognized humbug, the other.

If I am asked, 'What are your Politics?' I can truly answer, I have none; as I could were a similar question addressed to me by the inquisitive Moralist. That does not impose a profession of indifference to the spectacle of political obliquity; just as the other (its 'moral' counterpart) does not involve a person so answering in a doctrine of Art-for-Art's sake, or in an exhibition of diabolics or defiance of some useful code of social conduct.[4]

NOTES

1 'Editorial', *The Enemy*, No. 1, February, 1927, pp. ix-xv.
2 Wyndham Lewis, *Rude Assignment*. London: Hutchinson & Co. Ltd., 1950, p. 77.
3 Julien Benda, *Belphégor*. Paris: Emile-Paul Frères, 1947, pp. vii-viii. Italics L.'s. The book was first published in 1918. The critic referred to is Emile Faguet (1847–1916).
4 A reprint of *The Enemy* in full was published by Frank Cass & Co. Ltd., London, in 1968.

Truth and the Writer's Freedom

(From *The Writer and the Absolute,* 1952)

The Writer and the Absolute[1] dealt with the threat to literary freedom posed by absolutist politics—the 'big, ideologic currents, gaudily coloured, converging, dissolving, combining or contending'[2] which Lewis considered dominant features of twentieth century history. The book argued that the work of Sartre, Orwell, Malraux and others was distorted by absolutist pressures representing the fashionable mass politics of the Left. Wrote Lewis : 'A million people are far more concrete than is one person : paradoxically, it is that which is furthest removed from the Whole (i.e. the individual, the least part of the Whole) which is most capable of total comprehension.'[3]

———————

As far as I personally am concerned, I am paralysed the moment I try to write something I do not regard as true. I should be useless as a propagandist. My propaganda would so reek of insincerity that it would irretrievably damage the cause it was intended to further. Other writers have told me that it is like that with them too.

No moral scruple in writing something false would be present : for an understanding of the writer's dilemma what has to be recognized is the paralysis induced by the unreal—our nature's rootedness in *fact*. And the shoddy, the wooden style which finally would emerge were I to give myself up to propaganda would have an aspect at once repellent and spurious, corresponding as it did to nothing real, nor to the outright opposite of the real.

A writer whose country fell under the domination of a gang, was forced, he told me (his life and liberty in the balance), to write propaganda for a year or more. At the end of that period he made his escape into a free country. But he declared that as a consequence

31

of what he had been forced to do he became (sexually) impotent. I do not, however, advance this as a serious contribution to medical science. All I mean is that, whether true or not, it serves to demonstrate the attitude of the man of letters to the dragooning of his pen.

What holds the true apart from the false is a great force. This can be illustrated in the works of famous writers, but it is in the case of the great masters of painting that the operation of this instinct occurs with all the publicity of the visible, within sight of all of us, and so it is there that it may be studied to the best advantage. Chardin, with a bland intensity, fastens his eye, impacts his gaze forever, upon some object of daily use. Van Eyck, with the same intense animal absorption and austere tenacity, upon Arnolfini and his wife.[4] The *true* image must be put down. Delicate, minute, must be the inventory of truth. Is this imitation? Because of a pressure as irresistible as gravitation the artist cleaves to the truth. Writers are under identical compulsions in their creative life to those governing the practice of the masters of the visual arts I have just mentioned.

It would be an error, however, to regard these compulsions as privileged. Everyone, in one degree or another, experiences the kind of 'gravitationary pull' alluded to above. It is not only felt by some exquisitely sensitive person of the order of Chardin, Bach, or Crabbe. Truth is as necessary to everybody as the air we breathe. [. . . .]

It is dangerous to live, but to write is much more so.—That statement sums up the situation, though it would never have occurred to Bulwer Lytton, Ruskin, or Mrs. Gaskell, let us say, to look at writing in that way. Had you pointed out to them, indeed, that writing made living more dangerous, they would have wondered what on earth you were talking about. In the days of Guelph and Ghibelline, or of the Inquisition, or in XVIIth Century England, on the other hand, such a view of writing would have been accepted as a truism. *'Think what you like: but for heaven's sake do not write it down!'* —such an exhortation would have been received, too, as sound advice and greatly to the point.—We still trail clouds of glory, unfortunately, from the XIXth Century. Few have cleared their minds sufficiently of Victorian furniture; even today, when writing actually is *very* dangerous, people mostly take up the pen as if every rattle-snake bowed to the sanctity of free speech, and never bit a

man of letters or a journalist for fear it should be accused of inter-
fering with it.

Men do not take their lives because living is so risky, of course,
and has such a sinister conclusion; nor has there ever been a writer
who refrained from writing because he knew it made living more
dangerous. And I should add, perhaps, that this book is *not* like the
safety-first publicity campaigns of the Police, warning people to be
more circumspect when they are crossing the road—and admonish-
ing motorists to be a little more particular about killing pedestrians
—although it may seem like that at times. I should like to see writers
bolder, if anything, occasionally. They pursue this very risky calling
so warily that they are like men who take their carcass around as if
it were full of eggs which they fear the least jolt will break. It is a
long time since anyone in England said 'bo' to a goose.—All I
would do is to bring out the limits, and the true character, of liberty,
as that concerns the writer. Airing the misadventures of the free
mind, martyred for liberty—which involves truth—in the pursuit
of literature, may, who knows, improve the position a little. [. . . .]

Politics may, at any moment, bring to an end all serious creative
writing, just as religion can. In many times and places politics, as
much as religion, have done just that, or prevented it from ever
developing. Great literature depends altogether upon unobstructed
access to the true—upon licence to make use of the material which
appears to the writer to correspond to the truth. Naturally, the
ability to *perceive* the true—which is under everybody's nose but
not seen by everybody—is confined to people of considerable intelligence.

The factual is not just what lies there, to be picked up by anyone.
It is what is perceived by the wisest—and it at once is, and is not,
there for the short-sighted 'average man'. Indeed, it does not appear
to be the factual at all to the person devoid of insight: or, if you
like, there is *another* factual for him. Yet, of course, we are often
dealing with a more complicated situation than that; i.e. a matter of
the most rudimentary fact: such a fact, for instance, as the presence
in a field of a cow; present to all men equally, whatever their intelligence. There have been long periods in recorded history when the
cow was in the field, but no one mentioned the fact publicly because the writer was denied the right to do so. He was denied *verbal*
access to the cow—unless, that is, he were the padishah. These were

dark ages. The present is a private age in-the-making. It is all a question of how long we can fool ourselves, or others, that it is a public age : a *public* age, in my way of speaking, being a free age.

NOTES

1 Lewis, *The Writer and the Absolute*. London : Methuen, 1952. The excerpts here come from pp. 3-4, 9-10, 198.
2 Lewis, *Self Condemned*. London : Methuen, 1954, p. 90.
3 *The Writer and the Absolute*, p. 20.
4 The masterpiece by Jan van Eyck in the National Gallery, London.

The External Approach to Writing

(From *Men Without Art*, 1934)

The following section[1] summarizes Lewis's celebrated preference for the 'external' as against the 'internal' method of writing, a bias supposedly exemplified by his gargantuan 1930 satire, *The Apes of God*. In contrast with *Ulysses* or the works of Henry James, Gertrude Stein or D. H. Lawrence, *The Apes* 'is a book made of the outside of things', Lewis wrote. 'And it is also a book of *action*. By certain critics it was described, even, as an orgy of *the externals* of this life of ours. . . . But that is a compliment. Its author lays great store by that *externality*, in a world that is literally inundated with sexual viscera and the "dark" gushings of the tides of the Great Within.'[2] Indicating the significance to all this of Lewis's other career as a painter is his statement that 'I am an artist, and, through my eye, must confess to a tremendous bias. In my purely literary voyages my eye is always my compass.'[3]

———————

For an understanding of the literature of today and of tomorrow it is very necessary, I believe, to grasp the principles involved in this question; namely, that of the respective merits of the method of *internal* and *external* approach [. . . .]

My reasons for believing that the method of *external* approach is the method which, more and more, will be adopted in the art of writing are as follows :

(1) The *external* approach to things belongs to the 'classical' manner of apprehending : whereas the romantic outlook (though it may serve the turn of the 'transitionists') will not, I believe, attract

the best intelligences in the coming years, and will not survive the
period of 'transition'.

(2) The *external* approach to things (relying upon evidence of
the *eye* rather than of the more emotional organs of sense) can make
of 'the grotesque' a healthy and attractive companion. Other approaches cannot do this. The scarab can be accommodated—even
a crocodile's tears can be relieved of some of their repulsiveness. For
the requirements of the new world-order this is essential. And as for
pure satire—there the eye is supreme.

(3) All our instinctive æsthetic reactions are, in the west of
Europe, based upon Greek naturalist canons. Of the *internal*
method of approach in literature, Joyce or James are highly representative. Their art (consisting in 'telling from the inside', as it is
described) has for its backgrounds the naturalism (the flowing lines,
the absence of linear organization, and also the inveterate humanism) of the Hellenic pictorial culture. Stein is Teutonic music,
jazzed—Stein is just the German musical soul leering at itself in a
mirror, and sticking out at itself a stuttering welt of swollen tongue,
although perhaps, as she is not a pure Teuton, this is not quite fair
to the Teuton either—it is the mirror that is at fault.

(4) If you consider the naturalism of the Greek plastic as a
phenomenon of decadence (contrasted with the masculine formal-
ism of the Egyptian or the Chinese) then you will regard likewise
the method of the 'internal monologue' (or the romantic snapshot-
ting of the wandering stream of the Unconscious) as a phenomenon
of decadence.

(5) A tumultuous stream of evocative, spell-bearing, vocables,
launched at your head—or poured into your Unconscious—is,
finally, a dope only. It may be an auriferous mud, but it must remain mud—not a clear but a murky picture. As a literary medium
it is barbaric.

(6) If Henry James or if James Joyce were to paint pictures, it
would be, you feel, a very *literary* sort of picture that would result.
But also, in their *details*, these pictures would be lineal descendants
of the Hellenic naturalism. Only, such details, all jumbled up and
piled one against the other, would appear, at first sight, different,
and, for the Western Hellenic culture, exotic.—Neverthless, as in
the pictures of most Germans, all the plastic units would be suffused
with a romantic coloration. They would be overcharged with a

literary symbolism; their psyche would have got the better of their Gestalt—the result a sentiment, rather than an expressive form.

(7) We know what sort of picture D. H. Lawrence would paint if he took to the brush instead of the pen. For he did so, luckily, and even held exhibitions. As one might have expected, it turned out to be incompetent Gauguin! A bit more practice, and Lawrence would have been indistinguishable from that Pacific-Parisian Pierre Loti of Paint.[4]

(8) To turn once more to the renowned critic [. . .] Hazlitt. In reading Shakespeare, he said, 'we are let into the minds of his characters, we see the play of their thoughts. . . . His humour (so to speak) bubbles, sparkles, and finds its way in all directions, like a natural spring.'[5]—And that natural-spring-effect is the Greek *naturalism*, of course, as I have already indicated. That naturalism (whatever else may or may not happen) is bound to be superseded by something more akin to the classic of, say, the Chinese.

Shakespeare is the summit of the romantic, naturalist, European tradition. And there is a great deal more of that Rousseauish, *natural-springishness*, in much recent work in literature than is generally recognized. But especially, in the nature of things, is this the case with the *tellers-from-the-inside*—with the masters of the 'interior-monologue', with those Columbuses who have set sail towards the El Dorados of the Unconscious, or of the Great Within.

(9) Dogmatically, then, I am for the Great Without, for the method of *external* approach—for the wisdom of the eye, rather than that of the ear.

NOTES

1 From Lewis, *Men Without Art*, pp. 126-8.
2 Ibid., p. 123.
3 Lewis, *The Art of Being Ruled*. London: Chatto & Windus, 1926, p. 391.
4 Loti (1850-1923) wrote novels and other books saturated with the atmosphere of such exotic settings as Tahiti.
5 William Hazlitt, *Lectures on the English Comic Writers*. London: Dent (Everyman's Library), 1967, p. 39.

II

Satire

1

Satire Defended

(From 'Studies in the Art of Laughter', 1934)

The following[1] is one of many pronouncements by Lewis on satire and parts of it were incorporated in *Men Without Art*. Lewis always derided traditional English humour—for instance, in *The Mysterious Mr. Bull* (1938). There, satire is proudly paraded as 'a Hymn of Dispraise'.[2] The satirical impulse, Lewis emphasized, is an 'all purposeful activity', while the other is all quietist relaxation'.[3] The humorist 'surrounds himself in the soft dissolvent of a disarming mirth', Lewis continued. 'In cases of extremity, it may be regarded as a self-administered anaesthetic. . . . The satirist looks down upon the human scene, enlarges it for his peculiar ends, and by means of the sort of lenses employed by Swift in *Gulliver*, shows the earwig to be in fact a small-scale dragon, loudly demanding its St. George, and revealing what goes on in the jungle of a maiden's hair, or what rope-ends start out from her bare arm—though in the throes of our sexual suspicion we call it "down".'[4]

No one can be expected to love Satire exactly, at least no layman. For the technician it is otherwise : all writers worth their salt value the beloved 'Ben' as much as Herrick did, and would sell their shirt to be with him for a half-hour at the *Sun*, the *Dog*, the *Tunne*; and Gustave Flaubert attracts all penmen's ink-stained hearts—all who are authentic *hommes-plumes* as he called it, that is to say—and of course *in spite of* the fact that this outrageous Norman spent his days in word-sculpture of the besotted Bourgeois Man (lower than Neanderthal Man by far—an ape almost it seems) out of the very stuff and texture of mud, and of gutter-mud at that! His mud-images delight us just as much as the marmorial flattery of our kind

41

that the Greeks went in for. But that is *us* : if *we*, who are writers, do not give a damn whether it be god or a sewer-rat that comes out of the hat, provided that the man who elicits it be a superlative conjurer—as Flaubert was, or 'rare Ben Jonson'—that is not to say that the man of the great public (who is not interested at all in the 'shop' of the illusionist or even the most prodigious sleight-of-hand) is likely to feel that way about it. No : *your* face, *your* character, *your* behaviour—all that is most intimately *you*—is what the satirist takes for his target. And you do not thank him for it. Why should you? That would be too much to ask !

You cannot feel very warmly, therefore, towards his art : for what is *his* art after all, as you must see it, but the technique of human defamation? But Tragedy—take the art of tragedy : that is not in a much better case than Satire, perhaps, from the point of view of the mere onlooker—one of those who suffer the spell, not one of those who promote it. For the *destructive* element is not much more pleasant than the grotesque, if it comes to that : and the 'bitter' laughter of the satirist is at least no more humanly repellent than the weeping-and-gnashing-of-teeth, the howls of rage and bellows of sorrow, inseparable from the activities of the tragic muse.

Fortifying myself, at all events, with such arguments as these—and mollifying you, I hope, in the process—I will undertake the canvass of this rather sinister craft, and talk to you about Satire and satirists for a while. For Satire is very much in the news. It is (whether we like it or not) an art that is coming into fashion again, after a long eclipse.

Satire undoubtedly requires to be redefined somewhat. None of the traditional definitions will quite fit what the new schools of Satire that are arising—or have arisen—today would understand by that term. But when I say 'schools of satire', they are not referred to as schools, and *satire* is not how they would describe what they do, as a rule. In point of fact, the term 'satire' is never applied to a great deal of present-day artistic expression which, in any other period, would promptly, and as a matter of course, have been labelled Satire. The fact is that we are at once less sensitive and far more touchy than were people a century or two ago. It is this change which imposes upon us a new definition of Satire.

In the eighteenth century men were, on the one hand, far *more* exacting about delineations of Man in the abstract: but, on the other hand, far less exacting about delineations of their particular selves. No popular portrait-painter in 1934 could deal with his humblest sitter as did Goya (the great Spanish court-painter contemporary with Wellington) with his master the King of Spain. (And as to the Queen of Spain, to her he behaved, if anything, with less ceremony.) Should the contemporary portraitist take it into his head to do so, he would cease to be a 'popular portrait-painter' on the spot. [. . . .]

That for the artist there are two main orders of truth, that must always be insisted upon. There is (1) the 'truth' of Natural Science: and there is (2) the truth of Romance. As I have said elsewhere, it is people's vanity, nothing else, that causes them to use the term *satire* at all! It might be said that satire is the 'truth' of the intellect, whereas the 'truth' of the beauty-doctor is that of the average romantic sensualism. Your person, and your behaviour, as seen by the eye of Satire, would be very close to what it would appear to the eye of Science. In some cases, of course, it would be identical. It would be absurd to claim that *satiric* truth (or scientific truth) was the only truth. But it is equally absurd to say that 'Truth is beauty—beauty truth.'

Indeed 'truth' as that is understood in a Court of Law (of the 'truth and nothing but the truth' variety) and the sort of 'truth' we require of another man, to enable us to orientate ourselves in the practical transactions of life, is certainly satiric truth rather than romantic truth. 'This Desirable Residence For Sale' the house-agents' advertisement invariably runs. But usually a highly emotional truth is conveyed thereby. The *true* truth would as often as not run 'This *undesirable*—overpriced, inconvenient, ugly, damp, difficult-of-access, thoroughly out-of-date residence, etc., for sale.'

But, as I have said, if this great touchiness, or personal arrogance, is noticeable upon the part of the sitter for a contemporary portrait, it is quite the reverse regarding the same person's standards towards the pictorial presentation of Man in the abstract—or it is apt to be, where any pretensions to being 'abreast of the times' is in question. There (when we are dealing with a truly 'modern' man or woman) the greatest latitude is allowed, and even exacted. Indeed it could be said without exaggeration that the present day is the Satirists'

43

paradise! My dear sir, *this*—our epoch—should produce, sooner or later, a satiric art transcending any satire that has ever been done —Rome of the *Satyricon* and the France of Rabelais not excluded.

Whatever may be said for or against Satire in the absolute—and in such a time as ours he who sets his face against Satire brands himself as a racketeer or a fool—at least it must be allowed that Satire is very *cold*. And that is good! There is nothing of the hot innards of Freud-infected art—no 'Fantasias of the Unconscious'[5] about Satire, *that* you must allow. No, it is all constructed out of the dry shells and pelts of things. The surface of the visible machinery of life alone is used. The Quixotic technique—the wires that propel Volpone—the corybantics of Seithenin, in the pages of Peacock—the bustling manners of the satiric art do not lend themselves to swamp-effects, and to the smudgings of aura-lined spirit-pictures. All is metallic—all is external.

It is easier to achieve those polished and resistant surfaces of a great externalist art in Satire, or rather Satire lends itself to *nothing else*. More naturally than can be done beneath the troubled impulse of the lyrical afflatus, in Satire you reach the great classic lines of the skeleton of things. All the nineteenth-century poetry of France, for instance, from the *Fleurs du Mal* onwards, was stiffened with Satire too, as is all the best English poetry today. Messrs. T. S. Eliot, Roy Campbell, Auden, to name three of the most eminent among contemporary Anglo-Saxon poets, are satirists first and foremost. *The Hippopotamus, The Waste Land, Sweeny Agonistes, The Wayzgoose, The Georgiad, The Orators* are all works of Satire pure and simple. (And most contemporary painting and sculpture of any power is essentially Satire, too.)

But there is a stiffening of Satire in *everything* good, of 'the grotesque', which is the same thing—the non-human outlook must be there (beneath the fluff and pulp which is all that is seen by the majority) to correct our soft conceit. This cannot be gainsaid. Satire is *good*!

But I realize that, in these pæans to Satire, I shall be flying in the face of accepted opinion. And there is no opinion, on the subject of Satire, that is so firmly rooted, as that Satire should function ethically, or not at all. That I have been ignoring entirely; for no dogmatic moralist sanction seems to me required to play the critic and the artist in one—which is to be a *satirist*—or *scientist and artist* would perhaps be better; any more than a man has to take out a licence to be a landscape-painter, or to be a bio-chemist, though in due course that may come, I am quite aware.

*

How can Satire justify itself—its 'cruelty', its destructive values, its headman's rôle—without the *moral sanction*, it has repeatedly been asked. For Satire can only exist in contrast to something else —it is a shadow, and an ugly shadow at that, of some perfection. That is the idea. And it is so disagreeable, and so painful (at least in the austere sense in which we are to understand it here) that no one would pursue it *for its own sake*, or take up the occupation of the satirist from choice. The reply to this, of course, is to be sought, first and foremost, in that neglected factor, *style* (and, further, in the fact that the artist is compelled to some extent to supply his own police).

But it is my belief that in fact even Satire *for its own sake*—as much as anything else for its own sake—is possible : and that even the most virtuous and well-proportioned of men is only a shadow, after all, of some perfection; a shadow of an imperfect, and hence an 'ugly', sort. And as to *laughter*, if you allow it in one place you must, I think, allow it in another. Laughter—humour and wit—has a function in relation to our tender consciousness; a function similar to that of art. It is the preserver much more than the destroyer. And, in a sense, *everyone* should be laughed at or else *no one* should be laughed at. It seems that ultimately that is the alternative.

When Addison introduced the word 'genius', to take the place of the word used up to that time, 'wit', he did us all a disservice. Wit as a generic term for all those possessed of an excellent judgment, would tend (apart from the advantages resulting from its less pretentious sound) to marshal the gifted upon the *laughing* side of the world. But that little change of a popular monosyllable made all the difference, and today *the laugh* is not wholly respectable : it requires to be explained, if not excused.

But satire is a special sort of laughter : *the laugh* alone possesses great powers of magnification. But *the laugh* that magnified Falstaff till he grew to be a giant like Pantagruel, is not the laugh of the satirist, which threw up the Maids of Honour in Brobdingnag. Now, no one resents the size of Falstaff : he is a routine figure of fun, the jolly toper. But everyone resents the scale of the Maids of Honour in *Gulliver*, and resents all those sights and sounds that assail our senses in their gigantic company.

The text of Swift is bristling with very painful passages indeed. There is no question here of the mere he-man vulgarity of the egregious Scottish surgeon, Smollett. It is much more uncomfortable than that, not alone for the nice-minded but without exception for all the spokesmen of Mr. Everybody.

In this painful effect of true satire we might expect to find the main avenue of attack of the moralist—he might say that it was *illnatured* instead of *good-natured*, as is mere burlesque. But it is not to that that we must look today (when, as artists, we are taking our measures of defence) as being the spot likely to draw the fire of the ethical batteries.

The painful nature of satire was recognized by Hazlitt, but promptly misunderstood; for he was looking for something in satire which under no circumstances belongs there, and which in consequence he could not find.

'Bare-faced impudence, an idiot imbecility, are his dramatic commonplaces,' he writes of Ben Jonson. So, although one would have thought that Ben Jonson had acquitted himself to admiration of what is after all, in the narrowest sense, the satirist's job, the good Hazlitt finds fault with him for that very reason—because, in fact, Hazlitt did not at all like satire. Ben Jonson, the perfect satirist, was rebuked because he did not manage to fall short of that sinister ideal!

'Sheer ignorance, bare-faced impudence, or idiot imbecility, are his (Ben Jonson's) dramatic common-places—things that provoke pity or disgust, instead of laughter.'[6]

But why should not idiot imbecility provoke laughter? Obviously the answer is : Because, being found in a human being, it is 'letting down' the species, and so to laugh at it would be unethical and *inhuman*. Physical deformity, again, is often comic. Many dwarfs are highly grotesque (superbly grotesque, one may say without offence in the case of dwarfs). And they even relish the sensation of their funniness. But most people only laugh covertly at such spectacles, or sternly repress a smile. For, they would say, these are 'things'

46

which should 'provoke pity or disgust, instead of laughter.' Or such is the Anglo-Saxon point of view.

But the dago is different. Dwarfs, in Spain, are the object of constant mirth, on the part of their 'normal' fellow-citizens. Everyone pokes fun at them, there is no hypocrisy, as with us, and the dwarf gets on very well indeed. He is treated as a pet animal, and enjoys himself very much. Also, since he has a great deal of practice, from morning till night, he often ends by being a first-class clown. In short, neither disgust nor pity is experienced by these dagoes where their dwarfs are concerned. They feel, perhaps, that God has made them a present of these hideous oddities to be their sport: and the dwarf feels that too, and is quite puffed up with his own importance and proud of his god-sent job of joker or of public joke.

And, after all, pulling long faces at the dwarf, and surrounding him with an atmosphere of inhuman pity (or 'disgust') is bad for the dwarf. It is better to explode with laughter at the sight of him—better for all concerned.

So far so good: but what of the shell-shocked man, for instance? He is often very funny. Who has not on occasion (with shame) suppressed an involuntary laugh? But that is like laughing at the contortions of a dying man, and it would be too brutal a society that made a habit of laughing at its shell-shocked persons—especially as it would be to the society of the laughers to which ultimately the responsibility for these disfigurements would have to be brought home. Therefore there is no society that does not refrain from guffawing at the antics, however 'screamingly funny', of its shell-shocked men and war-idiots, and its poison-gas morons, and its mutilated battle-wrecks.

But here is also a principle, of use in the analysis of the comic, and so of use in considering Satire. *Perfect laughter*, if there could be such a thing, would be inhuman. And it would select as the objects of its mirth as much the antics dependent upon pathologic maladjustments, injury, or disease, as the antics of clumsy and imperfectly functioning healthy people.

At this point it is, perhaps, desirable to note that in general human beings display no delicacy about spiritual or mental shortcomings, in their neighbours, but only physical. To be a fool with a robust body can be no more pleasant for the person in question than being an intelligent dwarf: yet no one scruples to laugh at the former, but parades a genteel sensitiveness regarding the latter. Infinitely more pain is inflicted by laughter provoked by some non-physical cause than by that provoked by a physical one. So do not let us take too much for granted that we can put our finger blindfold upon *the supreme cad.*

Our deepest laughter is not, however, inhuman laughter. And yet it is non-personal and non-moral. And it enters fields which are commonly regarded as the preserve of more 'serious' forms of re-action. There is no reason at all why we should not burst out laughing at a fœtus, for instance. We should, after all, only be laughing *at ourselves!*—at ourselves early in our mortal career.

The wind that blows through satire *is* that same bleak element that we meet with in *King Lear,* in *Timon,* or in *Macbeth.* Which of Shakespeare's supreme plays but could, doctored a little by a competent satirist, be made into a typical specimen of the satiric art? Had Jules Laforgue (the author of *Moralités Légendaires*) been an Englishman, this would have been a job for him. He could have turned Hamlet into a titanic farce. It is almost that as it stands. And I question if it should be left to the Soviet authorities to rehandle Lear and Coriolanus, for instance. It could be done far better here, where English is spoken, and where there would be much less danger of damage to the original.

Satire, some satire, does undoubtedly stand half-way between Tragedy and Comedy. It may be a hybrid of these two. Or it may be a *grinning* tragedy, as it were. Or, yet again, it may be a comedy full of dangerous electrical action, and shattered with outbursts of tears.

But we all recognize *laughter* as an anti-toxin of the first order. As a matter of fact *no* man (as I have hinted above)—any more than the shell-shocked man—should be laughed at. It is unfair, therefore it is 'caddish', to laugh at *anybody* : we all, as much as the shell-shocked man, really could cry *cad*, or have cad cried at us, at any outburst of mirth at our expense. It is unnecessary to enumerate the tragic handicaps that our human condition involves : the glaring mechanical imperfections, the nervous tics, the prodigality of objectless movement—the, to other creatures, offensive smells, disagreeable moistures—the involuntary grimace—the lurch, roll, trot or stagger which we call our *walk*—it is only a matter of degree between us and the victim of locomotor-ataxy or St. Vitus's dance.

By making a great deal of noise ourselves we at least drown the alarming noise made by our neighbours. And the noise that, above all others, has been bestowed on us for this purpose is the bark which we describe as our *laugh*. I approve of a *barking man* myself—I find that I have less occasion, with his likes, to anticipate a really serious bite. So laughter is *per se* a healthy clatter—that is one of the first things to realize about it. [. . . .]

NOTES

1 Lewis, 'Studies in the Art of Laughter', *The London Mercury*, October, 1934, pp. 509–15.
2 Lewis, *The Mysterious Mr. Bull*. London: Robert Hale Ltd., 1938, p. 143.
3 Ibid., p. 150.
4 Ibid., p. 151.
5 A reference to D. H. Lawrence's *Fantasia of the Unconscious* (1922).
6 Hazlitt, *Lectures on the English Comic Writers*, p. 40.

III

Shakespeare and Shaw

Shakespeare

(From *The Lion and the Fox*, 1927)

Lewis's passionate interest in Shakespeare is reflected in both *The Lion and the Fox*[1] and his vivid 1914 portfolio of illustrations for *Timon of Athens*. One of the most intriguing facets of *The Lion and the Fox*, a study of—among other things—the hero and the nature of tragedy in Shakespeare, is the extent to which it casts light on the tragic in Lewis's own fiction and his theories about the attempted exaltation of the Little Man at the expense of the Great in modern society. Critics, in fact, might be inclined to suggest that the Shakespeare of *The Lion and the Fox* is mainly a reflection of Lewis's own creative preoccupations rather than an 'objective' study of The Bard. In any case, T. S. Eliot took exception to Lewis's interpretation. 'Mr. Lewis proposes a Shakespeare who is a *positive* nihilist, an intellectual force *willing* destruction,' Eliot wrote. 'I cannot see in Shakespeare either a deliberate scepticism, as of Montaigne, or a deliberate resignation, as of Seneca. . . . Mr. Lewis and other champions of Shakespeare as a great philosopher . . . fail to show that [Shakespeare] thought to any purpose; that he had any coherent view of life. . .'[2]

———————

The master-subject of Shakespeare's plays has its origin in the machiavellian obsession of his time: or rather, that is the form the deeper conflict takes. The figure used by Machiavelli to express this conflict is that of the *lion and the fox*; these two animals are chosen to represent the two forces in opposition, although his doctrine was directed to combining them. In Shakespeare, as in most of his contemporaries, with one foot in the old world of chivalrous romance and the other in the new one of commerce and science, they were imperfectly combined: for his was not an emancipated and scientific mind, like that of the great Italian in question. [. . . .]

[Machiavelli] was only known through the french of Gentillet,[3] if that : but he was the great character of supreme intrigue that, however taken, was at the back of every tudor mind. Elizabethan drama—'the first terror-stricken meeting of the England of Eliza- beth with the Italy of the late renaissance'—was more terrified of Machiavelli than of anybody. The Borgias, Sforzas, Baglionis, Mala- testas, Riartes were of far more importance to the elizabethan drama- tists than any of their own eminent countrymen. Familiarity bred contempt in the long run. But during its flourishing period the english stage went constantly to the schoolmaster of manslaughter, Machia- velli—and his political paradigms chosen in conformity with his Borgia worship—for its thrills. [. . . .]

All Shakespeare's work can be regarded as a criticism of action and of the agent-principle : though it is only in *Hamlet* that this mood becomes explicit, and as it were personal. This incomparable observer of the life around him 'had his opinions' of what he saw, although he had no gesture of rebellion against individual phases of it, but innumerable gestures against life itself. And, if against life itself, then against action itself. It was the *universality* or impersonal all-inclusiveness of this rebellion that makes him a 'universal' artist, as he is often called.

Whereas Machiavelli was the hypnotized advocate of a specific contemporary type of active life : and as Molière was—in a different way—its adversary and critic : Shakespeare was neither one nor the other. He was, if anything, the adversary of life itself (if to be the critic is to be the adversary, and that poetry is a criticism of life has been accepted as a good definition), and his works a beautifully impersonal outpouring of fury, bitter reflection, invective and com- plaint—complaint in the *Sonnets,* for instance; fury in *Timon,* or his other tragedies and histories. Of that sort of action—and that was the only action for which he had not a contempt—Shakespeare was a tremendous adept. In the tragic experiences of all his charac- ters he tragically participated : and they were much more mirrors held up to his tired and baffled mind than they were the mirrors of any nature that he objectively could know. *Tired with all these,* we find him, but there was something that attached him to them; and which, if he had left them, he would also have had to have left.

All that can strictly be described as his philosophy is contained

in Montaigne's *Essays*. There is the same curiosity and discourage-
ment, wonderful flexibility of expression, passionate friendship for
another man, humour and scepticism, in both. Both are the critics
of action, but Shakespeare paradoxically criticizes it by showing you
its adepts in *action*. [. . . .]

The phenomenon of the grand style is important in any discussion of Shakespeare's 'politics'—which Coleridge assures us exhibited a 'wonderfully philosophic impartiality'.[4] But making the
drawer or serving-woman speak in prose and the court official in
blank verse decides nothing about Shakespeare's political sentiments,
any more than would the appearance in a play of a legal document
in the pompous vernacular of the war, and a private letter in the
intimate undress natural in that case. [. . . .]

Of the long line of kings that came under his hand for dramatic
treatment, some had 'been deposed', 'some slain in war', 'some
haunted by the ghosts they had deposed', some had been 'poisoned
by their wives', 'some sleeping killed' : but most if not all had come
to a violent and stupid end, clamouring about their divine right and
their kingly ways, defiant or idiotically remorseful. He probably did
not think much more of these kings that passed though his hands
than Gibbon did of his gallery of despots. The image of the 'little
pin' which bored through the life-wall so easily, and then 'farewell
king!' was a reflection of the critical experiences of the poet, not
of Richard Plantagenet : *'For you have but mistook me all this
while!'* That great undressing of the dressed-up self in a simple
phrase is Shakespeare's, and has a universal application beyond the
royal disappointments of Richard II.

But for all his contempt for the individual being, it was not because
he was a king, but because he was human, that Shakespeare would
regard him as he did. Hence there is no occasion for surprise if
Shakespeare did not adopt a militant attitude toward those privileges.
He knew them too well to suppose that, dressed up differently, and
forbidden to deliver themselves in blank verse, or deprived of the
mechanism of royalty, they would change their skin. Nor was he
innocent enough to suppose that he was living beneath a more
oppressive system than the next, the next after that, or the one
before it. So he accepted his kings : but with a much worse grace
than is generally believed. [. . . .]

If the question were put categorically in this form : 'On whose side was Shakespeare in the conflict that played such an important part in his work, between the simple man and the Machiavel?' it could not, of course, be answered : or we should have to answer, if at all : 'On neither side.' For it would not be natural for Shakespeare to intervene in the eternal dispute of good and evil, or in the battles of the animal kingdom, where the foxes and lions perpetually manœuvre. It is impossible to make a fox-hunter of him : and he showed no tendency to wish to be a lion. So the answer would have to be complex, as is the phenomenon we are handling. One thing however can be decided at once where Othello, at least, is concerned; that with that first of his colossi (the series of titans of his third period, or the last phase of his career) he was not on the side of Othello's small destroyer. If most critics have tried to make of Iago a colossus, too, to match Othello, I do not think that Shakespeare ever did.

First of all, Shakespeare was no more the servant of the gods than he was of the populace. He was neither religious nor democratic, in any dogmatic sense, but philosophic. And so when he approached his hero in pursuance with his function of writer of tragedies, it was not with the frenzied intolerance either of a messenger of the gods or of a malignant emissary of the crowd. Noting his peaceable, hum-drum manner of life—rather like those hangmen who when not engaged on their terrible trade are grocers or barbers in some small provincial town—it is certainly natural to wonder how it was that he ever adopted such a profession.

With the exception of Chapman, Shakespeare is the only 'thinker' we meet with among the elizabethan dramatists.[5] By this is meant, of course, that his work contained, apart from poetry, phantasy, rhetoric or observation of manners, a body of matter representing explicit processes of the intellect which would have furnished a moral philosopher like Montaigne with the natural material for his essays. But the quality of this thinking—as it can be surprised springing naturally in the midst of the consummate movements of his art—is, as must be the case with such a man, of startling force sometimes. And if it is not systematic, at least a recognizable physiognomy is there [. . . .]

Shakespeare—the even, impartial spectator of life, quite undisturbed and without any personality—is often referred to in a flattering way (and to give an idea of the good impression this characterless

56

character has made on the person speaking of him) as a 'man of the world'. By this, of course, is meant 'one of us', a typical member of the minor, more fortunate, herd 'in the know'—what Nietzsche brands in his admirable description of 'the Cynic'.[6]

That he was in some profound way feminine we have already said. But, of the various figures that approximate to the feminine ideal, that of the 'man of the world' he has no claim on, I think— any more than he has on that of the jesuit. But the most illustrious 'men of the world' are almost invariably very unworldly : in short, they are anything but 'men of the world', although 'the world' has been their habitat. Machiavelli himself was no exception to this rule. Did he not, when accused of being the doctrinaire of every super-'wordly' duplicity, refer, with some point, to the great simplicity of his life, to his poverty and to the fact that as a result of his 'worldly' adroitness he was unable to obtain employment under any florentine government? [. . . .]

What is the solution of these contradictions? It seems to be that the qualities that make a man a successful theoretician are the opposite to those that make him a successful man of action : and that even if, as in the case of Machiavelli, he is a theoretician of *action*. The material of which the mirror destined to reflect action is made is at the other pole to the violent ferments providing the substance of *action*. Perhaps, as the *reflecting* mind is at all events living, it would be better to say that it must be both motionless and deep to reflect to the fullest advantage the conflict occurring in its world.

It is strange how many people consider themselves 'men of the world' : it is a very popular rôle. But it is the last thing, with its 'knowingness', its smartly advertising cynicism, herd-reclamation, mechanical snobbery, that even the smallest poet or philosopher could ever be, though no doubt they might affect it.

Like the woman, or the jesuit, the *man of the world*, if we erect him into a figure, is one of abnegation. His is essentially a system of defence and not of attack. He is a man who is himself small and weak, but who has acquired, who lives in the midst of, a powerful defensive machinery. He is in this sense the champion of the mechanical, and the constant adversary of the individual. His strategy is not the daring, ambitious, strategy of machiavellism; but a system of maxims that vary little from age to age in the freemasonry of 'the world'.

If the strategy of the world, however, has to be matched with its opposite (as many people wish, as we have said, to match Iago with Othello) it would not be the man of the world who would be chosen to be its champion, naturally enough; for with many a 'Thank-you!' he would hurry deeper into his labyrinth if approached to play the part of a champion, even of the most unheroic strategy. The great figure of human heroism, of the world's adversary and opposite, in such a match, could be found, I should say, in its fullest flower in the works of Shakespeare: though in the nature of things, since tragedy is a butchery and not a duel with equal arms, the ideal adversary is not introduced.

The ANTONY of *Antony and Cleopatra*, or CORIOLANUS, TIMON, OTHELLO or LEAR; all these great heroic children, who compass their *pathos* with such a pathetic magnificence, are the ideal saga types. The modernity of the language and the extreme subtlety of their creator make them more acceptable and more real to us than the great figures of what Professor Chadwick has called the 'heroic age'.[7]

Shakespeare's tremendous heroes, then, answer to the requirements of the contest on the heroes' side. But their tragedy is that they are involved in a *real* action: whereas they come from, and naturally inhabit, an ideal world.

They are struck down always by the puniest weapons; always by deceit, but quite ordinary deceit. The weapon has to be weak: for in the pessimism of tragedy not only have the great always to be vanquished; but they have always to be overcome by trivial opponents who substitute a poor and vulgar thing for the great and whole thing that they have destroyed. The point of the tragedy, like the ideal basis of christianity, is the 'strength of weakness', and the corresponding 'weakness of strength'. 'The first shall be last and the last shall be first', then, or 'He who humbleth himself shall be exalted', etc., in a dramatic action. But it is of course the exact opposite of christianity, inasmuch as the *pathos* of the Great is what fills it, in place of, as in christianity, the *pathos* of the Little. There the comparison ceases, because the *little* of christianity is not theoretically the same as that of tragedy, nor is its *great* the same. The Rich Man of christianity (who is its *great*) is never the hero of tragedy: or if tragedy consents to use him it loses its power over the mind: or its effect is greatest when its victim is least identifiable with him. Owing to this fact, the operation of tragedy resolves itself into something nearer to the christian spirit than would at first appear. It is as though the christian *little*, purified, exalted by the great simplicity of its faith, and become *great*, were vanquished by the christian *great* (the villain of the piece in that religion), degraded also by the magic of faith, but not altered.

Iago is very near to the man of the world, but he is far too 'honest'. He is a quite normal and commonplace worldly person complicated by an honesty *à la* Machiavel. He is not the unusual villain that he is often made out to be. With a little more intensity and resolution, most of the individuals composing any contemporary european 'educated' society would be very much like Iago. The tremendous intricacy of Shakespeare's art is well known in this treatment of Iago. The making of this villain Everyman is a supreme invention of genius. He is just the ordinary bluff, 'honest' man in the street, proud of his strategy, and the power it gives him; saying without any self-consciousness (pity almost coming to join with his envy) :

> The Moor is of a free and open nature,
> That thinks men honest that but seem to be so :
> And will as tenderly be led by the nose
> As asses are.

Iago is strictly the 'man of the world', with so much purpose and energy added as is required to be the David to Othello's Goliath in a predestined tragedy, where the dice are palpably loaded in the interest of the small and crooked. So Iago is the *small* destroyer, the eternal Charlie Chaplin figure of human myth, the gods on his side, their instrument in their struggle with the hero. . . . He is the ideal *little man* with the sling and the stone. Othello is the ideal human galleon, twenty storeys high, with his head in the clouds, that the little can vanquish. [. . . .]

Falstaff is a 'man of wit and pleasure', and could generally be described as a very good specimen of a 'man of the world'. But the same thing applies to him as Iago : the 'man of the world' is never so dramatically and openly cynical as Falstaff, any more than he is so candid as Machiavelli. He is not dramatic at all. To come to one of the necessary conclusions in this connexion, if the *Machiavel* were an Englishman he would be like Falstaff. This laziness, rascality and 'good fellow' quality, crafty in the brainless animal way, is the english way of being a 'deep-brained Machiavel'.

But Falstaff is a 'child', too, a *'naïf'*, as Ulrici says.[8] A worldly mixture of any strength is never without that ingredient. The vast compendium of worldly bluff that is Falstaff would have to contain that. It was like 'any christom child' that he 'went away', Mistress Quickly says.

He is armed from head to foot with sly feminine inferiorities, lovable weaknesses and instinctively cultivated charm. He is a big helpless bag of guts, exposing himself boldly to every risk on the child's, or the woman's, terms. When he runs away or lies down he is more adorable than any hero 'facing fearful odds'.

His immense girth and stature lends the greatest point, even, to his character. He is a hero run hugely to seed : he is actually heavier and bigger than the heaviest and biggest true colossus or hero. He is in that respect, physically, a mock-hero. Then this childishness is enhanced by his great physical scale, so much the opposite of the child's perquisite of smallness. And because of this meaningless, unmasculine immensity he always occupies the centre of the stage, he is the great landmark in any scene where he is. It all means nothing, and is a physical sham and trick put on the eye. And so he becomes the embodiment of bluff and worldly practice, the colossus of the *little*. [. . . .]

Since we possess a great deal of evidence as to what Shakespeare thought of military glory and martial events, we have no reason to suppose that the military heroics in *Coriolanus* are of a different order to what they are elsewhere. There is the curious demented sensuality that he is fond of attributing to military rivals, but which is not an element calculated to increase the atmosphere of respect at their feats of daring : it even makes them—the Hotspurs, Achilles, Hals and so forth—a little ridiculous. As to this feudal poet's courtly leanings, I do not think they are proved. He is quite ready to support his characters when the moment arrives for them to abuse the 'many-headed multitude' (which was the usual term—'we have been called so of many', the Citizen in Act II., scene 3, says). Shakespeare no doubt agreed with all the abuse his puppet Coriolanus was called upon to hurl at the roman crowd. It would very nearly describe what Shakespeare probably felt about the London crowd of his time, and especially as he came in contact with it at the theatre.

But from this to supposing that he had discriminated between this crowd and that other smaller crowd to which Coriolanus belonged —the crowd that thronged the more expensive seats of the Bankside theatres—is a long step of snobbish unreason and self-deception that we have no right to assume Shakespeare at all likely to have taken. For him *l'un vaudrait l'autre*, I expect. For it was human nature about which Shakespeare wrote, and he did not write on a tone of morals, nor on one of class-prejudice or class-illusion.

Coriolanus is no more a play to exhibit the virtues and destinies of the aristocrat (with a strong propaganda for a severe oligarchical form of government, and a strong snobbish illusion about the graceful advantages of the aristocratic life) than it is a play of educationist propaganda, whether for or against a certain type of training. It is a play about a conventional military hero, existing as the characteristic ornament of a strong aristocratic system. Shakespeare was neither for or against him, on propagandist, feudal or non-feudal grounds. He was quite ready to curse the crowd with him : and he was equally ready to examine with as little pleasure the child of a harsh practical system, abusing his many advantages, and showing to perfection how the top, as likewise the under, dog is unsatisfactory and foolish, the one very nearly worthy of the other— the violent, dull, conceited leader, and the resentful but cowardly slave. Meantime the play is charged with a magnificent rhetoric, as wherever any character utters Shakespeare's blank verse. Coriolanus speaks frequently like a god : also the *altofronto* tone is adopted by him from time to time, as by most Shakespeare heroes— his banter and bitterness being often just the same as that of Hamlet, Timon or Lear. But that is Shakespeare's own voice and manner that you hear, the central surge, that, wherever the music he is making excites him, comes out and is heard. What belongs properly to Coriolanus is not meant by Shakespeare to be attractive : he shows none of the sympathy for him that he does for Othello, Antony or Timon. Yet he is cast for the lion part; and Shakespeare gives him, as remarked above, his portion of magnificent music. Also he has to the full one of the great requisites of the shakespearian *lion*; he is completely helpless, childlike, truthful and unfortunate. So it is the rôle, rather than the figure filling it, that would set the tragic organ playing.

The *fox* is there too; the tribunes Sicinius and Brutus supply the

61

Iago element very adequately, except that no unpopularity is concentrated on them. [. . . .]

The one qualification that the life-history of a person must have to make it fit for tragedy is that it must abound in and express *action*. The really tragic hero must be *demented* : and there is nothing strange in all shakespearian colossi being demented, as was observed at the time we were reviewing them : where there is *only* action enough the person becomes demented automatically.

But it is impossible to be both a poet and a man of action, to be Homer and Hector, or Shakespeare and Cæsar; for, as we say, the man of action's self-expression or 'poetry' is his *action* (whereas, we could add, the traditional poet's—or that of the epic poet, like Shakespeare—is other people's actions); it is natural, we should also say, or even necessary, that the poet should be 'impersonal'. For he has to fit into the lives of his subjects and not they into his. The heroic appetite, even, of Hesiod is too much of something that is Hesiod's. The great *actions* must be harmonized and seen in the mirror of a dream, and its surface must be as smooth as glass. The vacuity of Shakespeare's face, even, is the receptive face of such a mirror, or a symbol of that inner condition that it was his function to affect. So to think of Homer as written by a woman, instead of by the blind and frowning Zeus of the Baiae bust, is, evidence apart, not such a wild notion.

Beneath the unruffled surface of this mirror, however, a drama is being enacted, too—namely, what could be termed the *drama of the mirror*—an Alice-through-the-Looking-Glass-like life. What is generally forgotten is that Shakespeare himself is a greater *hero* than any of the figures he depicted : that actually in spectacular glory and renown no physical achievement could surpass his. And yet he is *nobody* in his life; neither a norman king, a norman noble, a general or a statesman. He is a little actor, classed by the police of his day with 'sturdy beggars and vagabonds'. Christ's origin is not more singularly humble. He was at least well placed to have some of Christ's thoughts about the 'oppressor' and 'the proud man'.

To be a poet today (or in Shakespeare's time) is to be a tuneful writer of laments, principally connected with sex-experience; or the chronicler in some form of the heroic deeds of soldiers, royalties and statesmen. Since the numerous men and women fulfilling those duties in Shakespeare's time were very like those engaged in similar occupations today; or in combative, speculative finance—which is our equivalent for much that was then not so palpably connected with money—he can hardly have formed more favourable opinions of such personages than an outside observer, above the average in intelligence, would today. The only reason that we suppose he did is that he has been labelled at one time 'the feudal poet', and we are still inclined to be romantic about those 'spacious' days, and forget that, if nothing else, they had a renaissance, and we have not.

In spite of the placid and 'gentle' surface of this *mirror* of a man, we know the storms that raged beneath it; and we know that he must, personally, have suffered as much from the world about him as any of his heroes. If we take one of his great tragedies, *Timon of Athens*, for instance, and see what happens, in reality, in the progress of the play, the point of this protracted argument will be apparent. The Timon that a dispassionate observer would see (without the intervention of Shakespeare's poetry) would be the Timon seen by Apemantus. Shakespeare saw that one also—as he shows by means of the discourse of Apemantus. But Timon has to be sacrificed, to become *nothing* in a worldly sense, from having been *everything*; he has to suffer heroically and have a *pathos*. This does not happen to most men of the world—they know too much, are too prudent, or merely sufficiently lucky, in ordinary circumstances, to escape this degradation. In Timon's case, or Lear's, it was due expressly to some violent or child-like kink. It is when these figures *fall* to abjection that they reach the region of the Christs. But what is not so readily admitted is that that is also the region of the Shakespeares. If these figures had no *pathos* and humiliation they would never be clothed, as they are invariably by Shakespeare, for these occasions, in the most grand and mournful rhetoric of perhaps any poetry in the world. *Antony and Cleopatra, Othello, Lear, Timon,* and the rest, are all splendid masterpieces, all reproducing the same music of extinction and unbounded suffering. They are a gallery of sunsets : they are dream-storms in a single soul, with a piling up of vaster and vaster burdens with ever more colossal figures to carry them.

In this way the contradictions of these tragic creations have their immediate explanation. Shakespeare was, by reason of the tragic side of his dramatic function—the 'Shake-scene' side—something of a 'mute' and something of an executioner. His only interest in these great ones of this world was on account of their violent ends and the ceremonies arising in connexion with those events. Their worldly life, unclouded by catastrophe, did not interest him at all. So he was rather a pious and discreet executioner of feudal personages (but one showing great gusto) than a 'feudal poet'. And he had his favourites. No mother could have treated these more tenderly.

As the painter is fixed by opinion and public taste to the imitation of tables, lamp-posts, lord mayors, society beauties, regulation 'still-lifes', and so forth—although in reality his interest in these things *as such* is often very slight (his interests may plastically be of a more abstract description)—in the same way as a dramatic poet is fixed to the personages of the world of action. He has to make his world of thought out of elements of action, which in themselves and in their natural setting are almost meaningless. If a painter were able to make, and did, pillar-boxes and lamp-posts *think*, and *feel*, and subsequently or at the same time cause their thinking and feeling to issue in speech like the music of the spheres, he would then be doing what Shakespeare did. The action was the *being* the pillar-box or the lamp-post : the thinking, feeling and speech was Shakespeare's always, when the great interior action started, and the thing became transformed into a person. As action, in the sense used above, is function merely, it is when these figures turned from their function at last, and became alone, that they became a person. But without the personality of Shakespeare they would, from the moment of their functional demise, have ceased to exist. He gave them a short and brilliant existence, posthumous to the death of their function. He and the art he had perfected, especially that of heroic blank verse, performed this together.

NOTES

1   Excerpts here come from Lewis, *The Lion and the Fox*. London : Methuen (University Paperbacks), 1966, pp. 11, 64, 160, 162, 165, 178–9, 184, 186–9, 226–7, 244–6, 288–91.
2   T. S. Eliot, 'Shakespeare and the Stoicism of Seneca' in *Selected Essays*. London : Faber & Faber, 1951, pp. 134–5.
3   Gentillet's hostile commentary on Machiavelli, generally known as *Contre-Machiavel*, was published in 1576.
4   Samuel Taylor Coleridge, *Lectures and Notes on Shakespere and Other English Poets*. London : George Bell & Sons Ltd., 1900, p. 309.

5 Elsewhere in *The Lion and the Fox*, L. says of Chapman that 'the craft in statecraft and the problems of policy were even more present to him than to Shakespeare. . . . For he was one of the only tudor or stuart dramatists . . . who possessed an intelligence that could in any way be ranked with that of his greatest contemporary' (p. 265).
6 L. enlarges on this interpretation of Nietzsche in *The Art of Being Ruled*, p. 127.
7 Cf. H. Munro Chadwick, *The Heroic Age*. Cambridge: The University Press, 1912. This is a study of the heroic poetry of the Teutonic peoples (third to sixth centuries) and of the equivalent Hellenic period.
8 Hermann Ulrici, *Shakespeare's Dramatic Art and his Relation to Calderon and Goethe*. London: Chapman Brothers, 1846, p. 327.

George Bernard Shaw

(From *The Art of Being Ruled*, 1926)

In *Rude Assignment*, Lewis wrote that 'such men as Voltaire, or as Mr. Shaw, were very contradictory and contentious: but it was not their *time* they contradicted. . . . *They were perfectly in tune with the Zeitgeist*.'[1] The following attack[2] forms part of a general assault on the reaction of Shaw and Bertrand Russell to the human craving for power and mutual rivalry, compared by the philosopher to 'the dog's wolfish instincts'.[3] In a book singled out by Lewis, Russell wondered 'whether any method of strengthening kindly instincts exists.' Assuming that the strength or weakness of such impulses depends on the glands, Russell—perhaps with tongue in cheek—broached the idea of injections for world leaders designed to increase their benevolence towards other humans. 'But alas, the physiologists would first have to administer the love-philtre to themselves before they would undertake such a task. . . . And so we come back to the old dilemma: only kindliness can save the world, and even if we knew how to produce kindliness we should not do so unless we were already kindly. Failing that, it seems that the solutions which the Houyhnhnms adopted towards the Yahoos, namely extermination, is the only one; apparently the Yahoos are bent on applying it to each other.'[4] Commented Lewis: 'The possibility of "kindliness" becoming sufficiently prevalent for it to have any influence on the human race would never have occurred to anyone except an individual injected not with "kindliness" at all, necessarily, but with liberalism. And as to idly taunting the Yahoo with what he can never hope to possess, that is again a proceeding of the same political complexion. . . . The "kindliness" of Mr. Russell or Mr. Shaw has an unpleasant sound of moral charlatanism, of the virtue *à bon marché* of the immensely prosperous old liberal England.'[5]

In seeing Mr. Shaw's play, *St. Joan*, it was difficult to resist the suggestion that the cast had been furnished by the anglican clergy. The 'kindliness' of the Earl of Warwick, the 'kindliness' of the Bastard, the 'kindliness' in different ways, of everybody on the stage (with the exception of the admirable actor who took the part of the bishop of Beauvais) was overwhelming. It could have been produced by no machinery except that of anglo-saxon protestantism, livened up a little bit for the occasion by irish charm. The poorness of the language (when such things as 'green fields' had to be mentioned by Joan of Arc, who booed cheerlessly the thin journalese with which she was provided, this was forced on the attention)—the incessant rattle of stale, clever argumentation—the heartiness and 'kindliness' pervading everything—the chill of a soulless, arty, indefatigable 'rational' presentation of the theme—must have an increasingly depressing effect on the audience it seems destined to attract, if it is not softened or otherwise modified in new interpretations. It is the swan-song of english liberalism staged for the post-war suburbs of London. The 'kindly' twinkle in Mr. Lyall Sweete's eye, his massive gladstonian jaw and bulky person, is the symbol of that strange thing, part humbug, part fierce possessiveness, part real gentleness and goodness, that has served the white race so ill.

Why it is necessary to expose and condemn this humanitarianism, with the especial local colour conveyed for us in the word 'kindly' ('kindliness' having such a different sense to 'kind'), is because it is a sort of spiritual nineteenth-century vulgarization of the great fanatical compassion of which it is a degenerate, genial, tepid form; a half-measure, embalmed in rationalistic discourse.

It is always 'on the right tack': it never reaches any effective position. *St. Joan*, for example, has for its theme a very noble understanding of the unhappy situation of the saint. But Mr. Shaw, in spite of himself, desecrates it with his weak-minded, chilly wordliness, which is *plus fort que lui*. He seems to 'give away', to betray, at least artistically (which in a play is naturally everything), his heroine. He is resolved to show the world this situation, but he has not the power. He laughs, twinkles, and cackles to hide his incompetence where this task is concerned.

In the preface of *Back to Methuselah* there is similarly a fine humane motive at work. But what happens at the end? Well, of course, the play. But Adam and Eve are in the same predicament as Joan of Arc where their presentment by Mr. Shaw is concerned. They speak the jargon of the city tea-shop; as you read you fancy them in bathing drawers, a London bank clerk and his girl, great Wells readers, extemporizing in a studio the legend of the creation, prompted, mephistopheles-fashion, by Mr. Shaw : and the preface remains the play.

'Nobody noticed the new religion in the centre of the intellectual whirlpool,' he says, referring to the masterwork of his maturity.[6] He now reveals this latent 'new religion', which turns out to be Bergson's *élan vital.* He writes : 'Darwinism proclaimed that our true relation is that of competitors and combatants in a struggle for mere survival, and that every act of pity or loyalty to the old fellowship is a vain and mischievous attempt to lessen the severity of the struggle and preserve inferior varieties from the efforts of Nature to weed them out.'[7] But in the surplus life in which he suggests, as human creatures, we should live, he has nothing very positive to offer, except his 'new religion', that is, Bergson's *creative evolution.*

He misrepresents his hero Nietzsche, whom he interprets as follows : 'Nietzsche, for example . . . concluding that the final objective of this Will was power over self, and that the seekers after power over others and material possessions were on a false scent.'[8] This sense is certainly not obtained from a reading of Nietzsche's works. 'Power over others' came very vividly into the programme of that philosopher. Again, as a persuasive engine the exhortation to 'self-control' does not seem the best; it smacks of the Y.M.C.A. straight talks to young men. All his persuasiveness is haunted by this sort of vulgarity of mind : almost less than any famous english writer has he what Arnold would call a 'celtic' tact. He incessantly (when his criticism is finished and his persuasion begins) suggests the sunday school, or the 'straight and hearty, man to man' talk.

How, finally, these things can be summarized, is that both Mr. Shaw and Mr. Russell fail as artists, they have no dramatic sense above the rhetoric of the anglican pulpit. Although they can convince us of their sincerity, they would not be able to convince a stranger from some other system of things, because there is no vibration in their words or universal significance in their gestures. They are just words, opinions, that they have been unable to fuse, and which they have not the force to dramatically present. And their humanitarianism is a poor, prosaic food, meant for a cruder animal existence, and a much easier and more fortunate one, than ours. [. . . .]

To conclude, the vast mistake, exemplified so well by Mr. Shaw, is that he does not realize that men are tigers, wasps, and wolves, or parrots, geese, sheep, and asses, or the humdrum monkey, rather than men. He is, in short, too anthropomorphic. For all his lifetime of raillery and scolding he has not realized quite what sort of animal he has been talking to. 'The creatures that we see around us are not men : there is some perversion, the cause of which we cannot penetrate,' Rousseau would have told him. I think that his is a creditable and amiable mistake; but it puts him (and those of his persuasion) in a weak position where the science of life is concerned.

Sometimes, of course, he will pretend to understand, as when he is describing the embarrassments of the ruler : —

> Goodnatured unambitious men are cowards when they have no religion. They are dominated and exploited not only by greedy and often half-witted and half-alive weaklings who will do anything for cigars, champagne, motor cars, and the more childish and selfish uses of money, but by able and sound administrators who can do nothing else with them than dominate and exploit them. Government and exploitation become synonymous under such circumstances; and the world is finally ruled by the childish, the brigands, and the blackguards.[9]

That statement is full of confusions, because he has only half come out of his shell into the light of reality. For example, he admits that even 'able and sound administrators' can find nothing better to do with 'unambitious men' than *dominate* them. ('Exploit' is only an emotional redundancy : for who ever heard of a ruler not getting something out of his rule?) But then he winds up with his 'children and blackguards', immediately forgetting his admission of the 'able and sound administrators' into the picture. Yet (if such people exist, and he says they do) these 'able and sound' personages would surely have something to say to their 'childish and blackguardly' rivals, and not necessarily leave them to have the last word and the world to be 'finally ruled' by them?

What Mr. Shaw does not add, but should, is that 'unambitious men' would far rather be ruled by a 'brigand' or a 'child' (whom they can understand) than by Mr. Shaw. For that would require a measure of 'ambition' that is unfortunately by no means common.

That is the fallacy of the philosopher-king that we are brushing against.

Mr. Shaw has been a sort of mocking and 'mischievous' conscience to middle-class England for a good many years. People have put up with him because (in his capacity of 'a conscience') he was such a respectable thing to have He has been the one thing that has saved their face—while all the time he has been persuaded that he was putting them dreadfully out of countenance! But he has often been angrily accused of treating the public with contempt. The mistake emphasized above shows him, of course, in an opposite light—the mistake in virtue of which, bursting with optimism and friendliness, he approached the public brimming innocently with highly intellectual conversation, as though cheerily exclaiming, 'Ah, you old villain, I'll make a philosopher of you before I'm done with you!' The public has smiled and smiled—and remained a villain. Horatio wrote in his tablets in vain where Mr. Shaw is concerned.

In the nursery in which the 'blackguardly' children (who 'will do anything for cigars, champagne, and motor cars') rule the unambitious children (whose appetites do not aspire to these exciting luxuries), and in which Mr. Shaw has sat like a very genial uncle, a 'kindly' twinkle in his eye, humorously recommending the unambitious to revolt, there is a great deal of bloodshed. The game of government goes on, and it is a game that no philosopher has ever been able to interrupt seriously for a moment. The children die in shoals, the philosopher is aghast. But they hardly know they are dying—in the way, at least, that the philosopher understands it. The villains of the play (namely, the children fond of champagne and cigars) are as intent on the game, and as childlike, necessarily, as the others. The presence of a grown-up (a philosopher like Mr. Shaw) is useful; it enables them to be more ferocious than ever. The 'freedom of speech' in which he is able to indulge is their sanction, it gives an air of *fairness* to anything that happens. (Mr. Shaw especially, would give an air of *fairness* to almost anything. His mere presence at the most disgraceful spectacle would confer a certain respectability on it.) The philosopher stands wringing his hands, and the bloodshed redoubles in violence. A paroxysm of slaughter supervenes. When it abates, the voice of the philosopher is heard imploring the children not to cut off the tail of a mouse that they have caught : 'Ever since (Darwin) set up Circumstantial Selection as the creator and ruler of the universe, the scientific world has been the very citadel of stupidity and cruelty. Fearful as the tribal god of the Hebrews was, nobody ever shuddered as they passed even his meanest and narrowest Little Bethel or his proudest war-consecrating cathedral as we shudder now when we pass a physiological laboratory.'[10] In the listlessness and exhaustion ensuing on what was perhaps the biggest beano that has ever occurred, the voice is heard exclaiming : 'Neither the rulers nor the ruled understand high politics. They do not even know that there is such a branch of knowledge as political science; but between them they can coerce and enslave with the deadliest efficiency, even to the wiping out of civilization, because their education as slayers has been honestly and thoroughly carried out. Essentially the rulers are all defectives; and there is nothing worse than government by defectives who wield irresistible powers of physical coercion.'[11]

The scandal of these childish sports is, however, probably about to receive the attention of a more efficient principle of order than that of the irresponsible philosopher. Instead of the ineffective sporting 'fairness' of moral authority, there will be the justice of force. Let us suppose that that turns out worse than things have always been. At least the attempt is on novel lines, the old factors of failure are as far as possible eliminated. And at least the power engaged has shown from the start a sympathetic understanding of the adage, 'Boys will be boys!' which commutatively could be expressed, 'Animals will be animals!', which is more than can be said for the author whose views I have been discussing, who wishes that all the children would grow up, which is impossible. Animal life would never support the strain of his too ambitious programme.

NOTES

1 *Rude Assignment,* p. 202.
2 From *The Art of Being Ruled,* pp. 53–5, 59–62.
3 Bertrand Russell, *Icarus or the Future of Science.* London : Kegan Paul, Trench, Trubner & Co. Ltd., 1925, p. 13.
4 Ibid., pp. 61–2.
5 *The Art of Being Ruled,* pp. 50 and 52.
6 Bernard Shaw, 'Preface', *Back to Methuselah.* Harmondsworth, Middlesex : Penguin Books, 1971, p. 71.

71

7 Ibid., p. 43.
8 Ibid., p. 44.
9 Ibid., p. 9.
10 Ibid., pp. 42–3.
11 Ibid., p. 13.

IV

Novelists

1

Cervantes

(From *The Lion and the Fox*, 1927)

In the chapter from which the following excerpt is taken,[1] Lewis argues that Cervantes derived force and point from the same struggle as was depicted by Shakespeare—that 'between chivalry, "celtism", christian mysticism, on the one hand, and the "scientific spirit" of the renaissance mind and of the modern world on the other'.[2] Lewis adds that 'this preoccupation as manifested in Shakespeare could be styled the battle of the lion and the fox : the contest or the tragedy arising from the meeting of the *Simpleton* and the *Machiavel*, the Fool and the Knave.'[3] Lewis suggests that Cervantes, rather than satirizing Don Quixote, revered this Fool as embodying 'the chivalrous characteristics of bravery, simple-heartedness, generosity, good faith and exalted and romantic love'.[4]

Don Quixote advertises and perpetuates chivalry, does it not, far more than any *Amadis de Gaula* or the *Gesta* of the Cid? And Cervantes betrays a tenderness for this *hijo seco*, this mournful and stately child of his, in a wild and commonplace world, which cannot be missed, and which no burlesque can displace; and which is certainly not the handling of political satire. The millionaire monsters of roman satire, cheap and dull, swimming in a sewer of disfiguring luxury, are not on the same side of the battle as this penniless, sober, solemn gentleman, setting out on a haggard horse to relieve distress and uphold his empty dream.

For if Miguel Cervantes were *attacking* Don Quixote—the very statement of this unnatural event disposes of it—it would be the one lonely and conspicuous case of an attack by a great artist on the poor, the unfortunate, the mocked-at, insulted and despised. Which (applying the euclidean formula, and remembering our earlier axiom that 'Satire is always directed at the fortunate and successful') *is impossible.*

Therefore, if we had nothing else to guide us, we should know that Cervantes was identifying himself with Don Quixote, rather than with the world besetting his knight. It would be identifying all that he admired most with his hero, at the same time that he understood its melancholy destiny: the laughter and mockery that he stirred up around this noble fiction he knew that violence alone could silence, and that for its depravity and foolishness the bitterest laughter would be too light a thing. And in that violence he was not disposed to deal. The violence that stamped out periodically all the foolishness was the rage of a thing of the same flesh and blood as itself, fighting it on its own material ground with material weapons. The rage behind the satire of Juvenal or Persius would easily take the form of a murderous violence and eclipse in one suffocating blow the image of itself that it hated. But the poor lunatic gentleman of La Mancha—no real rage ever came near him, at most the impatient buffeting of things he mistook for something they were not (as Roland, when he went mad, charged flocks of sheep in place of the infidel): he is as remote from life as an image of the Buddha. He is one of the greatest productions of the western imagination: he is not a postulant but a complete initiate—but far more dissociated from his world than the high things of the asiatic imagination have been from theirs.

Taken as a satire, then, all the satire is concentrated not upon the palpable object of its activity, but just upon those assistants it conjures up to help it with its supposed victim. The stupid go-between, the half-hearted devotee, Sancho Panza, the faithful dog dazzled by something it cannot understand, its scepticism delivering constant assaults upon its infatuation, this fragment of the alien world sticking to the saint, is the focus for the satire in reality. The senseless turning of the windmills, even, is included in the mechanical personality of the homely and cunning spanish Hodge.

NOTES

1 From *The Lion and the Fox*, pp. 206–7.
2 Ibid., p. 201.
3 Ibid., pp. 201–2.
4 Ibid., p. 206.

The Russians

(From *Rude Assignment*, 1950)

This autobiographical chapter, called 'The Puritans of the Steppes',[1] was based on a radio talk given by Lewis on the BBC in March, 1947. A recording of the talk is kept at the British Institute of Recorded Sound, London. Although Lewis here suggests that 'on the surface, at least', the Russian influences on him had vanished in the Twenties, the intentions of his 1937 novel *The Revenge for Love* may be compared in some respects with those of Dostoevsky in *The Possessed*. And a later Lewis novel, *Self Condemned*, abounds in minor characters of Russian-like vitality, while its final chapter evokes the Diabolical dimension to a Dostoevskean degree. Lewis recalls that as a young man he was not interested in problems of good and evil; but the conflict between these principles, or at least between the Divine and the Diabolical, comes to dominate *The Human Age*, the most ambitious fictional work of his last years.

Asked to describe what influences were decisive in my life as a writer —indeed in the question addressed to me the somewhat alarming word *crisis* was used, what, I was asked, had constituted for me the crisis as a result of which I became what I am—I was at first at a loss to know what to say. It had to be a book, too, which raised a further obstacle : for no book I could think of had mastered my mind in the way required by the question.

There had been nothing violent about the birth of my mind. There was no dramatic and sudden enlightenment, but a long series of enlightening experiences—with the steady accretion of the technical means for the communication of the burden of experience. It seemed at first quite impossible to point to any one influence responsible for my development; though no doubt I could sort out the sources of enlightenment into weaker and stronger impressions.—However, for the purposes of the talk I had agreed to give it would be better if I could identify something that could be said, as an impression, to exceed all the others, and to have left a permanent mark.

So I went on a search, backwards into my young life, keeping my eyes open for the intellectual *coup de foudre*. For guidance I divided my activity into the creative and the critical : and since— as I believe I have already remarked—the critical with me grew out of the creative, it must be to the source of the latter that I must give especial attention.—And at last, stepping warily as I moved about in the misty youthful scene (everything before world war i has become almost an alien land) I came up against a solid mass of books—not *one* book, as I had thought I might—which supplied the answer. This was something that revolutionized my technique of approach to experience—that did not merely give me a great kick at the moment, and then quickly fade, as most things do.— The mass of books to which I have referred is the creative litera- ture of Russia. And when I took down some of these half-forgotten volumes—went again with Pierre in his incongruous white hat and green coat on to the field of Borodino, and with Raskolnikov lifted the axe to strike down the aged usurer—I very nearly had *another* crisis, hardened as I am now to such influences.

For the purposes of my broadcast the search was ended. I had no occasion to go any farther, and I started at once to write out what I proposed to say. But for anyone who has read *The Apes of God* or *Childermass*, it will be obvious that these influences however strong, were not the last : on the surface, at least, all trace of them had vanished in the twenties. But in my earliest essay in the writing of fiction, *Tarr*, it is another matter : and it is to that story this chapter and the next [of *Rude Assignment*] are devoted.

Dostoevsky, on the European continent, continues to exert a magical influence; as an instance of which I may cite the Swiss theologian, Barth, who acknowledges two main sources of inspira- tion, namely Dostoevsky and Kierkegaard. I have noted several in- stances, by the way, in which these two names have been bracketed in this manner. In England there has been a decline in sympathy with the Nineteenth Century Russian novelists, which partly is fashion, and in part to do with the long infatuation of British intellectuals for everything Russian of a much more recent date. This raised an ideologic barrier to enjoyment. But these great novelists of Tsarist days should not be looked upon as a sort of rival of the contemporary Russian. A careful reading of their books assists, on the contrary, to an understanding of the Russians of today. Stalin dancing upon the table at a victory banquet is a page from Gogol. The unexpectedly able Russian generals, beating off the Panzers, at Smolensk, or before the capital itself, one recognizes as one reads of Kutuzov at Borodino, more than a match for Bonaparte.

As a student in Paris, in French translations, I first read all these Russian books, and I lived for some time wholly in that Russian world—of *Poor Folk* : in the tragic family circle of the Karamazovs; with Verhovensky, Shigalev, and the nihilists; with Rudin, losing interest and departing when he saw the spell he had cast had collapsed; listening to the Kreutzer Sonata and noting the big hips of the lady's-man; or submissively assisting at all the exclamatory archness of those Varvaras and Natalies.

So my 'crisis'—if we wish to retain that over-forcible expression —was even more than a collection of books : it was a world. As I have described myself as doing, tracing my steps back, I was not suddenly stoped by a wall of books. Rather I passed imperceptibly into a warmer, richer, atmosphere—as crossing the Atlantic one enters the area of the Gulf Stream; I heard again the raucous voice of La Baboulenka crying : 'You do not know *what*? By heavens, are you *never* going to drop that roulette of yours? Are you going to whistle *all* your property away?'[2]

And I saw the ruined General wilt before the glare of his aged mother, borne aloft like a carnival figure in an arm-chair.

Paris was full of Russian students (this of course was before the Russian Revolution), who walked about in pairs, in tight black semi-military jackets. They conversed with no one—they were contemptuous of Western levity, stern and self-absorbed. It has been said that when Dostoevsky wrote *The Possessed* there were in Russia no Stavrogins or Verhovenskys, that they came much later and this was a divination of the future. In that case these characters, now become flesh and blood, were met by me every day on the Boulevards, and they decidedly looked the part.

These were the new Puritans, who were to dominate Europe : a generation with many points of resemblance with the black-coated sectaries who began to swarm in England in the first days of the Seventeenth Century and who subsequently transmitted their passionate disciplines to, and became the genius of, the North American continent, the 'New World'.

The world of imagination I inhabited at that time, however, was anything but puritan, taken as a whole. For this great volume of creation produced in the Nineteenth Century by a group of men over a space of fifty or sixty years there is no parallel since the Renaissance—to which the Tudor stage, of course, was the greatest English contribution. The impression conveyed is of a release on the grand scale of prodigal energies.

All the writers, it seems to me, responsible for this new world of the spirit are of the same half-Western, half-Eastern, ethos; which, among other things, gives them a peculiar value—like everything about Russia. They must, in consequence, for the Western European, remain a great universalizing influence. And all the Russians, Tolstoy almost as much as Dostoevsky, were conscious of their curious relationship to the West—of it, and yet not of it : conscious also of something like a mission with regard to it, namely as the purveyors of sincerity to the over-institutionalized European. We find this missionary spirit, itself institutionalized, its ethical passion dimmed in the process, in the contemporary Russian.

A cultural see-saw, of westernizing and anti-westernizing, proceeded among the intellectual leaders : but to hold themselves apart from the West—a little contemptuously apart—was by far the more popular attitude.—From *The Gambler* and elsewhere in the pages of Dostoevsky a very shrewd analysis of the Western European could be compiled. There is for instance the Junker : 'He had legs which seemed to begin almost at his chest—or rather, at his chin ! Yet, for all his air of peacock-like conceit . . . his face wore a sheepish air'.[3] Then there is the Frenchman : 'He was a true Frenchman in so far as, though he could be lively and engaging when it suited him, he became insufferably dull and wearisome as soon as ever the need for being lively and engaging had passed. Seldom is a Frenchman naturally civil : he is civil only as to order and of set purpose. Also, if he thinks it incumbent upon him to be fanciful and original, his fancy always assumes a foolish, unnatural vein, compounded of trite, hackneyed forms. In short, the natural Frenchman is a conglomeration of commonplace, petty, everyday positive-ness.'[4]—No more today than yesterday, I think, do we appreciate how genuine sincerity can take even a self-righteous form, and how insincere and untrustworthy, in many respects, the West must seem to these Puritans of the Steppes, whose lineaments already are visible in the dramatis personæ of the Nineteenth Century Russian classics. When, however, self-righteousness grows so extreme that it violently liquidates all whom it regards as sinful, it is natural it should awaken hatred and alarm.

A great deal of what I read as a student I either did not under-stand, or took no interest in. I knew, for instance, what I was wit-nessing everywhere in Dostoevsky; namely the almost muscular struggle of the human will to repulse evil and cleave to the good— or to embrace evil with a convulsive violence, and then to repent, with more convulsions. It was the unrelievedly gloomy epic of spiritual freedom—which the further you went, got to look more and more like predestination.—But in the first place I was not my-self of a gloomy temperament : also since I was not interested in problems of good and evil, I did not read these books so much as sinister homilies as monstrous character patterns, often of miraculous insight.

I am inclined, I find, to attribute to myself less understanding, when I first read all these books, than I in fact had. But what is quite certain is that the politics in Dostoevsky—almost as distinctive a feature of his work as the mysticism, and, I now am of the opinion, far too much influenced by it—these very unusual politics were entirely lost upon me at that time. Three years ago I read again *The Possessed*. There were all the names and scenes, just as in the past, when first I read it. But it was a very different book. Evidently as a student I had read it somewhat as a child reads *Through the Looking Glass*. That is the only possible explana-tion.

Dostoevsky was an arch counter-revolutionary, and it is not only in *The Possessed*—which is the highwater-mark, almost a counter-revolutionary tract—that this passionate reaction is to be found. But when in his letters one reads that he thought of postponing a journey owing to the news, which had greatly upset him, of the death of the Tsar's aunt, that makes one feel that when he refers to himself in his diary as a 'conservative', in this one particular he was right. Yet what an extraordinary work *The Possessed* is! Stavrogin, Tihon, Verhovensky, Shatov—what a prodigious company.

Allowing for a great deal that was unintelligible, the impact of such books was due to much more than their vitality. Perhaps Ivan Karamazov supplies the correct answer, where he is speaking of the young men who sat drinking and talking in the corners of the Russian taverns. 'They've never met before, and when they go out of here they won't see each other again for the next forty years. But what do they talk about for the moment that they're here? Nothing but universal problems: Is there a God? Does the immortal soul exist? Those who don't believe in God discuss socialism and anarchism, and the reorganization of mankind on a new pattern; which are the same questions, only tackled from the other way up.'[5]

That was what 'Russian boys' had their minds filled with apparently, and what these books showed them ardently discussing in taverns as they drank, as if the fate of the universe hung upon their words. Well, what do young Englishmen discuss under similar circumstances? Probably 'the Dogs', or football. What do young Frenchmen discuss? Undoubtedly women, and their smartness in handling same.—So it was in everything. Here was a more serious world altogether, thought I. Then what consummate realists these people were!—with their slovenly old gentlemen with a great reputation for sanctity—the 'saintly fools' of the monasteries, with their embarrassed 'bashful' smiles, smelling slightly of vodka; the police commissioners who behaved like a Marx Brother; Napoleon Bonaparte persuaded that he was directing a battle, while in fact everyone had forgotten his existence and fought it in their own way: the Chagall-like figures skimming along the surface of the water in pursuit of the river-steamer; or the celebrated cloak of Gogol, or his walking Nose.

I too 'came out of that mantle of Gogol': a lot of things have happened to me since, but there was a time when I did not follow my own nose, but *his*. Paris for me is partly the creation of these books. I now realize that if I had not had Tchekov in my pocket I should not have enjoyed my Dubonnet at the 'Lilas' so much or the beautiful dusty trees and beyond them the Bal Bullier. It was really as a character in Tolstoy—I remember now—that I visited a *bal musette.* And the hero of the first novel I wrote reminded a very perceptive critic of Stavrogin.

In view of all this I think we may really say that the first time, moving down the rue des Ecoles, I arrived at my particular book-shop, opposite the 'Montague', to find a book by Faguet, and took away *Tales from the Underworld* as well, *crisis* was at hand.

NOTES

1 From *Rude Assignment*, pp. 144–7.
2 This passage appears in a different translation in Fyodor Dostoevsky, *The Gambler and Other Stories*. Translated by Constance Garnett. London: Heinemann & Zolnay Ltd., 1949 impression, p. 56.
3 Cf. Ibid., p. 32.
4 Cf. Ibid., p. 38–9.
5 Cf. Dostoevsky, *The Brothers Karamazov*. Garnett translation. London: Heinemann, 1968 reprint, p. 239.

3

Russian Novelists and Trollope

(From ' "Detachment" and the Fictionist', 1934)

The essay of which this except forms a part[1] deals with, among other subjects, the literary atmosphere of the Thirties—'so bitterly "in earnest" and so impatient of anything that looks at all like an ivory tower'. Lewis emphasizes here the contrast between Victorian fiction and the sombre high-seriousness of Russian literature in the nineteenth century. After 1914, he added, English fiction underwent a transformation. 'I do not mean, of course, to say that the English Public have arrived at the unquiet and piercing vision of the slavonic mind, which, partly Asiatic, is prone to feel that nothing can be separated from anything else. . . . But they have moved very appreciably away from the light-hearted pigeon-holing of their grandfathers.'[2]

––––––––––

Consider the great Russian novelists of the nineteenth century. They were very political animals, indeed. The great English novelists of the same century were in comparison mere animals *tout court*, or else blandly genteel. The reason for this difference is to be sought, I think, in the different attitude to art existing in the respective publics of Russia and England. A Mr. Micawber, a man languishing in the Marshalsea, was the father of Dickens—a Dostoevsky-like figure, certainly; but the spiritual father of Dostoevsky was Fyodor Karamazov, a very different kettle of fish.

For the Englishman of tradition, taking his cue from a fox-hunting aristocracy ('for thinking they have no great turn', in the words of Matthew Arnold, these territorial masters of 'the unphilosophic race', as they contemptuously were described by Nietzsche) for the average Englishman art has been *a sport*. So has politics, of course—a sort of eternal boxing-match, under Queensberry Rules, between

84

a Tory and a Whig; and, outside the political prize-ring—where the most 'hotly-contested' bout always must terminate in a hearty handshake, Mr. Left and Mr. Right have always been the best of friends. But politics is one sort of sport, art is another sort of sport. For an 'artist-fellow' therefore like Tolstoy or Dostoevsky, to marry politics into art would be an impropriety—a hybrid must result; a piece of *Tory fiction*, or a piece of *Whig fiction*, would have been, to the traditional John Bull, an abomination—if you like a similar order of joke as 'A Radical Tennis-player', or 'A Seventh Day Adventist Bisley Marksman', or 'A Baptist Rowing Blue'.

The great Russian novelists of the nineteenth century prepared the way for the Soviet Revolution. The great English novelists of the same century—whether this is to their credit or no, is not the question at this stage—could have been held no more responsible for a barricade, had such a thing made its appearance, than for an Ice Age, had such a phenomenon occurred. For Thackeray, a nostalgic *pasticheur*, the French Revolution was abolished—in 1850 he was back in the days of *The Bee* and *The Rambler*. The politics of Trollope were the ecclesiastical disturbances of a sleepy county-capital, no more; the 'high' and the 'low' churchmen were his white guards and his red guards. And the politics of Conrad, the last of that line, were the politics of the clipper and confined to the grouses of 'the greaser' or the supercargo; his economics were those of Daniel Defoe. That takes up to 1914.

But before proceeding I had better meet a possible objection, for I suppose that Trollope may be regarded by some people as a peculiarly political writer. There is his *Phineas Finn*, for instance; that is ostensibly a political book. But it was not political in the sense intended here. *Phineas Finn* is all about the House of Commons, certainly, and the lives of Cabinet Ministers and M.P.'s whereas *The Brothers Karamazov*, to turn to a famous Russian novel, is all about a murder in a Russian country house; it is not ostensibly about politics at all. Yet *The Brothers Karamazov* is far more political, in the most vital sense, than is *Phineas Finn*.

Phineas Finn was written rather to introduce the political world of London, as a possible narrative subject-matter, into the English novel, than to stage a political issue in a book of fiction; and Trollope worked very hard on his local colour, going to the House of

Commons every day for several months to get the correct 'atmosphere' for this experiment. The 'Radicalism' talked in Lady Laura Kennedy's drawing-room, by 'that most inveterate politician, Lady Glencora',[3] and the rest, is the *same* Radicalism that we have all heard in the London drawing-rooms of a so much later day; a genteel self-advertisement, indulged in by sheltered and wealthy people, desirous of contriving a little identity for themselves, and of sending a shudder down some country flunkey's back—and down their own as well, of course.

These salon reds, of high degree, are well observed, for Trollope had an excellent pair of eyes in his head; but (to his credit or not) he was so little of a politician, this reporter of parts, and so much the professional romancer, that he supplies us with a good photograph, not a living artistic organism. The letter of Mr. Joshua Monk, certainly, is an excellent statement of the theory of English democracy; the M.P.'s should not be 'the best possible 658 Members of Parliament'—that is 'a most repulsive idea', indeed, for the true democrat! thinks Mr. Joshua Monk.[4] No, they should be like a faithful portrait gallery: 'As a portrait should be like the person portrayed, so should a representative House be like the people whom it represents.'[5] But there are some, Mr. Monk tells Phineas in his letter, who do not at all understand the principle of *representation*; who 'declare to themselves that this wicked, half-barbarous, idle people should be *controlled* and not *represented*.[6] And when the simple Phineas shows Mr. Monk's letter to his friends, Mr. and Mrs. Low, the latter exclaims: 'It's what I call downright Radical nonsense. . . . Portrait indeed! Why should we want a *portrait* of ignorance and ugliness?'[7] Mrs. Low's rejoinder to the argument in the letter of Mr. Monk is based upon the type of reasoning of those hostile to democratic institutions, to be met with upon all sides today. And it is evident that Trollope had pondered a little upon all these matters. But *Phineas Finn* is not a political book, in anything but subject-matter, for all that; it is in the main an entertainment novel, packed with the stilted sex-interest of the time, and, as for politics, must be regarded as the daring experiment of a professional purveyor of entertainment (of a high order) intended to put across that super-novelty, *the political hero*, of all ungodly things! So he explains it, indeed, more or less, in his autobiography.

NOTES

1 Lewis, ' "Detachment" and the Fictionist', *The English Review*, October, December, 1934. This excerpt comes from the October number, pp. **448–51.**
2 Ibid., pp. 451–2.
3 Anthony Trollope, *Phineas Finn: The Irish Member*. London: Panther Books Ltd., 1973, p. 320.
4 Ibid.
5 Ibid., p. 303.
6 Ibid., p. 304. Italics L.'s.
7 Ibid., p. 305. Italics L.'s.

Henry James

(From *Men Without Art*, 1934)

The following[1] may be viewed as a continuation of Lewis's advocacy of the external method (see p. 35 of this volume) and an attempt to explain why Henry James came to represent the opposite approach to writing. Lewis here places great stress on the 'visual medium' in which the young James was brought up—America as 'a sort of desert', topographically and otherwise. As Lewis wrote in the course of his commentary on James in *Men Without Art* : 'The frequently remarked "asceticism" of the American, which we usually attribute to the shadow of the old conventicles of the early Puritan settler, is much more the immediate result of living in a desert—for even *within* the towns, or for that matter cities, there has, of necessity, always been an absence of the urbanity to which the European is accustomed : a breathless business hustle has left no room for its development' (p. 150).

———————

To be 'dogmatically for the great *Without*'—to set up the Shell as your shield, against the Dark Within, in a *parti-pris* for the rigours of the sun—in favour of its *public* values, in contrast to the *private* values of the half-lighted places of the mind—to evince more interest in the actor, and in action, than about the daydreams of a dilettante scene-shifter, or the brutal trances of the mob; all this must forever compromise you with the either disguised or overt doctrinaires of a disembodied, a non-corporeal, artistic expression. You have in the most unmistakable way come down upon the side of what is material, if you have accepted in the main my contentions—over against those people who prefer the mind's eye, as an instrument, to the eye upon the outside of their head. The mind's eye I refer to is that organ which looks out equally upon the past and present, but perceives the actual scene a little dimly, at the best *peeps* out upon the contemporary scene: it is the *time-eye*, as it might be called, the eye of Proust.

Proust is the archetype of the internal traveller. Walter Pater and Marcel Proust are patently of kindred intelligence. Joyce is far more robust and spacious, at his best. But James is, for us, in the field of investigation here being opened up, more important than either. For 'æstheticism', though in truth rampant and ubiquitous, is on all hands violently disowned: and although the manner of Pater is today constantly imitated, on the sly, and his teaching absorbed along with his style, he is scarcely *respectable*, in the intellectual sense. But there is nothing against James. He has played, in the Anglo-Saxon world, much the part monopolized by Flaubert upon the continent—though, in detail, with all the difference that there is between the robust culture of the French and the rather anæmic and uneasy culture of the modern Anglo-Saxon. [. . . .]

But as a creative artist he was led into the field of his predilection, which was a twilight feminine universe—of little direct action, and of no gross substance at all. Yet how much better had he relieved this mass of finicks with even an occasional *direct* gesture or an explosion of some sort (not necessarily too elemental) to dispel the stuffiness. And then the rather ponderous phantoms of his ratiocination might quite often, with advantage, have been taken out for an airing: and there is not one of them that would not have been a more compelling personage if approached from that end—the externalist end.

That James was technically capable of this who can doubt, for he had an excellent eye in his head, when he consented to use it. But as a matter of fact James did not leave North America quite soon enough: he was twenty-seven years old before he finally passed over into Europe. And for the over-delicate mind of the New Englander this meant that all his senses were confirmed in the abstractness which is such a feature of the North American continent.

One of the facts of which the 'visual' intelligence is peculiarly aware is the importance of the geographic background—the *visual medium*, as it were, in which men exist. This factor is for us of critical moment. But today it is a commonplace that our European urban life is being 'Americanized'. It is impossible, on the other hand, to 'Americanize' our countryside, short of making it into a

89

desert. Still the 'Americanization', with a difference, is there. So I think we may decide with advantage, at this point, to hold up our argument, in order to obtain a clearer notion of what 'America' implies. For the romantically selected backgrounds of the Hollywood films does not supply the analytic picture we require. [. . . .]

Undeniably, the 'American scene' is of the utmost barrenness, physically and socially. It is planted in the midst of a relative wilderness, beneath a surprisingly hard and penetrating light. The American is still the white settler, except for the dense swarms in the great cities, and he has not been able to furnish, except in a sketchy fashion, his slice of the great New Land. It remains very empty looking: there are no nuances on the North American continent. But equally—until, I imagine, you get to the frontiers of Latin America, that is Mexico—the hardness and the crudity is not inspiring, in the way that the barrenness of northern Africa certainly is, or the centre of Spain. The actual physical landscape has something of a Swiss frigidity and emptiness.

'Boston! And, beyond Boston, that great unendowed, unfurnished, unentertained, and unentertaining continent where one sniffed as it were the very earth of one's foundations! "I shall freeze after this sun," said Albrecht Dürer, as he turned homeward across the Alps from Italy. And where was James to turn for warmth, he whose every fibre longed for that other gracious world, that soft, harmonious, picturesque "Europe" of his imagination, that paradise of form, color, style. . . ?"² This is from the pages of Mr. Van Wyck Brooks' *Pilgrimage of Henry James*, a good account of his life and work, told as far as possible in his own words, or, if not that, his jargon. In this account, in James's account, of the 'American Scene', always the two elements are mingled, the physical and the mental elements. The 'return of the native' was like a return into a Sahara. 'One felt like a traveller in the desert, deprived of water and subject to the terrible mirage, the torment of illusion, of the thirst-fever. . . . And then this emptiness, this implacable emptiness: not a shadow, nothing but the glare of a commonplace prosperity.'³ As to the city streets—'how deficient somehow in weight, volume, and resonance were the souls one discerned in these hurrying passers-by!'⁴ This emptiness, this implacable emptiness! It is the sense of that that I have been attempting to convey.

But I will insist no more: I have said enough to indicate the background, and James's attitude to that background: and a visit to North America today would be found by any European to confirm to some extent this account by James of the waste places of his birth. Of course, in the year 1934, there are few Americans of the type of Henry James in existence—they are as rare as the Redskin! The new United States will be a very different affair. But it will still be desertic. [. . . .]

No one, of the last hundred years, writing in English, is more worthy of serious consideration than Henry James. But from a cause as concrete—and regrettable—as a serious and crippling accident in boyhood would have been, his activities were all turned *inwards* instead of *outwards*. That is the point that I would make. He was, by force of circumstances, led to conceive of art as a disembodied statement of abstract values, rather than as a sensuous interpretation of values, participating in a surface life. 'America, to James, signified failure and destruction. *It was the dark country, the sinister country, where the earth was a quicksand . . . where men were turned into machines . . .* The American artist, in the American air, was a doomed man: pitfalls surrounded him on every side.'[5]

And he early acquired the habit of living underground, and this habit he took with him from the 'American Scene' into the 'European Scene'. As a pattern of life for the artist this is scarcely to be universally recommended. Is it not in fact the best way to extinguish the artistic impulse altogether, if taken to its bitter and barren, logical conclusion? Admiration for the finest of such achievements should not blind us critically to that pretty obvious fact.

As a contemporary illustration to all this, imagine Mr. T. S. Eliot's horror, just as he was doubtless congratulating himself upon his timely escape from that 'dark country', that 'sinister country', that country 'where the earth is a quicksand', and his timely establishment in a land that is still fairly 'well-furnished', where every blade of grass possesses an historic identity—in pre-war Britain in fine, to behold all this orderly little cosmos turning into ashes beneath hs feet, at the blast of war, and then progressively assuming more and more, socially, the dread physiognomy of the desert from which he was in flight!—We do not, indeed, have to look very far for the origin of *The Waste Land*.

Before leaving this subject let me quote the father of Henry James, a very interesting man indeed, who fully realized the dangers besetting the future novelist (there was of course no danger for the philosopher—North America is an admirable place for a philosopher). In 1849 he wrote to Emerson as follows (I take this from the same excellent book by Mr. Van Wyck Brooks):

'Considering with much pity our four stout boys, who have no playroom within doors and import shocking bad manners from the street, we gravely ponder whether it wouldn't be better to go abroad for a few years with them, allowing them to absorb French and German, and get such a sensuous education as they cannot get here.'[6]

That 'sensuous education' which formerly Europe could be depended upon to supply is assuming more tenuous proportions every day. But where that sensuous education is lacking entirely, it must be very difficult to make good the loss. And later a hatred, or at all events a distrust, of 'the sensuous' is liable to develop. A great talent can make a powerful if eccentric something out of this vacuum. But it is not an influence likely to promote the general health of the arts, and the pagan robustness most suitable for artistic production. [....]

[Henry James] was the modern Anglo-Saxon *par excellence*—a moralist, an 'introvert'; although himself a large bull-like person, a man of timid mind; chary of embarking without a thousand precautions amid the menacing objects of the external world, as introduced, gingerly, into his world of art; as frightened to commit himself as the most cautious peasant; a social-snob, that is a believer in mob-values; a beauty-doctor in words—hence his style of an elaborate German *friseur,* which was an elephantine attempt at being verbally seductive—for he actually believed it to be 'beautiful'; and withal, of course, *the best* of his order, a *petit maître* on a portentous scale.

NOTES

1   *Men Without Art*, pp. 145, 149–52, 153–4, 231.
2   Van Wyck Brooks, *The Pilgrimage of Henry James*. New York: E. P. Dutton & Co., 1925, p. 36.
3   Ibid., p. 37.
4   Ibid.
5   Ibid., p. 29. Italics L.'s.
6   Ibid., p. 1.

Virginia Woolf

(From *Men Without Art,* 1934)

The following[1] comes from a Lewis chapter which caused Virginia Woolf the most intense foreboding.[2] Stephen Spender defended her in a *Spectator* review on October 19, 1934, accusing Lewis of a malicious attack on Mrs. Woolf. In a counter-attack, Lewis conceded that Mrs. Woolf was 'charming, scholarly, intelligent, everything that you will : but here we *have* not a Jane Austen.' And he added that his book's remark about having 'taken the cow by the horns' (p. 97 here) referred not to Mrs. Woolf but to 'the Feminine Principle'.[3] Mrs. Woolf is treated unfavourably, by implication, in the lampooning of 'Mrs. Rhoda Hyman', the fictional monarch of literary London in *The Roaring Queen* (1936). As a leading light of the Bloomsbury group, a circle accused by Lewis of being a malefic, ambitious and jealous cabal exercising a destructive influence on English intellectual life, Mrs. Woolf would inevitably have been an Enemy target. In an unpublished attack on the Bloomsbury group, written about 1934, Lewis noted how 'they played at being "geniuses" with each other. But it was a tremuously exciting impersonation : for the "Genius" aimed at was the heavily-sentimental and perfectly silly valuation proper to the mid-victorian child-mind. . . . There survives the quite unreal veneration . . . for the quite second-rate, although pleasant and delicate, literary output of Mrs. Woolf, the original female counterpart of the *Führer* Lytton [Strachey].'[4] In *Men Without Art,* Lewis seized on a quotation from Mrs. Woolf's literary parable, *Mr. Bennett and Mrs. Brown* : 'We must reconcile ourselves to a season of failures and fragments. We must reflect that where so much strength is spent on finding a way of telling the truth, the truth itself is bound to reach us in rather an exhausted and chaotic condition.' Mrs. Woolf also suggested that the figures of Ulysses, Queen Victoria and Mr. Prufrock in modern literature were thus 'a little pale and dishevelled'.[5]

But let us at once repudiate, as false and artificial, this account of the contemporary situation in the 'Mrs. Brown' fable. Joyce's *Ulysses* may be 'a disaster'—a failure—as Mrs. Woolf calls it in her Plain Reader. But it is not a fragment. It is, of its kind, somewhat more robustly 'complete' than most of the classical examples of the novel, in our tongue certainly. It is not the half-work in short, 'pale' and 'dishevelled', of a crippled interregnum. Nor is there anything *half-there* about D. H. Lawrence's books. Far from being 'pale', they are much too much the reverse.

If you ask : Do you mean then there is nothing in this view at all, of ours being a period of *Sturm und Drang*, in which new methods are being tried out, and in which the artistic production is in consequence tentative? I reply : There is nothing new in the idea at all, if you mean that the present time differs from any other in being experimental and in seeking new forms : or if you seek to use that argument to account for mediocrity, or smallness of output, or any of the other individual 'failures' that occur as a result of the natural inequality of men, and the certain precariousness of the creative instinct—subject, in the case of those over-susceptible to nervous shock, to intermittency of output, and, in extreme cases, to extinction.

Then why, you may enquire, is it an opinion that is so widely held?—Because—I again make answer—the people who have been most influential in literary criticism, for a number of years now, have been interested in the propagation of this account of things—just as the orthodox economists have, consciously or not, from interested motives, maintained in its place the traditional picture—that of superhuman *difficulty*—of some *absolute* obstructing the free circulation of the good things of life.

Those most influential in the literary world, as far as the 'highbrow' side of the racket was concerned, have mostly been minor personalities, who were impelled to arrange a sort of bogus 'time' to take the place of the real 'time'—to bring into being an imaginary 'time', small enough and 'pale' enough to accommodate their not very robust talents. That has, consistently, been the so-called 'Bloomsbury' technique, both in the field of writing and of painting, as I think is now becoming generally recognized. And, needless to say, it has been very much to the disadvantage of any vigorous manifestation in the arts; for anything above the *salon* scale is what

94

this sort of person most dislikes and is at some pains to stifle. And also, necessarily, it brings into being a quite false picture of the true aspect of our scene.

So we have been invited, all of us, to instal ourselves in a very dim Venusberg indeed: but Venus has become an introverted matriarch, brooding over a subterraneous 'stream of consciousness' —a feminine phenomenon after all—and we are a pretty sorry set of knights too, it must be confessed,—at least in Mrs. Woolf's particular version of the affair.

> *I saw pale kings, and princes too,*
> *Pale warriors, death-pale were they all . . .*

It is a myopic humanity, that threads its way in and out of this 'unreal city', whose objective obstacles are in theory unsubstantial, but in practice require a delicate negotiation. In our local exponents of this method there is none of the realistic vigour of Mr. Joyce, though often the incidents in the local 'masterpieces' are exact and puerile copies of the scenes in his Dublin drama (cf. the Viceroy's progress through Dublin in *Ulysses* with the Queen's progress through London in *Mrs. Dalloway*—the latter is a sort of undergraduate imitation of the former, winding up with a smoke-writing in the sky, a pathetic 'crib' of the firework display and the rocket that is the culmination of Mr. Bloom's beach-ecstasy). But to appreciate the sort of fashionable dimness to which I am referring, let us turn for a moment to Mrs. Woolf, where she is apeeping in the half-light.

'She had reached the park gates. She stood for a moment, looking at the omnibuses in Piccadilly.' She should really have written *peeping* at the omnibuses in Piccadilly!—for 'she would not say of anyone in the world now that they were this or were that. She felt very young; at the same time unspeakably aged. She sliced like a knife through everything; at the same time was outside, looking on. She had a perpetual sense, as she watched the taxicabs, of being out, out, far out to sea and alone; she always had the feeling that it was very, very dangerous to live even one day.' To live *outside*, of course that means. Outside it is terribly *dangerous*—in that great and coarse Without, where all the he-men and he-girls 'livedangerously' with a brutal insensibility to all the *risks* that they run, forever in the public places. But this *dangerousness* does, after all, make it all very *thrilling*, when peeped-out at, from the security of the private mind : 'and yet to her it was absolutely absorbing; all this; the cabs passing.'[6]

Those are the half-lighted places of the mind—in which, quivering with a timid excitement, this sort of intelligence shrinks, thrilled to the marrow, at all the wild goings-on ! A little old-maidish, are the Prousts and sub-Prousts I think. And when two old maids—or a company of old maids—shrink and cluster together, they titter in each other's ears and delicately tee-hee, pointing out to each other the red-blood antics of this or that upstanding figure, treading the perilous Without. That was that manner in which the late Lytton Strachey lived—peeping more into the past than into the present, it is true, and it is that of most of those associated with him. And—minus the shrinking and tittering, and with a commendable habit of standing, half-concealed, but alone—it was the way of life of Marcel Proust.

But it has also, in one degree or another, been the way of life of many a recent figure in our literature—as in the case of Marius the Epicurean, 'made easy by his natural Epicureanism . . . prompting him to conceive of himself as but the passive spectator of the world around him.'[7] Some, not content with retreating into the ambulatories of their inner consciousness, will instal there a sort of private oratory. From this fate 'the fleshly school' of the last century was saved, not much to its credit certainly, by the pagan impulses which still lingered in Europe. And it became ultimately the 'art-for-art's-sake' cult of the Naughty Nineties. Walter Pater was, of course, the fountain-head of that cult. And he shows us his hero, Marius—escaping from that particular trap, waiting upon the introverted—in the following passage :

> At this time, by his poetic and inward temper, he might have fallen a prey to the enervating mysticism, then in wait for ardent souls in many a melodramatic revival of old religion or theosophy. From all this, fascinating as it might actually be to one side of his character, he was kept by a genuine virility there, effective in him, among other results, as a hatred of what was theatrical, and the instinctive recognition that in vigorous intelligence, after all, divinity was most likely to be found a resident.[8]

That is, from the horse's mouth, the rationale of the non-religious, untheosophic, pleasure-cult, of which—in that ninetyish pocket at

96

the end of the nineteenth century, in full, more than Stracheyish, reaction against Victorian manners—Oscar Wilde was the high-priest. And there is, of course, a very much closer connection than people suppose between the æsthetic movement presided over by Oscar Wilde, and that presided over in the first post-war decade by Mrs. Woolf and Miss Sitwell. (Miss Sitwell has recently been rather overshadowed by Mrs. Woolf, but she once played an equally important part—if it can be called important—in these events.)[9] It has been with considerable shaking in my shoes, and a feeling of treading upon a carpet of eggs, that I have taken the cow by the horns in this chapter, and broached the subject of the part that the feminine mind has played—and minds as well, deeply feminized, not technically on the distaff side—in the erection of our present criteria. For fifteen years I have subsisted in this to me suffocating atmosphere. I have felt very much a fish out of water, very alien to all the standards that I saw being built up around me. I have defended myself as best I could against the influences of what I felt to be a tyrannical inverted orthodoxy-in-the-making. With the minimum of duplicity I have held my own: I have constantly assailed the swarms of infatuated builders. So, having found myself in a peculiarly isolated position, I had begun to take for granted that these habits of mind had come to stay, in those about me, and that I must get used to the life of the outlaw, for there was nothing else to do. But it seems that I was perhaps mistaken. There is, to judge from all the signs, a good chance that a reversal of these values—the values of decay—is at hand.

NOTES

1 From *Men Without Art*, pp. 167–71.
2 See Virginia Woolf, *A Writer's Diary*. London: The Hogarth Press, 1953, pp. 228–9.
3 W. K. Rose, ed., *The Letters of Wyndham Lewis*. London: Methuen, 1963, pp. 224–5.
4 Lewis, 'Say It With Leaves' (or 'The Bloomsburies'), a typescript in the Lewis collection, Cornell University, pp. 21–2.
5 Woolf, *Collected Essays*, Vol. I. London: The Hogarth Press, 1966, pp. 335–6.
6 Woolf, *Mrs. Dalloway*. London: The Hogarth Press, 1968, pp. 10–11.
7 Walter Pater, *Marius the Epicurean*. London: Jonathan Cape, 1931, p. 102.

8   Ibid.
9   In the same year, L. blasted Miss Sitwell's book, *Aspects of Modern Poetry.*
    He wrote in a review of the book that it 'will remain a collector's piece I
    fear—for those interested in the history of publicity. . . . The patter is
    frankly poor, the jests are very "old favourites" indeed : and with so much
    wild stuff hurtling about in the air, there is, it must be confessed, a certain
    danger for the public—or there would be if there *were* a public.' (Lewis,
    'Sitwell Circus', *Time and Tide* November 17, 1934.)

6

James Joyce

(From *Time and Western Man*, 1927)

Lewis first met Joyce in 1920 and the two enjoyed some excellent nocturnal outings together in Paris during subsequent months. In a 1922 letter to Joyce, Lewis described himself as 'your devoted friend'[1] and intellectual admiration for the Irish writer is obvious in the series of superb pencil drawings of him done by Lewis in that period. Lewis also joined in a protest against an American pirating of *Ulysses*. When Lewis's 1927 attack on Joyce appeared, from which the following section is excerpted,[2] Joyce was stung, though he acknowledged later that it was by far the best hostile criticism published about his work. He added, however: 'Allowing that the whole of what Lewis says about my book is true, is it more than 10 per cent of the truth?'[3] By 1928, his official reply to Lewis was appearing as part of his serialized *Work in Progress*, notably its fable of the 'Ondt and the Gracehoper'. Thus the final work, *Finnegans Wake*, contains numerous parodies of the Lewis message and manner as exhibited in the book Joyce chose to call *Spice and Westend Woman*. Lewis, in turn, parodied Joyce, in *The Childermass* (1928), having much verbal fun at the expense of 'Joys of Jingles'. But argument over the *Time and Western Man* attack erupted again when a book on Joyce by Professor Harry Levin accused Lewis of malice towards the Irishman's work.[4] Lewis's indignant response to this appears in *Rude Assignment*, where he also enlarges, by way of a personal recollection, on his 1927 assault against the 'chaotic mosaic' of *Ulysses*. He and Joyce were discussing the heavily encumbered façade of Rouen cathedral: 'I had said I did not like it, rather as Indian or Indonesian sacred buildings are a fussy multiplication of accents, demonstrating a belief in the virtue of *quantity*, I said. All such quantitative expression I have at all times found boring, I pointed out. I continued to talk against Gothic altogether, and its "scholasticism in stone" : the dissolving of the solid shell—the spatial intemperance, the nervous multiplication of detail. Joyce listened and then remarked that he, on the contrary, liked this multiplication of detail, adding that he himself, as a matter of fact, in words, did something of that sort.'[5]

———————

[. . . .] To start with, Joyce is not a homologue of Swift. That is a strange mistake. There is very little of the specific power of that terrible personage, that *terribilità*, in the amiable author of *Ulysses*. Another writer with whom he has been compared, and whom he is peculiarly unlike, is Flaubert. But to mention all the authors with whom Joyce has been matched would take an appreciable time. So I will rather attempt to find his true affinities. The choice would lie, to my mind, somewhere between Robert Louis Stevenson and Laurence Sterne, if you imagine those writers transplanted into a heavily-freudianized milieu, and subjected to all the influences resulting in the rich, confused ferment of *Ulysses*.

Contact with any of his writing must, to begin with, show that we are not in the presence of a tragic writer, of the description of Dostoevsky or of Flaubert. He is genial and comic; a humorous writer of the traditional English School—in temper, at his best, very like Sterne. But he has the technical itch of the 'sedulous ape'—the figure under which Stevenson (with peculiar modesty, it is true) revealed himself to his readers. The impression produced by his earlier books, merely as writing, is very like that of a page of Stevenson—not of Stevenson 'apeing', but of the finished, a little too finished, article.

Ulysses, on the technical side, is an immense exercise in style, an orgy of 'apeishness', decidedly 'sedulous'. It is an encyclopaedia of english literary technique, as well as a general-knowledge paper. The schoolmaster in Joyce is in great evidence throughout its pages. [. . . .]

Mr. Joyce is by no means without the 'personal touch'. But in a sense he is not the 'personality' that Shaw or Yeats is, or that Wilde was. But that is in conformity with his rôle, which is a very different one from theirs. Joyce is the poet of the shabby-genteel, impoverished intellectualism of Dublin. His world is the small middle-class one, decorated with a little futile 'culture', of the supper and dance-party in 'The Dead'. Wilde, more brilliantly situated, was an extremely metropolitan personage, a man of the great social world, a great lion of the London drawing-room. Joyce is steeped in the sadness and the shabbiness of the pathetic gentility of the upper shopkeeping class, slumbering at the bottom of a neglected province; never far, in its snobbishly circumscribed despair, from the pawn-shop and the 'pub'. [. . . .]

It is at this point that we reach one of the fundamental questions of value brought out by his work. Although entertaining the most studied contempt for his compatriots—individually and in the mass —whom he did not regard at all as exceptionally brilliant and sympathetic creatures (in a green historical costume, with a fairy hovering near), but as average human cattle with an irish accent instead of a scotch or welsh, it will yet be insisted on that his irishness is an important feature of his talent; and he certainly also does exploit his irishness and theirs. [. . . .]

The romantic persons who go picking about in the Arran Islands, Shetlands, the Basque Provinces, or elsewhere, for genuine human 'antiques', are today on a wild-goose chase; because the sphinx of the Past, in the person of some elder dug out of such remote neighbourhoods, will at length, when he has found his tongue, probably commence addressing them in the vernacular of the *Daily Mail*. For better or for worse, local colour is now a thin mixture; it does not inhere in what it embellishes, but is painted on, often with a clumsy insolence. It suits the political intelligence with its immemorial device, *divide et impera*, to encourage it, but its application to the conditions of mind and to the external nature of the machine-age becomes more and more fantastic.

There is nothing for it today, if you have an appetite for the beautiful, but *to create new beauty*. You can no longer nourish yourself upon the Past; its stock is exhausted, the Past is nowhere a reality. The only place where it is a reality is in *time*, not certainly in space. So the mental world of time offers a solution. More and more it is used as a compensating principle. [. . . .]

Mr. Joyce is very strictly of the school of Bergson-Einstein, Stein-Proust. He is of the great time-school they represent. His book is a *time-book*, as I have said, in that sense. He has embraced the time-doctrine very completely. And it is as the critic of that doctrine and of that school that I have approached the analysis of his writings up to date. (I insert this last time-clause because there is no reason at all to suppose that he may not be influenced in turn by my criticism; and, indeed, I hope it may be so, for he would be a very valuable adherent.)

Yet that the time-sense is really exasperated in Joyce in the fashion that it is in Proust, Dada, Pound or Miss Stein, may be doubted. He has a very keen preoccupation with the Past it is certain; he does lay things down side by side, carefully dated; and added to that, he has some rather loosely and romantically held notion of periodicity. But [what] I believe that all these things amount to with him is this: as a careful, even meticulous, craftsman, with a long training of doctrinaire naturalism, the detail—the time-detail as much as anything else—assumes an exaggerated importance for him. And I am sure that he would be put to his trumps to say how he came by much of the time-machinery that he possesses. Until he was told, I dare say that he did not know he had it, even; for he is 'an instinctive', like Pound, in that respect; there is not very much reflection going on at any time inside the head of Mr. James Joyce. That is indeed the characteristic condition of *the craftsman*, pure and simple.

And that is what Joyce is above all things, essentially the craftsman. It is a thing more common, perhaps, in painting or the plastic arts than in literature. I do not mean by this that he works harder or more thoroughly than other people, but that he is not so much an inventive intelligence as an executant. He is certainly very 'shoppy', and professional to a fault, though in the midst of the amateurism of the day it is a fault that can easily be forgiven.

What stimulates him is *ways of doing things*, and technical processes, and not *things to be done*. Between the various things to be done he shows a true craftsman's impartiality. He is become so much a writing-specialist that it matters very little to him *what* he writes, or what idea or world-view he expresses, so long as he is trying his hand at this manner and that, and displaying his enjoyable virtuosity. Strictly speaking, he has none at all, no special point of view, or none worth mentioning. It is such people that the creative intelligence fecundates and uses; and at present that intelligence is political, and its stimuli are masked ideologies. He is only a tool, an instrument, in short. That is why such a sensitive medium as Joyce, working in such a period, requires the attention of the independent critic.

102

So perhaps it is easy to see how, without much realizing what was happening, Joyce arrived where he did. We can regard it as a diathetic phenomenon partly—the craftsman is susceptible and unprotected. There are even slight, though not very grave, symptoms of disorder in his art. The painful preoccupation with the *exact* place of things in a room, for instance, could be mildly matched in his writing. The *things themselves* by which he is surrounded lose, for the hysterical subject, their importance, or even meaning. Their *position* absorbs all the attention of his mind. Some such uneasy pedantry, in a mild form, is likely to assail any conscientious craftsman—especially in an intensive 'space-time' atmosphere, surrounded by fanatical space-timeists. The poor craftsman has never been in such peril as today, for it is a frantic hornpipe indeed that his obedient legs are compelled to execute. But otherwise Joyce, with his highly-developed *physical* basis, is essentially sane.

The method that underlies *Ulysses* is known as the 'telling from the inside'. As that description denotes, it is psychological. Carried out in the particular manner used in *Ulysses*, it lands the reader inside an Aladdin's cave of incredible bric-à-brac in which a dense mass of dead stuff is collected, from 1901 toothpaste, a bar or two of Sweet Rosie O'Grady, to pre-nordic architecture. An immense *nature-morte* is the result. This ensues from the method of confining the reader in a circumscribed psychological space into which several encyclopaedias have been emptied. It results from the constipation induced in the movement of the narrative.

The amount of *stuff*—unorganized brute material—that the more active principle of drama has to wade through, under the circumstances, slows it down to the pace at which, inevitably, the sluggish tide of the author's bric-à-brac passes the observer, at the saluting post, or in this case, the reader. It is a suffocating, mœotic expanse of objects, all of them lifeless, the sewage of a Past twenty years old, all neatly arranged in a meticulous sequence. The newspaper in which Mr. Bloom's bloater is wrapped up, say, must press on to the cold body of the fish, reversed, the account of the bicycle accident that was reported on the fated day chosen for this Odyssey; or that at least is the idea.

At the end of a long reading of *Ulysses* you feel that it is the very nightmare of the naturalistic method that you have been experienc-

103

ing. Much as you may cherish the merely physical enthusiasm that expresses itself in this stupendous outpouring of *matter*, or *stuff*, you wish, on the spot, to be transported to some more abstract region for a time, where the dates of the various toothpastes, the brewery and laundry receipts, the growing pile of punched 'bus-tickets, the growing holes in the baby's socks and the darn that repairs them, assume less importance. It is your impulse perhaps quickly to get your mind where there is nothing but air and rock, however inhospitable and featureless, and a little timeless, too. You will have had a glut, for the moment (if you have really persevered), of *matter*, procured you by the turning on of all this river of what now is rubbish, but which was not *then*, by the obsessional application of the naturalistic method associated with the exacerbated time-sense. And the fact that you were not in the open air, but closed up inside somebody else's head, will not make things any better. It will have been your catharsis of the objective accumulations that obstinately collect in even the most active mind.

Now in the graphic and plastic arts that stage of fanatic naturalism long ago has been passed. All the machinery appropriate to its production has long since been discarded, luckily for the pure creative impulse of the artist. The nineteenth-century naturalism of that obsessional, fanatical order is what you find on the one hand in *Ulysses*. On the other, you have a great variety of recent influences enabling Mr. Joyce to use it in the way that he did.

The effect of this rather fortunate confusion was highly stimulating to Joyce, who really got the maximum out of it, with an appetite that certainly will never be matched again for the actual *matter* revealed in his composition, or proved to have been lengthily secreted there. It is like a gigantic victorian quilt or antimacassar. Or it is the voluminous curtain that fell, belated (with the alarming momentum of a ton or two of personally organized rubbish), upon the victorian scene. So rich was its delivery, its pent-up outpouring so vehement, that it will remain, eternally cathartic, a monument like a record diarrhœa. No one who looks *at* it will ever want to look *behind* it. It is the sardonic catafalque of the victorian world.

Two opposite things were required for this result. Mr. Joyce could never have performed this particular feat if he had not been, in his make-up, extremely immobile; and yet, in contradiction to that, very open to new technical influences. It is the *craftsman* in Joyce that is progressive; but the *man* has not moved since his early days in Dublin. He is on that side a 'young man' in some way embalmed. His technical adventures do not, apparently, stimulate him to think. On the contrary, what he thinks seems to be of a conventional and fixed order, as though perhaps not to embarrass the neighbouring evolution of his highly progressive and eclectic craftsmanship.

So he collected like a cistern in his youth the last stagnant pumpings of victorian anglo-irish life. This he held steadfastly intact for fifteen years or more—then when he was ripe, as it were, he discharged it, in a dense mass, to his eternal glory. That was *Ulysses*. Had the twenty-year-old Joyce of the *Dubliners* not remained almost miraculously intact, we should never have witnessed this peculiar spectacle.

That is, I believe, the true account of how this creative event occurred with Joyce; and, if that is so, it will be evident that we are in the presence of a very different phenomenon from Proust. Proust *returned* to the *temps perdu*. Joyce never left them. He discharged it as freshly as though the time he wrote about were still present, because it was *his* present. It rolled out with all the aplomb and vivacity of a contemporary experience, assisted in its slick discharge by the latest technical devices. [. . . .]

There are several other things that have to be noted as characteristic of Joyce for a full understanding of a technique that has grown into a very complex, overcharged façade. The craftsman, pure and simple, is at the bottom of his work. I have already insisted upon that; and in that connection it almost appears, I have said, that he has practised sabotage where his intellect was concerned, in order to leave his craftsman's hand freer for its stylistic exercises. That is a phenomenon very commonly met with in the painter's craft. Daring or unusual speculation, or an unwonted intensity of outlook, is not good for technical display, that is certain, and they are seldom found together. The intellect is in one sense the rival of the hand, and is apt to hamper rather than assist it. It interferes, at all events, with its showing-off, and affords no encouragement to the hand's 'sedulous apeishness'; or so would say the hand.

The extreme conventionality of Joyce's mind and outlook is per-

haps due to this. In *Ulysses*, if you strip away the technical com-
plexities that envelop it, the surprises of style and unconventional
attitudes that prevail in it, the figures underneath are of a remarkable simplicity, and of the most orthodoxly comic outline. Indeed,
it is not too much to say that they are, most of them, walking
clichés. So much is this the case, that your attention is inevitably
drawn to the evident paradox that ensues; namely, that of an intelligence so alive to purely verbal clichés that it hunts them like fleas,
with remarkable success, and yet that leaves the most gigantic
ready-made and well-worn dummies enthroned everywhere, in the
form of the actual personnel of the book. [. . . .]

But if they are clichés, Stephen Dedalus is a worse or a far more
glaring one. He is the really wooden figure. He is 'the poet' to an
uncomfortable, a dismal, a ridiculous, even a pulverizing degree.
His movements in the Martello-tower, his theatrical 'bitterness', his
cheerless, priggish stateliness, his gazings into the blue distance, his
Irish Accent, his exquisite sensitiveness, his 'pride' that is so crude
as to be almost indecent, the incredible slowness which which he
gets about from place to place, up the stairs, down the stairs, like
a funereal stage-king; the time required for him to move his neck,
how he raises his hand, passes it over his aching eyes, or his damp
brow, even more wearily drops it, closes his dismal little shutters
against his rollicking irish-type of a friend (in his capacity of a type-
poet), and remains sententiously secluded, shut up in his own personal Martello-tower—a Martello-tower within a Martello-tower
—until he consents to issue out, tempted by the opportunity of
making a 'bitter'—a very 'bitter'—jest, to show up against the
ideally idiotic background provided by Haines; all this has to be
read to be believed—but read, of course, with a deaf ear to the
really charming workmanship with which it is presented. *Written*
on a level with its conception, and it would be as dull stuff as you
could easily find.

The stage-directions with which the novelist in general pursues
his craft are usually tell-tale, and *Ulysses* is no exception to that
rule. The stage-directions for getting Stephen Dedalus, the irritating hero, about, sitting him down, giving accent to his voice, are all
painfully enlightening.

This is how the hero of *Ulysses* first appears on page 2 of the
book :

Stephen Dedalus stepped up, followed him (Mulligan) *wearily* halfway and sat down. . . .[6]

He does almost everything 'wearily'. He 'sits down' always before he has got far. He moves with such dignified and 'weary' slowness, that he never gets further than *half-way* under any circumstances as compared with any other less dignified, less 'weary', figure in the book—that is to say, any of the many figures introduced to show off his dismal supremacy. This is where (page 2) Stephen Dedalus first speaks :

'. . . Tell me, Mulligan,' Stephen said quietly.[7]

In this *quiet* 'Tell me, Mulligan'—(irish accent, please)—you have the soul of this small, pointless, oppressive character in its entirety. You wonder for some pages what can be the cause of this weighty inanition. There is perhaps some plausible reason for it, which will be revealed in the sequel. That would make things a little better. But nothing happens of that sort. You slowly find out what it is. *The hero is trying to be a gentleman!* That is the secret —nothing less, nothing more. The 'artist as a young man' has 'the real Oxford manner', you are informed; and you eventually realize that his oppressive mannerisms have been due in the first instance to an attempt to produce the impression of 'an Oxford manner'. [. . . .]

Turning to Mr. Bloom, we find an unsatisfactory figure, too, but of an opposite sort and in a very different degree. He possesses all the recognized theatrical properties of 'the Jew' up-to-date—he is more feminine than *la femme*, shares her couvade, the periodicity of her intimate existence is repeated mildly in his own; he counts the beer bottles stacked in a yard he is passing, computing with glee the profit to be extracted from that commerce; but such a Jew as Bloom, taken altogether, has never been seen outside the pages of Mr. Joyce's book. And he is not even a Jew most of the time, but his talented irish author.

In reality there is no Mr. Bloom at all, of course, except at certain moments. Usually the author, carelessly disguised beneath what other people have observed about Jews, or yet other people have believed that they have seen, is alone performing before us. There is no sign throughout the book that he has ever directly and intelligently observed any *individual* Jew. He has merely out of books

107

and conversations collected facts, witticisms and generalizations about Jews, and wrapped up his own kindly person with these, till he has bloated himself into a thousand pages of heterogeneous, peculiarly unjewish, matter. So he has certainly contributed nothing to the literature of the Jew, for which task he is in any case quite unsuited.

This inability to observe directly, a habit of always looking at people through other people's eyes and not through his own, is deeply rooted with Joyce. Where a multitude of little details or some obvious idiosyncrasy are concerned, he may be said to be observant; but the secret of an *entire* organism escapes him. Not being observant where entire people (that is, people at all) are concerned, he depicts them conventionally always, under some general label. For it is in the fragmentation of a personality—by isolating some characteristic weakness, mood, or time-self—that you arrive at the mechanical and abstract, the opposite of the living. This, however, leaves him free to achieve with a mass of detail a superficial appearance of life; and also to exercise his imitative talents without check where the technical problem is concerned. [. . . .]

In *Ulysses* you have a deliberate display, on the grand scale, of technical virtuosity and literary scholarship. What is underneath this overcharged surface, few people, so far, have seriously inquired. In reality it is rather an apologuical than a real landscape; and the two main characters, Bloom and Dedalus, are lay-figures (the latter a sadly ill-chosen one) on which such a mass of dead stuff is hung, that if ever they had any organic life of their own, it would speedily have been overwhelmed in this torrent of matter, of *nature-morte.* [. . . .]

Another thing that can be dismissed even more summarily is the claim that Bloom is a creation, a great *homme moyen sensuel* of fiction. That side of Bloom would never have existed had it not been for the Bouvard and Pécuchet of Flaubert, which very intense creation Joyce merely takes over, spins out, and translates into the relaxed medium of anglo-irish humour. Where Bloom is being Bouvard and Pécuchet, it is a translation, nothing more.

Nor really can the admirable Goya-like fantasia in the middle of the book, in which all the characters enjoy a free metaphysical existence (released from the last remnants of the nineteenth-century restraint of the doctrine of naturalism), be compared for original power of conception with the *Tentation*. As to the homeric framework, that is only an entertaining structural device or conceit.

In *The Art of Being Ruled* (chap. vi. part xii.), I have analysed in passing one aspect of the 'telling from the inside' method, where that method is based upon a flaubertian naturalism, and used by an english writer brought up in the anglo-saxon humorous tradition. There my remarks were called forth by the nature of the more general analysis I was at the time engaged upon, which included what I described as the 'sort of gargantuan mental stutter' employed by Miss Stein, in the course of her exploitation of the processes of the demented. I shall now quote what is essential to my present purpose from that chapter relative to Mr. Joyce:

> . . . the repetition (used by Miss Stein) is also in the nature of a photograph of the unorganized word-dreaming of the mind when not concentrated for some logical functional purpose. Mr. Joyce employed this method with success (not so radically and rather differently) in *Ulysses*. The thought-stream or word-stream of his hero's mind was supposed to be photographed. The effect was not unlike the conversation of Mr. Jingle in *Pickwick*.
>
> The reason why you get this Mr. Jingle effect is that, in *Ulysses*, a considerable degree of naturalism being aimed at, Mr. Joyce had not the freedom of movement possessed by the more ostensibly personal, semi-lyrical utterances of Miss Stein. He had to pretend that we were really surprising the private thought of a real and average human creature, Mr. Bloom. But the fact is that Mr. Bloom was abnormally *wordy*. He *thought in words*, not images, for our benefit, in a fashion as unreal, from the point of view of the strictest naturalist dogma, as a Hamlet soliloquy. And yet the *pretence* of naturalism involved Mr. Joyce in something less satisfying than Miss Stein's more direct and arbitrary arrangements.
>
> For Mr. Joyce's use of Miss Stein's method the following passage[s] will suffice (it is of the more genial, Mr. Jingle, order):

> 'Provost's house. The reverend Dr. Salmon : tinned salmon. Well tinned in there. Wouldn't live in it if they paid me. Hope they have liver and bacon today. Nature abhors a vacuum. . . .
>
> 'There he is : the brother. Image of him. Haunting face. Now that's a coincidence. Course hundreds of times you think of a person,' etc.[8]

'Feel better. Burgundy. Good pick me up. Who distilled first. Some chap in the blues. Dutch courage. That *Kilkenny People* in the national library now I must.'[9]

Here is Mr. Jingle, from *Pickwick* :

'Rather short in the waist, ain't it? . . . Like a general postman's coat—queer coats those—made by contract—no measuring—mysterious dispensations of Providence—all the short men get long coats—all the long men short ones. . . .'[10]

'Come . . . stopping at Crown—Crown at Muggleton—met a party—flannel jackets—white trousers—anchovy standwiches—devilled kidneys—splendid fellows—glorious.'[11]

So by the devious route of a fashionable naturalist device—that usually described as 'presenting the character from the *inside*'—and the influence exercised on him by Miss Stein's technique of picturesque dementia—Mr. Joyce reaches the half-demented *crank* figure of traditional english humour.[12]

The clowning and horseplay of english humour play a very important part in the later work of Joyce. In *Ulysses* Rabelais is also put under contribution to reinforce this vein, though it is the manner of Rabelais that is parodied, and the matter of that unusually profound writer is not very much disturbed. Since *Ulysses* (but still in the manner of that book) Mr. Joyce has written a certain amount— the gathering material of a new book, which, altogether almost, employs the manner of Nash—though again somewhat varied with echoes of Urquhart's[13] translations. He has fallen almost entirely into a literary horseplay on the one side, and Steinesque child-play on the other.

As to the Nash factor, when read in the original, the brilliant rattle of that Elizabethan's high-spirited ingenuity can in time grow tiresome, and is of a stupefying monotony. What Nash says, from start to finish, is nothing. The mind demands some special substance from a writer, for words open into the region of ideas; and the requirements of that region, where it is words you are using, must somehow be met. Chapman, Donne or Shakespeare, with as splendid a mastery of language, supply this demand, whereas Nash does not.

But Nash is a great prose-writer, one of the greatest as far as sheer execution is concerned, and in that over-ornate bustling field. Yet his emptiness has resulted in his work falling into neglect, which, if you read much of him, is not difficult to understand. His great appetite for words, their punning potentialities, along with a power of compressing them into pungent arabesques, is admirable enough to have made him more remembered than he is. But certainly some instinct in Posterity turned it away from this *too* physical, too merely high-spirited and muscular, verbal performer. He tired it like a child with his empty energy, I suppose.

Nash appears to be at present the chief source of Joyce's inspiration—associated with his old friend Rabelais, and some of the mannerisms of Miss Stein, those easiest assimilated without its showing. There is a further source now, it appears; he has evidently concluded that the epistolary style of Ezra Pound should not be born to blush unseen, but should be made a more public use of than Pound has done. So in it has gone with the rest. [. . . .]

The *Portrait of the Artist* is an extremely carefully written book; but it is not technically swept and tidied to the extent that is *Ulysses*. For instance, this passage from the opening of chapter ii. would not have remained in the later book :

> Every morning, therefore, uncle Charles *repaired* to his outhouse but not before he had creased and *brushed scrupulously* his back hair, etc.[14]

People *repair* to places in works of fiction of the humblest order or in newspaper articles; and *brushed scrupulously*, though harmless certainly, is a conjunction that the fastidious eye would reject, provided it had time to exercise its function. But elsewhere in the *Portrait of the Artist*, in the scene on the seashore with the bird-girl, for instance, the conventional emotion calls to itself and clothes itself with a conventional expression; which, however merely technically pruned, leaves a taste of well-used sentiment in the mind, definitely of the cliché order. The more full-blooded humour of *Ulysses* prevents that from happening so often.

It is in tracking this other sort of cliché—the cliché of feeling, of thought, and in a less detailed sense, of expression—that you will find everywhere beneath the surface in Joyce a conventional basis or framework. And until you get down to that framework or bed, you will not understand what is built over it, nor realize why, in a sense, it is so dead.

NOTES

1 Lewis, *Letters*, p. 131.
2 From Lewis, *Time and Western Man*. London; Chatto & Windus, 1927, pp. 92, 93, 95, 99, 106–9, 112, 113–15, 117–18, 119, 121–3, 126.
3 Richard Ellman, *James Joyce*. New York: Oxford University Press, 1965, pp. 607-8.
4 Harry Levin, *James Joyce: A Critical Introduction*. London: Faber & Faber, 1944. Professor Levin made several barbed references to Lewis's analysis of Joyce. Commenting on part of *Ulysses*, he remarked: 'This staccato diction, as the malice of Wyndham Lewis did not fail to observe, makes a startling appearance in the very first novel of Charles Dickens.' (*James Joyce*, p. 69)
5 *Rude Assignment*, p. 56.
6 James Joyce, *Ulysses*. London: The Bodley Head, reset 1960 edition, p. 2. L.'s italics.
7 Ibid.
8 Ibid., p. 209.
9 Ibid., p. 229.
10 Charles Dickens, *The Posthumous Papers of the Pickwick Club*. London: Oxford University Press, 1964, p. 18.
11 Ibid., p. 90.
12 *The Art of Being Ruled*, pp. 400-2.
13 Sir Thomas Urquhart (1611–60?), translator of Rabelais and author of books written in a unique jargon.
14 Joyce, *A Portrait of the Artist as a Young Man*. London: The Egoist Limited, 1918, p. 65. L.'s italics, as is also the 'etc'.

7

Gertrude Stein

(From *Time and Western Man*, 1927)

The year before the attack reproduced here,[1] Lewis had described Miss Stein as 'the best-known exponent of a literary system that consists in a sort of gargantuan mental stutter'. She was exploiting in her method the processes of the demented, he claimed.[2] He argued that this constituted one of the main weapons in what he called 'the war against the conceptual stronghold of the intellect'.[3] Lewis's disdain for Stein 'and the various stammering, squinting, punning group who followed her'[4] rumbles through many of his books. In one of them, he declared : *'Miss Stein should get out of english* . . . The stammer would promptly die down . . . and english would be at peace'.[5]

[Miss Stein] has never needed to be a best-seller, luckily for herself —had that been so, she would have opened our eyes, I suspect. But in her earlier books [. . .] she, too, *became* the people she wrote about, adopting their illiteracies and colloquialisms. The other main factor in her method resulted in her story taking the form of *a prose-song*.

It is in a thick, monotonous prose-song that Miss Stein characteristically expresses her fatigue, her energy, and the bitter fatalism of her nature. Her stories are very often long—all the longer, too, because everything has to be repeated half a dozen times over. In the end the most wearisome dirge it is possible to imagine results, as slab after slab of this heavy, insensitive, common prose-song churns and lumbers by.

To an Antheil[6] tempest of jazz it is the entire body that responds, after all. The executant tires; its duration does not exceed ten minutes or so, consecutively. But it is *the tongue*—only the poor, worried, hard-worked tongue—inside the reader's head, or his laryngeal apparatus, that responds to the prose-song of Miss Stein.

At present I am referring to what I have read of Miss Stein at the *Three Lives* stage of her technical evolution.[7] What is the matter with it is, probably, that it is so *dead*. Gertrude Stein's prose-song is a cold, black suet-pudding. We can represent it as a cold suet-roll of fabulously-reptilian length. Cut it at any point, it is the same thing; the same heavy, sticky, opaque mass all through, and all along. It is weighted, projected, with a sibylline urge. It is mournful and monstrous, composed of dead and inanimate material. It is all fat, without nerve. Or the evident vitality that informs it is vegetable rather than animal. Its life is a low-grade, if tenacious, one; of the sausage, by-the-yard, variety.

That is one aspect of the question, the technical one. There is another which has a certain reference to the political ideology I have been analysing. In adopting the simplicity, the illiterateness, of the mass-average of the Melancthas and Annas, Miss Stein gives proof of all the false 'revolutionary', propagandist *plainmanism* of her time. The monstrous, desperate, soggy *lengths* of primitive mass-life, chopped off and presented to us as a never-ending prose-song, is undoubtedly intended as an epic contribution to the present mass-democracy. The texture of the language has to be jumbled, cheap, slangy and thick to suit. It must be written in a slovenly, straight-off fashion, so that it may appear to be more 'real'. Only the metre of an obsessing *time* has to be put into it. It has to be rhythmatized; and this proclivity both of Miss Stein, and of all the characteristic fashions of those for whom she writes, destroys the 'reality' at least, giving to the life it patronizes the mechanical bias of its creator.

Next we will take up the fashionable child-factor as it is found in the work of Miss Stein, and in most art today, from Sir James Barrie to Charlie Chaplin. Her latest book, a vast one, I hear, I have not read. But many slighter, or at least shorter, more recent pieces, I know. In these, where she is not personifying a negress or some small american bourgeoise, but playing her own personal literary game (she may be described as the reverse of Patience sitting on a monument—she appears, that is, as a Monument sitting upon patience), this capable, colossal authoress relapses into the rôle and mental habits of childhood. Fact is thrown to the winds;

114

the irresponsible, light-hearted madness of ignorance is wooed, and the full-fledged *Child* emerges. This child (often an idiot-child as it happens, but none the less sweet to itself for that) throws big, heavy words up and catches them; or letting them slip through its fingers, they break in pieces; and down it squats with a grunt, and begins sticking them together again. Else this far-too-intellectual infant chases the chosen word, like a moth, through many pages, worrying the delicate life out of it. The larynx and tongue of the reader meantime suffer acutely. Every word uttered threatens to obsess and stick to his tongue. Having come, wrongly spelt, wrongly pronounced, or wrongly according to usage, it refuses to move till it has been put right; yet will not come right in Miss Stein's hands.

It is in these occasional pieces that the *child-personality* of Miss Stein is discovered in its acutest form. But *the child* with her is always overshadowed by the imbecile. That is to say, that very clever, very resourceful Gertrude Stein is heavily indebted to the poor honest lunatic for her mannerisms. All the regions between the dull stupor or complete imbecility—which is splendidly portrayed in Picasso's pneumatic giantesses—and the relatively disciplined, alert, fixed condition, which is humanly regarded as the other pole to imbecility, she has thoroughly explored. The massive silence of the full idiot is, unfortunately, out of her reach, of course. In her capacity of writer, or wordknitter, she has to stop short of that, and leave it to her friend Picasso. For words, idle words, have one terrible limitation—they must represent human speech in some form. The silent canvas is their master there.

That, very briefly, is Miss Stein's rôle in the child-cult, and the kindred one (Freud-inspired or not) of *the demented*. She is herself a robust intelligence, a colossus among the practitioners of infancy; a huge, lowering, dogmatic Child. The point of her writing is best seen, perhaps, in less intelligent imitators or homologues. Even by taking a quite flimsy writer in the same movement (both on account of psychology and technique) like Miss Loos, you will be helped to that essential simplification.[8]

My general objection, then, to the work of Miss Stein is that it is *dead*. My second objection is that it is *romantic*. As to the latter count, for all its force I feel it to be *unreal* in the same way that I feel Conrad or Zola to be, but without the rationale of the fictionist. It is the personal rhythm, the obvious bias, that of a peculiar rather than a universal nature, that produces this sensation. The dull frantic vitality of Zola is that of an inferior, a brutal, not a highly-organized, nature. The chocolate-cream richness of Conrad, the *romance* laid on with a shovel—best revealed where Mr. Hueffer helped him in the book specifically named *Romance*—all this excess, this tropical unreality, I find (of course, to some extent concealed in an elaborate intellectualist technique) in Miss Stein.[9]

As to the quality of deadness, that can be matched most exactly by comparison with contemporary painting, even the best. In *The Caliph's Design* I have named this the *nature-mortiste* school of painting.[10]

In Miss Stein you get a temperament on the grand scale, as you do in Picasso; they both enjoy the colossal. But if you compare one of Picasso's giantesses (the first born about 1920, I believe) with a giant from the Sistine Ceiling, you will at once find that the Picasso figure is a beautifully executed, imposing, human *doll*. Its fixed imbecility of expression, its immense, bloated, eunuchoid limbs, suggest the mental clinic immediately. They are all opaque fat, without nerve or muscle. The figures of Michelangelo, on the other hand—the most supremely noble and terrible creations of the dramatic genius of the West—are creatures of an infectious life. Between the outstretched forefinger of Adam and the finger of the hurrying Jehovah, there is an electric force in suspense of a magnitude that no vegetative imbecility, however well done or however colossal, on one side and on the other, would be able to convey.

The *weight*, then, that is characteristic of the work of Miss Stein —like the sluggish weight of the figures, or the sultry oppressiveness of the chocolate-cream tropics in which they move, of Conrad; or of the unintelligent, catastrophic heaviness of Zola—is, to me, of a dead order of things. But this kind of doll-like *deadness*, the torpid fatal *heaviness*, is so prevalent, in one form or another, as to dominate in a peculiar way the productions of the present time. Now that we have enough of it to generalize what was at first a sense only of the assembling of a peculiar consciousness into a formularized mass, we can study it as a very definite, clearly marked thing. It is the hall-mark of a great school. Wherever a member of the school grows ambitious—and in consequence colossal—he or she betrays this essential *deadness*. The reasons, of a sociologic order, for this, it is not my business here, to analyse.

116

NOTES

1 From *Time and Western Man*, pp. 77–80.
2 Lewis, *The Art of Being Ruled*, p. 400.
3 Ibid., p. 401.
4 Ibid., p. 397.
5 Lewis, *The Diabolical Principle and the Dithyrambic Spectator*. London: Chatto & Windus, 1931, pp. 7–8.
6 George Antheil (b. 1900) was a pioneer of jazz themes in symphonic composition. Though an American, he spent much time in Paris during the Twenties, when he also knew L.
7 *Three Lives*, with its stories about Anna, Melanctha and the Gentle Lena, was first published in 1909.
8 Anita Loos (b. 1893) whose *Gentlemen Prefer Blondes* had appeared in 1925.
9 Ford Madox Hueffer (later Ford) had collaborated with Joseph Conrad on *Romance*, an historical adventure story published in 1903.
10 A pamphlet published in 1919 and reprinted in Walter Michel and C. J. Fox, eds., *Wyndham Lewis on Art*. London: Thames & Hudson, 1969. See p. 132 of that book.

D. H. Lawrence

(From *Paleface*, 1929)

Lawrence was a constant target for Lewis.[1] The antagonism was mutual. In 1929, Lawrence attacked Lewis who, he said, retreated into the intellect and there displayed 'the utterly repulsive effect people have on him'. According to Lawrence, Lewis's attitude to humanity was tantamount to exclaiming, 'My God, they stink!'[2] However, as William Pritchard has remarked in suggesting similarities between these mutually hostile masters, 'we need and should insist on having both Lawrence and Lewis, one against the other, yes, but also together against others: as invaluable critics of literature and society, and as the two most significant English novelists of our century'.[3] For all the broadsides he discharged against Lawrence, Lewis clearly acknowledged his antagonist's stature as a writer: 'The terrible disease that at last accounted for him, and which hunted him through life (much more than "the world of men")—it was *that* also which was responsible (so it seems to me) for a good deal that was most hysterical and feeble in his work.'[4] Lewis concentrated some of his fire on the Laurentian cultists rather than on the man they hailed as a prophet. 'It is not as a "prophet" that I should praise Lawrence—it seems to me a finer thing to wish "to be among the English poets" after you are dead than "to be among prophets". And if you extend the term "Poet" to include romance, autobiography and travel-sketch, then D. H. Lawrence is certainly in the former class.'[5]

———

I will now turn to Mr. D. H. Lawrence's account of the Mexican Indian, and especially to his chapter 'Indians and Entertainment':

It is almost impossible for the white people to approach the Indian without either sentimentality or dislike.[6]

(Mr. Lawrence proves himself in this respect a *good White Man,* I think, in his book about the Indian. There is no sign of dislike, so he is the other sort of conventional White Man.)

> The common healthy vulgar white usually feels a certain native dislike of these drumming aboriginals.[7]

Mr. Lawrence we can at once agree is not 'a common healthy vulgar white'; he has nothing very 'native' about him, either white or dark.

> The highbrow invariably lapses into sentimentalism like the smell of bad eggs.[8]

Mr. Lawrence is a 'highbrow', about that I think there cannot be two opinions. And a 'sentimentalism like the smell of bad eggs', I am sorry to have to say, rises from all the work of Mr. Lawrence. It is all slightly 'high' and *faisandé* in a sentimental way.

Anyhow, far from 'disliking' the 'drumming' of these 'aboriginals', there is no question that he likes it very much; and heavily implied in all his descriptions is the notion that these drumming and other 'native' habits are far superior to ours; the dark ones to the white. If we followed Mr. Lawrence to the ultimate conclusion of his romantic teaching, we should allow our 'consciousness' to be overpowered by the alien 'consciousness' of the Indian. And we know what he thinks that would involve: for he has told us that 'the Indian way of consciousness is different from and fatal to our way of consciousness'.[9]

We will now turn to his account of the specific way in which this 'consciousness' of the Mexican Indian differs from ours.

The 'commonest entertainment among the Indians', we are told (that is I suppose among the 'common healthy vulgar' Indians, if Mr. Lawrence's romantic soul could bring itself to admit that a Toltec or a Hopi *could* be 'common' or 'vulgar'), 'is singing round the drum, at evening'.[10]

There are fishermen in the Outer Hebrides, he says, who do something of this sort, 'approaching the indian way', but of course, being mere Whites, they do not reach or equal it. Still, the Outer Hebrideans do succeed in suggesting to Mr. Lawrence a realm inhabited by 'beasts that . . . stare through . . . vivid, *mindless* eyes'.[11]

119

They do manage to become *mindless* : though not so *mindless* as the Indian, therefore inferior.

> This is *approaching* the Indian song. But even this is *pictorial, cenceptual* far beyond the Indian point. *The Hebridean still sees himself human,* and *outside* the great naturalistic influences. . . .[12]

The poor White Hebridean still, alas, remains *human*, he is not totally *mindless*, though more nearly so than any other White Mr. Lawrence offhand can bring to mind.

The important thing to note in all these accounts is the insistence upon *mindlessness* as an essential quality of what is admirable. The Hebridean is not to be admired so much as the Mexican Indian because he still deals in 'conceptual', 'pictorial' things; whereas the Mexican Indian is purely emotional—'musical', in a word, in the Spengler sense. (For the full analysis of this type of thinking I refer you to *Time and Western Man*, where there is a detailed account of spenglerism.) And the first impulse to the anti-conceptualist, anti-intellectual, anti-pictorial point of view in philosophy, and thinking generally, was given by Bergson : just as in Berman's account of Behaviourism we saw him attributing the genesis of *Gestalt* to Bergson.[13] So at last we know just where we are, philosophically, with Mr. Lawrence. Mr. D. H. Lawrence is a distinguished artist— member of the great and flourishing society of 'Emergent Evolution', 'Creative Evolution', 'Gestalt', 'World-as-History', etc. etc.

I will go on quoting to show how completely Mr. Lawrence is beneath the spell of this evolutionist, emotional, non-human, 'mindless' philosophy : and how thoroughly he reads it into and applies it to the manifestations of the Indian 'consciousness'.

> The Indian, singing, sings *without words or vision*.[14]

I am italicizing the expressions that it is particularly necessary to mark in what I am quoting. How the attitude to 'words', on the one hand, and to 'vision' and the things of vision, 'pictorial' things, on the other, is pure Spengler !

> Face lifted and *sightless*, eyes half closed and *visionless*, mouth open and *speechless*, the *sounds* arise in his chest, from the *consciousness in the abdomen*.[15]

A 'consciousness in the abdomen' or a visceral consciousness (which otherwise is 'sightless', 'visionless', and 'speechless') is what we commonly should call *unconsciousness*. And indeed that is what —if we were to capitalize it under one word—we should take as describing the kernel of this propagandist account. It is as a servant of the great *philosophy of the Unconscious* (which began as 'Will' with Schopenhauer, became 'The Philosophy of the Unconscious' with von Hartmann,[16] launched all that 'the Unconscious' means in Psychoanalysis, and was 'Intuition' for Bergson, which is 'Time' for Spengler, and 'Space-Time' for Professor Alexander)[17] that Mr. Lawrence is writing.

'*The consciousness in the abdomen*' removes the vital centre into the viscera, and takes the privilege of leadership away from the hated 'mind' or 'intellect', established up above in the head. [. . . .]

One of the rhythmical patterns of 'sound' produced by the Indian the latter describes as a 'bear hunt', Mr. Lawrence tells us.

'But,' says Mr. Lawrence, 'the man coming home from the bear hunt is any man, all men, the bear is any bear, every bear, all bear. *There is no individual, isolated experience.* It is the hunting . . . demon of manhood which has won against the . . . demon of all bears. The experience is generic, non-individual.'[18]

So we reach Mr. Lawrence's *communism*, cast into the anthropologic moulds first prepared by Sir Henry Maine.[19] For Mr. Lawrence is, in full hysterical flower, perhaps our most accomplished english communist. He is *the natural communist*, as it were, as distinguished from the indoctrinated, or theoretic, one.

(1) The Unconscious; (2) The Feminine; (3) The Communist; those are the main principles of action of the mind of Mr. Lawrence, linked in a hot and piping trinity of rough-stuff primitivism, and freudian hot-sex-stuff. With *Sons and Lovers*, his first book, he was at once hot-foot upon the fashionable trail of incest; the book is an eloquent wallowing mass of Mother-love and Sex-idolatry. His *Women in Love* is again the same thick, sentimental, luscious stew. The 'Homo'-motive, how could that be absent from such a compendium, as is the nature of Mr. Lawrence, of all that has long passed for 'revolutionary', reposing mainly for its popular effectiveness upon the meaty, succulent levers of sex and supersex, to bait those politically-innocent, romantic, anglo-saxon simpletons dreaming their 'anglo-saxon dreams', whether in America or the native country of Mr. Lawrence? The motif of the 'child-cult', which is usually found prominently in any 'revolutionary' mixture, is echoed,

and indeed screamed, wept and bellowed, throughout *Sons and Lovers*.

At first sight, I am afraid, many of the *rapprochements* that I make here may sound strained, since, I am sorry to say, if things do not lie obviously together and publish their conjunction explicitly and prominently, it is not considered quite respectable to suggest that they have any vital connection. The suggestion of anything 'illicit' shocks, even where ideas are concerned. That one idea should have a hidden liaison or be in communication with another idea, without ever approaching it in public, or any one even *mentioning them together*—that is the sort of thing that is never admitted in polite society.

So the majority of people are deeply unconscious of the affiliations of the various phenomena of our time, which on the surface look so very autonomous, and even hostile; yet, existing under quite a different label, in a quite different region of time and space, they are often closely and organically related to one another. If you test this you will be surprised to find how many things do belong together, in fact, in our highly contentious and separatist time.

Yet it is our business—especially, it appears, mine—to establish these essential liaisons, and to lay bare the widely-flung system of cables connecting up this maze-like and destructive system in the midst of which we live—destructive, that is of course, to something essential that we should clutch and be careful not to lose, on our way to the Melting-pot.

What, you might say, for instance, has Mr. Lawrence's remark about the 'mindlessness' of the Mexican songs got to do with communism? Or, again, 'mindlessness' or 'communism' to do with 'the Feminine Principle' (as opposed to the Masculine)? I can show you at once what 'mindlessness' has to do with 'communism'. I will quote the latest european advocate of Bolshevism, René Fülöp-Miller, from his book *The Mind and Face of Bolshevism*. It should really be called *The Face of Bolshevism*, since we learn that 'Mind' is of all things what Bolshevism is concerned to deny and prohibit. He is relating how the 'higher type of humanity' is to be produced, the super-humanity of which Bolshevism is the religion.

> It is only by such external functions as the millions have in common, their uniform and simultaneous movements, that the many can be united in a higher unity : marching, keeping in step, shout-

ing 'hurrah' in unison, festal singing in chorus, united attacks on the enemy, these are the manifestations of life which are to give birth to the new and superior type of humanity. *Everything that divides the many from each other, that fosters the illusion of the individual importance of man, especially the 'soul', hinders this higher evolution, and must consequently be destroyed*. . . . organization is to be substituted for the soul. . . . the vague mystery of the 'soul', with that evil handed down from an accursed individualistic past. . . .[20]

Let us now continue with our quotations from Mr. Lawrence.

There is no individual isolated experience. . . . *It is an experience of the human bloodstream, not of the mind or spirit*. Hence the subtle incessant, insistent rhythm of the drum, which is pulsated like the heart, and *soulless* and inescapable. Hence the strange blind unanimity of the . . . men's voices.[21]

As you see, it might equally be Mr. Fülöp-Miller on the beauties of Bolshevism. The Mexican Indian of Mr. Lawrence is the perfect Bolshevik. The 'blind unanimity of the men's voices' (the 'keeping in step . . . festal singing in chorus' of Fülöp-Miller) assures 'soullessness'. The 'soul . . . must be destroyed' says the apostle of Bolshevism. '——the real Indian song is non-individual. . . . Strange, clapping, crowing, gurgling sounds, in an unseizable subtle rhythm, the rhythm of the heart in her throes : . . . from an abdomen where the great bloodstream surges in the dark, and surges in its own generic experiences.'[22]

To witness all this is, to Mr. Lawrence, heaven. '—— perhaps it is the most stirring sight in the world in the dark, near the fire, with the drums going,' etc. etc.

It is the dark blood falling back from the mind, from sight and speech and knowing, back to the great central source where is rest and unspeakable renewal.[23]

On the same principle as 'Back to the Land', the cry of Mr. Lawrence (good little Freudian that he has always been) is 'Back to the Womb!' For although a natural communist and born feminist, it required the directive brain of Freud and others to reveal him to himself.

'We Whites, creatures of spirit!' he cries. Ah, the 'strange' things we 'never realize'! (such as the 'strange falling back of the dark blood . . . the *downward* rhythm, the rhythm of pure forgetting and pure renewal').²⁴ [. . . .]

What is *virtue* in woman? Mr. Lawrence becomes very Western at once, under the shadow of a kind of suffragist-chivalry, at the mere thought of 'Woman'.

'In woman (virtue) is the putting forth of all herself in a delicate, marvellous sensitiveness, which draws forth the wonder to herself,' etc.²⁵ (To 'draw the wonder to herself' is to be a witch, surely? So virtue and wickedness would get a little mixed up.)

What would the Indian think if he heard his squaw being written about in that strain—'delicate, marvellous sensitiveness'. He would probably say 'Chuck it, Archie!' in Hopi. At least he would be considerably surprised, and probably squint very hard, under his 'dark' brows, at Mr. Lawrence. [. . . .]

The emotion throughout the book from which I have quoted is the dogmatism of 'revolution', of political revolution, to be precise. In contrast to the White Overlord of this world in which we live, Mr. Lawrence shows us a more primitive type of 'consciousness', which has been physically defeated by the White 'consciousness', and assures us that that defeated 'consciousness' is the better of the two. But, since the 'consciousness' of the Indian is death to the 'consciousness' of the White, and eventually, if it prevailed, to the White, physically, as well, it is (however indirectly, and in the form of an entertainment, a book of 'fiction') an invitation to suicide addressed to the White Man. 'Give up, lay down, your White "consciousness",' it says. 'Capitulate to the mystical communistic Pan of the Primitive Man! Be Savage!'

Not only the opposition as between beasts and men, or Black and White, is stressed (with, always, the rebellious hypnotic accompaniment of the revolutionary drum, the primitive tom-tom, and always, that is the important thing, all the sympathy of the reader engaged on the side of the oppressed and superseded, the underdog—or, in the above instance, of the under-parrot); also we are taken into the dark-backward, to more exaggerated oppositions. Once we have got to the earliest birds, and, most ancient of all the dispossessed, the serpent (whom Mr. Lawrence sees biting his tail with an immemorial rage, and remarking, as he glances malevolently up at Man, 'I will bruise his heel!'), beyond this we reach *things*—beyond the earliest amœba. Mr. Lawrence does not take us

124

as far as that. But the philosophers who mainly influence him do.

This will be without meaning perhaps for some readers. Elsewhere I have shown how *that* most fundamental of all revolutionary impulses works, too. Mr. Bertrand Russell, for instance, obedient to his liberalist traditions, which he imports into his physics, attempts to stir up the tables and chairs against us and lead them in revolt against the overweening overlord, Man, who sits upon them, and uses them to write books at, without even asking himself if they may not resent his behaviour, and have their private thoughts about *him*— as he flings himself down upon them, or rests his elbows upon them and scratches his head.

The reason why I direct an adverse analysis against this type of 'revolutionary' emotionality, is not, once more, because I believe that the White Man as he stands today is the last word in animal life, or in spiritual perfection, or that he is not often quite as ridiculous as Mr. Lawrence's parrots would have him, and in any case he is engaged in the road to the Melting-pot. I will not here enumerate my reasons for hostility where this revolutionary picture is concerned: I will say, only, that most Aztecs are probably fairly bored with being Aztecs: that the average Hopi, like the average cat, is rather negatively admirable and exceedingly mechanical: that admiration for savages and cats is really an expression of the worst side of the Machine Age—that Machine-Age Man is effusive about them *because they are machines* like himself; and Mr. Lawrence, at least, makes no pretence of admiring his savages because they are *free*—they are no longer for the contemporary 'revolutionary' doctrinaire 'the noble savage' in the rousseauesque or Fenimore Cooper sense, at least not for the best informed doctrinaire: and, lastly, what such gospels as those of Mr. Lawrence or of Sherwood Anderson really amount to is an emotional, and not quite disinterested, exaltation (indirectly) of the *average man*, l'homme moyen sensuel—though in this case *the average Hopi*.

I find the average White European (such as Chekhov depicted) often exceedingly ridiculous, no doubt, but much more interesting than the average Hopi, or the average Negro. I would rather have the least man that *thinks*, than the average man that squats and drums and drums, with 'sightless', 'soulless' eyes : I would rather have an ounce of human 'consciousness' than a universe full of 'abdominal' afflatus and hot, unconscious, 'soulless', mystical throbbing.

125

NOTES

1 This attack comes from Lewis, *Paleface*. London: Chatto & Windus, 1929, pp. 174–7, 180–84, 185–6, 193–6.
2 From a 1929 essay reprinted in D. H. Lawrence, *Selected Literary Criticism*. London: Heinemann, 1964, pp. 411–12.
3 William Pritchard, 'Lawrence and Lewis', *Agenda* magazine, London, Autumn-Winter, 1969–70 (Wyndham Lewis Special Issue), p. 147.
4 Lewis, 'The Son of Woman', *Time and Tide*, London, April 18, 1931, p. 470.
5 Ibid., p. 472. In *Rude Assignment*, Lewis continued to deride Lawrence's 'arty voodooism' (p. 206) and his 'abdominal raptures about the Mexican Indian' (p. 204) but also called him 'that novelist of genius' (p. 106).
6 D. H. Lawrence, *Mornings in Mexico and Etruscan Places*. Harmondsworth: Penguin Books Ltd., 1974, p. 54.
7 Ibid.
8 Ibid.
9 Ibid., p. 55.
10 Ibid., p. 56.
11 Ibid., L.'s italics.
12 Ibid. All italics L.'s except *outside*.
13 Louis Berman, author of *The Glands and Human Personality*, attacked in *Time and Western Man*, pp. 354–9.
14 *Mornings in Mexico*, p. 56. L.'s italics.
15 Ibid. L.'s italics.
16 Eduard von Hartmann, author of *Philosophy of the Unconscious*, another target of *Time and Western Man* (pp. 334–9) for his theories on the unconscious as the driving force of human life.
17 Samuel Alexander (1859–1938), the philosopher whose theories of an evolving cosmic order—set out in *Space, Time and Deity* (1920)—Lewis assailed in *Time and Western Man*.
18 *Mornings in Mexico*, p. 56. L.'s italics.
19 Nineteenth-century author of *Ancient Law*.
20 René Fülöp-Miller, *The Mind and Face of Bolshevism*. London: G. P. Putnam's & Sons, Ltd., 1927, p. 2. L.'s italics.
21 *Mornings in Mexico*, pp. 56–7. L.'s italics.
22 Ibid., p. 57.
23 Ibid., p. 58.
24 Ibid. L.'s italics.
25 Ibid., p. 63.

9

Sherwood Anderson

(From *Paleface*, 1929)

In an introduction to the 1964 English edition of Ernest Hemingway's celebrated spoof on Sherwood Anderson, *The Torrents of Spring*, David Garnett wrote of the *Paleface* section from which the excerpts below[1] are taken: 'In a brilliant critical essay Wyndham Lewis analysed in detail the ideas underlying Anderson's *Dark Laughter* and compared them with Lawrence's ideas in *Mornings in Mexico*. Nothing could be better than Wyndham Lewis's exposure of the stupidity of these ideas, and the painstaking reader would do well to look up *Paleface*. The only fault to be found with Lewis is that he was an alarmist who saw a deadly danger lurking round every corner. But I myself cannot see in Anderson's ideas . . . anything very original.'[2] *Paleface* as a whole marked a turning point in Lewis's career, after which he speedily lost much of the favour he had previously enjoyed with the liberal intelligentsia. To charges that the book was anti-Coloured, he protested that he had sought merely 'to attack the Paleface sentimentalizing about the dark skin . . . and *not* the Asiatic or the African.'[3] D. G. Bridson, in *The Filibuster*, his comprehensive study of Lewis's political ideas, notes that it was mainly from books by Sherwood Anderson that Lewis gathered quotations to show how the Black American was being romanticized—and debased. The Black American as depicted by Anderson is 'the archetypal Uncle Tom', Bridson writes, 'and Lewis is to be credited with recognizing Uncle Tommery long before it was officially denounced by the Black militants.'[4]

I am now going over into the books of Sherwood Anderson : and I assure you that, if you have followed my analysis of the passages in *Mornings in Mexico*, you will be in a much better position to understand exactly what Mr. Anderson wants to say to you, at the same time that he spins you an excellent yarn.

I will begin with *Dark Laughter* (it pairs very well with *Mornings in Mexico*, though, as a book, in every way inferior, and not even a 'good yarn'); and I will take my leave of Mexico with a quotation describing the parrots in the patio mocking Rosalino the indian servant, with *their* 'dark laughter'. In this way the two types of 'dark laughter' will be brought into the nearest possible contact, so that any reader will be able to see how very near they are together in spirit, as well.

The two parrots 'a quite commonplace pair of green birds' sit or hang there, with their 'flat disillusioned eyes', their 'heavy overhanging noses', their 'sad old long-jowled faces', and *watch* the ridiculous human beings underneath hour after hour, bursting into mockery when tired of watching and noting.

> The parrots whistle exactly like Rosalino, only a little more so . . . Rosalino, sweeping the *patio* with his twig broom . . . covers himself more and more with the cloud of his own obscurity. . . . Up goes the wild, sliding Indian whistle into the morning. . . .[5]

Mr. Sherwood Anderson's book, *Dark Laughter*, ends as follows :

> Why couldn't Fred laugh? He kept trying but failed. In the road before the house one of the negro women now laughed. There was a shuffling sound. The older negro woman tried to quiet the younger, blacker woman, but she kept laughing the high shrill laughter of the negress. 'I knowed it, I knowed it, all the time I knowed it,' she cried, and the high shrill laughter ran through the garden and into the room where Fred sat upright and rigid in bed.
> The End.[6]

The negresses in *Dark Laughter* (they are the black servants, and their mocking laughter usually rises from the scullery or kitchen) perpetually release their 'high shrill laughter of the negress', as they observe with astonishment and derision the feebleness and absurdity of their White Overlords up in the parlour and out on the lawn. 'Up goes the wild, sliding Indian whistle in the morning' from the parrots (mocking the human beings in the court beneath, from which, owing to the overlordship of the human species, they are excluded, and forced to pass their time hanging upon the trees) in Mr. Lawrence's *Mornings in Mexico* : and up goes the 'high shrill laughter' of the negroes in Mr. Sherwood Anderson's *Dark Laughter*. The *negresses* in Mr. Anderson's book are in the rôle of the *parrots* in Mr. Lawrence's book: and the White Overlords in Mr. Anderson's book are in the rôle of Homo Sapiens in Mr. Lawrence's book. But in Mr. Lawrence's book, as in Mr. Anderson's, the *White Overlord*, rather than the more abstract and fundamental Human Being, is the true objective. And the Mexican Indian in *Mornings in Mexico* plays the part of the Negro in *Dark Laughter*. I think this parallel can be missed by no one. So there is a good deal of truth, it seems, in the 'moron' critic's gibe, 'Sherwood Lawrence', in Mr. Mencken's *Americana*.[7]

Dark Laughter is the story of a journalist who, having escaped from his wife in Chicago, gets employment in a small town in the South. He finds his employer's wife ('Fred' is the employer) attractive. She returns his love. She advertises for a gardener. He takes on the job. After what seems a very long time to the negro woman watching from the kitchen and other menial vantage points, Fred's wife and the hired man go up to the bedroom of the wife of Fred, the employer, during Fred's absence, and the 'deed of darkness' is at last consummated.

A high-pitched negro laugh rang through the house.—(End of Book Ten.)[8]

That is the story. It proceeds to the mocking accompaniment of the laughter of the negro servants who find their masters a great joke. Fred's wife finds their laughter disquieting, but she dismisses it as follows:

Soon it would be evening, the negro women come home. . . . About the negro women it did not matter. They would think as their natures led them to think, feel as their natures led them to feel. You can't ever tell what a negro woman thinks or feels. They are like children looking at you. . . . White eyes, white teeth in a brown face—laughter.[9]

But *we*, the readers of *Dark Laughter*, know what the negresses think more or less, for we have the following enlightenment, which resolves itself into a sort of 'Attaboy' chorus—the manly straightforward advice of the divinely-inspired black child of nature: 'Get down to it! Get to business! Hurry up! Have her quick! Don't hang and moon about!'

Negroes singing—

> And the Lord said . . .
> Hurry, Hurry.

Negroes singing had sometimes a way of getting at the ultimate truth of things. Two negro women sang in the kitchen of the house. . . . The two negro women in the house sang, did their work, looked and listened.[10]

That is the situation. 'Spring was coming on fast in southern Indiana.'[11] But the specimen of the White race depicted for us, called upon to be the 'man in the case 'or third side to the triangle, and to accommodate Freds' wife, is slow, slow—as slow, in fact, as *the spring in southern Indiana* is fast. And—

> The two negro women in the house watched and waited. Often they looked at each other and giggled. The air on the hill top was filled with laughter—*dark laughter.*
> 'Oh, Lord! Oh, Lord! Oh, Lord!' one of them cried to the other. She laughed—a high-pitched negro laugh.[12]

It is the 'Spring' motif of *Dark Laughter* that Mr. Ernest Hemingway has so ably caricatured in his *Torrents of Spring.* [. . . .]

Mr. Hemingway's book, it is to be hoped, will put a stop to *Dark Laughter* for the time, at least, on the part of Mr. Anderson. But some form or other of it (and it becomes, with people more sophisticated than Mr. Anderson, though otherwise much the same, White laughter or imitation-'dark') is sure to abound and to multiply, since it has struck root in the anglo-saxon mind : and one swallow, that is one Hemingway, does not either make or mar an andersonian spring—that teutonic zolaesque, meaty, maudlin, sexish spring, heralding a communist summer—in which, delirious with the 'chinook', creatures are rhetorically invited to *merge* in the 'dark' juicy matrix of Mother Nature in colossal, 'direct', 'soulless' abandons.

The dread of sexual impotence, thoughts about impotence, taunts about impotence, anxious appeals to the 'chinook'—of such cheerful and 'manly' material as this are many of the pages of Mr. Lawrence and Mr. Sherwood Anderson composed. But there is a strain of frank and free modesty in Mr. Anderson, whenever he casts a glance in the direction of his own 'maleness'. It leaves much to be desired, in his eyes. Throughout his books Mr. Anderson indeed is comparing himself unfavourably, on the score of his 'manhood', with other men (his brother, for instance in the account of his childhood). In his *Story Teller's Story*,[13] and indeed everywhere when he appears in a more or less veiled form, these dark doubts beset him. The adulterous Bruce in *Dark Laughter* feels that a *real man* would behave quite different from what he does in most things. He would make less fuss, *think* about things less, *act*. He is a bit of a poet, really, that is what it is, not a man of action he says to himself. Perhaps Mr. Anderson is over-modest. He is probably as 'manly' as most men : but, however that may be, he is very much puzzled and befuddled : he is a poor henpecked, beFreuded, bewildered White, with a brand-new 'inferiority complex'.

Mr. Lawrence is quite a different story. He is in full and exultant enjoyment of a full battery of 'complexes' of every possible shade and shape of sexiness. He possesses them *en connaisseur*, and any new one that is suggested to him he receives with an experienced delight. He is *l'homme moyen sensuel* gloating over the savouriness and variety of the contemporary fare. Beside him Anderson strikes one as a rather muddle-headed, clumsy, in some ways very stupid sensationalist, doing his best for a group of 'dark' influences which he very imperfectly understands, and often misinterprets.

NOTES

1 From *Paleface*, pp. 196–200, 202–4.
2 Ernest Hemingway, *The Torrents of Spring*. (Published 1926). London : Jonathan Cape, 1964, introduction by David Garnett, pp. 14–15.
3 *Rude Assignment*, p. 206.
4 D. G. Bridson, *The Filibuster*. London : Cassell, 1972, p. 85.
5 Lawrence, *Mornings in Mexico*, p. 10.
6 Sherwood Anderson, *Dark Laughter*. London : Jarrolds, 1926, p. 288.
7 H. L. Mencken, ed., *Americana 1925*. London : Martin Hopkinson & Co. Ltd., 1925, p. 1.
8 *Dark Laughter*, p. 243.
9 Ibid., p. 241.
10 Ibid., pp. 224–5.
11 Ibid., p. 203.
12 Ibid., p. 229. L.'s italics.
13 *A Story Teller's Story* (1924), Anderson's semi-fictional autobiography.

Ernest Hemingway

(From *Men Without Art*, 1934)

Despite Hemingway's violent reaction to the chapter—subtitled 'The "Dumb Ox" '—from which the following excerpts are taken,[1] Lewis consistently admired the American writer. 'I have always had a great respect for Hemingway,' he wrote in *Rude Assignment*, where he also quoted a letter from Hemingway to himself as saying, '[I] thought you destroyed the Red and Black Enthusiasm very finely in *Paleface*'.[2] But the 'Dumb Ox' essay left Hemingway 'so much enraged that he punched a vase of tulips' in a Paris bookshop where he was shown Lewis's chapter.[3] Hemingway tried to wreak his final revenge with personal abuse of Lewis in his memoir of Paris in the Twenties, *A Moveable Feast* (1964). In an article for a Toronto magazine in 1942, Lewis contrasted the work of fiction-writer Morley Callaghan—wrongly billed 'The Canadian Hemingway'—with that of the American. In Callaghan's 1936 collection, *Now That April's Here and Other Stories*, Lewis found, not the 'crude dynamism' he had been led to expect, but 'discrete miniature dramas' which ended softly and gently. 'The plot, however tragic, is *not* some diabolic and meaningless phantasy, in other words—which is the fatal conclusion that we are required to draw from the perusal of a story, say of Mr. Hemingway's. There is good and evil—not merely *good luck* and *bad luck*.' Thus Lewis was pleasantly surprised by what he called Callaghan's 'gently-stepping, gravely resigned, little parables of everyday life'.[4]

Ernest Hemingway is a very considerable artist in prose-fiction. Besides this, or with this, his work possesses a penetrating quality, like an animal speaking. Compared often with Hemingway, William Faulkner is an excellent, big-strong, novelist : but a conscious artist he cannot be said to be. Artists are made, not born : but he is considerably older, I believe, than Hemingway, so it is not that. But my motive for discussing these two novelists has not been to arrive at estimates of that sort.

A quality in the work of the author of *Men Without Women* suggests that we are in the presence of a writer who is not merely a conspicuous chessman in the big-business book-game of the moment, but something much finer than that. Let me attempt to isolate that quality for you, in such a way as not to damage it too much : for having set out to demonstrate the political significance of this artist's work, I shall, in the course of that demonstration, resort to a dissection of it—not the best way, I am afraid, to bring out the beauties of the finished product. This dissection is, however, necessary for my purpose here. 'I have a weakness for Hemingway,' as the egregious Miss Stein says :[5] it is not agreeable to me to pry into his craft, but there is no help for it if I am to reach certain important conclusions.

But *political significance!* That is surely the last thing one would expect to find in such books as *In Our Time, The Sun Also Rises, Men Without Women,* or *A Farewell to Arms.* And indeed it is difficult to imagine a writer whose mind is more entirely closed to politics than is Hemingway's. I do not suppose he has ever heard of the Five-Year Plan, though I dare say he knows that artists pay no income tax in Mexico, and is quite likely to be following closely the agitation of the Mexican matadors to get themselves recognized as 'artists' so that they may pay no income tax. I expect he has heard of Hitler, but thinks of him mainly, if he is acquainted with the story, as the Boche who went down into a cellar with another Boche and captured thirty Frogs and came back with an Iron Cross. He probably knows that his friend Pound writes a good many letters every week to American papers on the subject of Social Credit, but I am sure Pound has never succeeded in making him read a line of *Credit-power and Democracy.*[6] He is interested in the sports of death, in the sad things that happen to those engaged in the sports of love—in sand-sharks and in Wilsonspoons—in war, but *not* in the things that cause war, or the people who profit by it, or in the ultimate human destinies involved in it. He lives, or affects to live, *submerged.* He is in the multitudinous ranks of *those to whom things happen*—terrible things of course, and of course stoically borne. He has never heard, or affects never to have heard, that there is another and superior element, inhabited by a type of unnatural men which preys upon that of the submerged type. Or perhaps it is not quite a submerged mankind to which he belongs, or affects to belong, but to something of the sort described in one of Faulkner's war stories : 'But after twelve years,' Faulkner writes, 'I think of us as bugs in the surface of the water, isolant and aimless and unflagging. Not on the surface; in it, within that line of demarcation not air and not water, sometimes submerged, sometimes not.'[7] (What a stupid and unpleasant word 'isolant' is ! Hemingway would be incapable of using such a word.) But—twelve, fifteen years afterwards—to be *submerged*, most of the time, is Hemingway's idea. It is a little bit of an *art pur* notion, but it is, I think, extremely effective, in his case. Faulkner is much less preoccupied with art for its own sake, and although he has obtained his best successes by submerging himself again (in an intoxicating and hysterical fluid) he does not like being submerged quite as well as Hemingway, and dives rather because he is compelled to dive by public opinion, I imagine, than because he feels at home in the stupid medium of the sub-world, the *bêtise* of the herd. Hemingway has really taken up his quarters there, and has mastered the medium entirely, so that he is of it and yet not of it in a very satisfactory way.

Another manner of looking at it would be to say that Ernest Hemingway is the Noble Savage of Rousseau, but a white version, the simple American man. That is at all events the rôle that he has chosen, and he plays it with an imperturbable art and grace beyond praise.

It is not perhaps necessary to say that Hemingway's art is an art of the surface—and, as I look at it, none the worse for that. It is almost purely an art of action, and of very violent action, which is another qualification. Faulkner's is that too : but violence with Hemingway is deadly matter-of-fact (as if there were only violent action and nothing else in the world) : whereas with Faulkner it is an excited crescendo of psychological working-up of a sluggish and not ungentle universe, where there *might* be something else than high-explosive—if it were given a Chinaman's chance, which it is not. The latter is a far less artistic purveyor of violence. He does it well : but as to the manner, he does it in a way that any fool could do it. Hemingway, on the other hand, serves it up like the master of this form of art that he is, immeasurably more effective than

Faulkner—good as he is; or than say the Irish novelist O'Flaherty[8] —who is a *raffiné* too, or rather a two-gun man; Hemingway really banishes melodrama (except for his absurd escapes, on a Hollywood pattern, in *A Farewell to Arms*).

To find a parallel to *In Our Time* or *A Farewell to Arms* you have to go to *Colomba* or to *Chronique du Règne de Charles IX* : and in one sense Prosper Mérimée supplies the historical key to these two ex-soldiers—married, in their literary craft, to a theatre of action *à l'outrance*. The scenes at the siege of La Rochelle in the *Chronique du Règne de Charles IX* for instance : in the burning of the mill when the ensign is roasted in the window, that is the Hemingway subjects-matter to perfection—a man melted in his armour like a shell-fish in its shell—melted lobster in its red armour.

> S'ils tentaient de sauter par les fenêtres, ils tombaient dans les flammes, ou bien étaient reçus sur la pointe des piques. . . . Un enseigne, revêtu d'une armure complète, essaya de sauter comme les autres par une fenêtre étroite. Sa cuirasse se terminait, suivant une mode alors assez commune, par une espèce de jupon en fer qui couvrait les cuisses et le ventre, et s'élargissait comme le haut d'un entonnoir, de manière à permettre de marcher facilement. La fenêtre n'était pas assez large pour laisser passer cette partie de son armure, et l'enseigne, dans son trouble, s'y était précipité avec tant de violence, qu'il se trouva avoir la plus grande partie du corps en dehors sans pouvoir remuer, et pris comme dans un étau. Cependant les flammes montaient jusqu'à lui, échauffaient son armure, et l'y brûlaient lentement comme dans une fournaise ou dans ce fameux taureau d'airain inventé par Phalaris.[9]

Compare this with the following :

> We were in a garden at Mons. Young Buckley came in with his patrol from across the river. The first German I saw climbed up over the garden wall. We waited till he got one leg over and then potted him. He had so much equipment on and looked awfully surprised and fell down into the garden. Then three more came over farther down the wall. We shot them. They all came just like that.[10]

'In no century would Prosper Mérimée have been a theologian or metaphysician,' and if that is true of Mérimée, it is at least equally true of his American prototype. But their 'formulas' sound rather the same, 'indifferent in politics . . . all the while he is feeding all his scholarly curiosity, his imagination, the very eye, with the, to him ever delightful, relieving, reassuring spectacle, of those straightforward forces in human nature, which are also matters of fact.There is the formula of Mérimée! the enthusiastic amateur of rude, crude, naked force in men and women wherever it could be found . . . there are no half-lights. . . . Sylla, the false Demetrius, Carmen, Colomba, that impassioned self within himself, have no atmosphere. Painfully distinct in outline, inevitable to sight, un-relieved, there they stand, like solitary mountain forms on some hard, perfectly transparent day. What Mérimée gets around his singularly sculpturesque creations is neither more nor less than empty space.'[11]

I have quoted the whole of this passage because it gives you 'the formula', equally for the author of *Carmen* and of *The Sun Also Rises*—namely *the enthusiastic amateur of rude, crude, naked force in men and women:* but it also brings out very well, subsequently, the nature of the radical and exteremely significant *difference* exist-ing between these two men, of differing nations and epochs—sharing so singularly a taste for physical violence and for fine writing, but nothing else. Between them there is this deep gulf fixed : that gifted he of today is 'the man that things are done to'—even the 'I' in *The Sun Also Rises* allows his Jew puppet to knock him about and 'put him to sleep' with a crash on the jaw, and this first person singular covers a very aimless, will-less person, to say the least of it : whereas that *he* of the world of *Carmen* (so much admired by Nietzsche for its bright Latin violence and directness—*la gaya scienza*) or of Corsi-can vendetta, he was in love with *will*, as much as with violence : he did not celebrate in his stories a spirit that suffered bodily injury and mental disaster with the stoicism of an athletic clown in a par-ticularly brutal circus—or of oxen (however robust) beneath a crush-ing yoke : *he*, the inventor of Colomba, belonged to a race of men for whom action meant *their* acting, with all the weight and momentum of the whole of their being : *he* of post-Napoleonic France cele-brated intense spiritual energy and purpose, using physical violence as a mere means to that only half-animal ideal. *Sylla, Demetrius, Colomba*, even *de Mergy*, summon to our mind a world bursting with purpose—even if always upon the personal and very animal plane, and with no more universal ends : while Hemingway's

136

books, on the other hand, scarcely contain a figure who is not in some way futile, clown-like, passive, and above all *purposeless*. His world of men and women (*in violent action*, certainly) is completely empty of will. His puppets are leaves, *very violently* blown hither and thither; drugged or at least deeply intoxicated phantoms of a sort of matter-of-fact shell-shock.

In *A Farewell to Arms* the hero is a young American who has come over to Europe for the fun of the thing, as an alternative to baseball, to take part in the Sport of Kings. It has not occurred to him that it is no longer the sport of kings, but the turning-point in the history of the earth at which he is assisting, when men must either cease thinking like children and abandon such sports, or else lose their freedom for ever, much more effectively than any mere *king* could ever cause them to lose it. For him, it remains 'war' in the old-fashioned semi-sporting sense. Throughout this ghastly event, he proves himself a thorough-going sport, makes several hair-breadth, Fenimore Cooper-like, escapes, but never from first to last betrays a spark of intelligence. Indeed, his physical stoicism, admir-able as it is, is as nothing to his really heroic imperviousness to thought. This 'war'—Gallipoli, Paschendaele, Caporetto—is just another 'scrap'. The Anglo-Saxon American—the 'Doughboy'—and the Anglo-Saxon Tommy—join hands, in fact, outrival each other in a stolid determination absolutely to ignore, come what way, what all this is about. Whoever may be in the secrets of destiny—may indeed be destiny itself—*they* are not nor ever will be. They are an integral part of that world *to whom things happen* : they are not those who cause or connive at the happenings, and that is per-fectly clear.

> *Pack up your troubles in your old kit bag,*
> *Smile boys, that's the style*

and *keep smiling*, what's more, from ear to ear, a *should-I-worry?* 'good sport' smile, as do the Hollywood Stars when they are being photographed, as did the poor Bairnsfather 'Tommy'— the 'mud-died oaf at the goal'—of all oafishness![12]

I hope this does not seem irrelevant to you : it is not, let me re-assure you, but very much the contrary. The roots of all these books are in the War of 1914-1918, as much those of Faulkner as those of Hemingway : it would be ridiculous of course to say that either of these two highly intelligent ex-soldiers shared the 'oafish' mentality altogether : but the war-years were a democratic, a *levelling*, school, and both come from a pretty thoroughly 'levelled' nation, where personality is the thing least liked. The rigid organization of the communal life as revealed in *Middletown*, for instance[13] (or such a phenomenon as N.R.A.)[14] is akin to the military state. So *will*, as expressed in the expansion of the individual, is not a thing we should expect to find illustrated by a deliberately typical American writer.

Those foci of passionate personal energy which we find in Mérimée, we should look for in vain in the pages of Hemingway or Faulkner : in place of Don José or of Colomba we get a pack of drugged or intoxicated marionettes. These differences are exceedingly important. [. . . .]

So any attempt to indentify 'the formula' for Prosper Mérimée with that of Ernest Hemingway would break down. You are led at once to a realization of the critical difference between these two universes of discourse, both employing nothing but physical terms; of how an appetite for the extremity of violence exists in both, but in the one case it is personal ambition, family pride, romantic love that are at stake, and their satisfaction is violently sought and undertaken, whereas in the other case purposeless violence, for the sake of the 'kick', is pursued and recorded, and the 'thinking subject' is to regard himself as nothing more significant than a ripple beneath the breeze upon a pond.

If we come down to the manner, specifically to the style, in which these sensational impressions are conveyed, again most interesting discoveries await us : for, especially with Mr. Hemingway, the story is told in the tone, and with the vocabulary, of the persons described. The rhythm is the anonymous folk-rhythm of the urban proletariat. Mr. Hemingway is, self-consciously, a folk-prose-poet in the way that Robert Burns was a folk-poet. But what is curious about this is that the modified *Beach-la-mar*[15] in which he writes, is, more or less, the speech that is proposed for everybody in the future —it is a volapuk which probably will be ours tomorrow. For if the chief executive of the United States greets the Roman Catholic democratic leader (Al Smith) with the exclamation 'Hallo old potato !' today, the English political leaders will be doing so the day after tomorrow. And the Anglo-Saxon *Beach-la-mar* of the future will not be quite the same thing as Chaucer or Dante, contrasted with the learned tongue. For the latter was the speech of a race rather than of a class, whereas our 'vulgar tongue' will really be *vulgar*.

But in the case of Hemingway the folk-business is very seriously complicated by a really surprising fact. He has suffered an over-mastering influence, which cuts his work off from any other, except that of his mistress (for his master has been a *mistress*!). So much is this the case, that their destinies (his and that of the person who so strangely hypnotized him with her repeating habits and her *faux-naif* prattle) are for ever interlocked. His receptivity was so abnor-mally pronounced (even as a craftsman, this capacity for being *the person that things are done to* rather than the person who naturally initiates what is to be done to others, was so marked) and the affinity thus disclosed was found so powerful! I don't like speaking about this, for it is such a first-class complication, and yet it is in a way so irrelevant to the spirit which informs his work and must have in-formed it had he never made this apparently overwhelming 'con-tact.' But there it is : if you ask yourself how you would be able to tell a page of Hemingway, if it were unexpectedly placed before you, you would be compelled to answer, *Because it would be like Miss Stein!* And if you were asked how you would know it was not by Miss Stein, you would say, *Because it would probably be about prize-fighting, war, or the bull-ring, and Miss Stein does not write about war, boxing or bull-fighting!*

It is very uncomfortable in real life when people become so cap-tivated with somebody else's tricks that they become a sort of cari-cature or echo of the other : and it is no less embarrassing in books, at least when one entertains any respect for the victim of the fascina-tion. [. . . .]

[Lewis then quotes a long passage from Hemingway's story 'In Our Time', on the girl fantasies of the central character, Krebs, juxtapos-ing it with quotations from Stein's *Three Lives* and *Composition as Explanation*.]

There is no possibility, I am afraid, of slurring over this. It is just a thing that you have to accept as an unfortunate handicap in an artist who is in some respects above praise. Sometimes it is less pro-nounced, there are occasions when it is *almost* absent—Krebs, for instance, is a full-blooded example of Hemingway steining away for all he is worth. But it is never quite absent.

How much does it matter? If we blot out Gertrude Stein, and suppose she does not exist, does this part of Hemingway's equipment help or not? We must answer *Yes* I think. It does seem to help a good deal : many of his best effects are obtained by means of it. It is so much a part of his craft, indeed, that it is difficult now to imagine Hemingway without this mannerism. He has never taken it over into a gibbering and baboonish stage as has Miss Stein. He has kept it as a valuable oddity, even if a flagrantly borrowed one —ever present it is true, but one to which we can easily get used and come to like even as a delightfully clumsy engine of innocence. I don't mind it very much.

To say that, near to communism as we all are, it cannot matter, and is indeed praiseworthy, for a celebrated artist to take over, lock, stock and barrel from another artist the very thing for which he is mainly known, seems to me to be going too far in the denial of the person, or the individual—especially as in a case of this sort, the trick is after all, in the first instance, a *personal* trick. Such a practice must result, if universally indulged in, in hybrid forms or monstrosities.

And my main criticism, indeed, of the *steining* of Hemingway is that it does impose upon him an ethos—*the Stein ethos*, as it might be called. With Stein's bag of tricks he also takes over a *Weltanshauung*, which may not at all be his, and does in fact seem to contradict his major personal quality. This infantile, dull-witted, dreamy stutter compels whoever uses it to conform to the infantile, dull-witted type. He passes over into the category of *those to whom things are done*, from that of those who execute—if the latter is indeed where he originally belonged. One might even go so far as to say that this brilliant Jewish lady had made a *clown* of him by teaching Ernest Hemingway her baby-talk! So it is a pity. And it is very difficult to know where Hemingway proper begins and Stein leaves off as an artist. It is an uncomfortable situation for the critic, especially for one who 'has a weakness' for the male member of this strange spiritual partnership, and very much prefers him to the female.

Hemingway's two principal books. *The Sun Also Rises* (for English publication called *Fiesta*) and *A Farewell to Arms*, are delivered in the first person singular. What that involves may not be at once apparent to those who have not given much attention to literary composition. But it is not at all difficult to explain. Suppose you, Raymond Robinson, sit down to write a romance; subject-matter, the War. You get your 'I' started off, say just before the outbreak of war, and then there is the outbreak, and then 'I flew to the nearest recruiting station and joined the army' you write. Then the 'I' goes off to the Western Front (or the Italian Front) and you will find yourself writing 'I seized the Boche by the throat with one hand and shot him in the stomach with the other,' or whatever it is you imagine your 'I' as doing. But this 'I', the reader will learn, does not bear the name on the title page, namely Raymond Robinson. He is called Geoffrey Jones. The reader will think, 'That is only a thin disguise. It is Robinson's personal experience all right!'

Now this difficulty (if it be a difficulty) is very much enhanced if (for some reason) Geoffrey Jones is *always* doing exactly the things that Raymond Robinson is known to have done. If Raymond Robinson fought gallantly at Caporetto, for instance, then Geoffrey Jones—with the choice of a whole earth at war to choose from—is at Caporetto too. If Raymond Robinson takes to the sport of bull-fighting, sure enough Geoffrey Jones—the 'I' of the novel—is there in the bull-ring too, as the night follows day. This, in fine, has been the case with Hemingway and *his* First-person-singular.

Evidently, in this situation—possessing a First-person-singular that invariably copies you in this flattering way—something must be done about it. The *First-person-singular* has to be endowed so palpably with qualities that could by no stretch of the imagination belong to its author that no confusion is possible. Upon this principle the 'I' of *The Sun Also Rises* is described as sexually impotent, which is a complete alibi, of course, for Hemingway.

But there is more than this. The sort of First-person-singular that Hemingway invariably invokes is a dull-witted, bovine, monosyllabic simpleton. This lethargic and stuttering dummy he conducts, or pushes from behind, through all the scenes that interest him. This burlesque First-person-singular behaves in them like a moronesque version of his brilliant author. He *Steins* up and down the world, with the big lustreless ruminatory orbs of a Picasso doll-woman (of the semi-classic type Picasso patented, with enormous hands and feet). It is, in short, the very dummy that is required for the literary

141

mannerism of Miss Stein! It is the incarnation of the Stein-stutter
—the male incarnation, it is understood.

But this constipated, baffled 'frustrated'—yes, deeply and Freud-
ianly 'frustrated'—this wooden-headed, leaden-witted, heavy-
footed, loutish and oafish marionette—peering dully out into the
surrounding universe like a great big bloated five-year-old—pointing at this and pointing at that—uttering simply 'CAT!'—'HAT!'
—'FOOD!'—'SWEETIE!'—is, as a companion, infectious. His author
has perhaps not been quite immune. Seen for ever through his
nursery spectacles, the values of life accommodate themselves, even
in the mind of his author, to the limitations and peculiar requirements of this highly idiosyncratic puppet.

So the political aspects of Hemingway's work (if, as I started by
saying, one can employ such a word as *political* in connection with
a thing that is so divorced from reality as a super-innocent, queerly-
sensitive, village-idiot of a few words and fewer ideas) have to be
sought, if anywhere, in the personality of this *First-person-singular*,
imposed upon him largely by the Stein-manner. [. . . .]

If you place side by side the unfortunate impressionability of
Hemingway, which caused him to adopt integrally the half-wit
simplicity of repetitive biblical diction patented by Miss Stein, and
that other fact that Mr. Hemingway, being an American nationalist
by temperament, is inclined to gravitate stylistically towards the
national underdog dialect, in the last resort to the kind of *Beach-la-
mar* I have been discussing, you have the two principal factors in
Hemingway as artist in prose-fiction, to make of what you can.

Take up any book of his, again, and open it at random: you will
find a page of stuff that is, considered in isolation, valueless as
writing. It is not written: it is lifted out of Nature and very artfully
and adroitly tumbled out upon the page: it is the brute material
of every-day proletarian speech and feeling. The *matière* is cheap
and coarse: but not because it is proletarian speech merely, but because it is *the prose of reality*—the prose of the street-car or the
provincial newspaper or the five and ten cent store. [. . . .]

[Lewis then quotes a lengthy dialogue between the wounded hero
and hospital nurses in *A Farewell to Arms*.]

It is not writing, if you like. When I read *A Farewell to Arms*
doubtless I read this page as I came to it, just as I should watch

scenes unfolding on the screen in the cinema, without pictorial criticism; and it, page eighty-three, contributed its fraction to the general effect: and when I had finished the book I thought it a very good book. By that I meant that the cumulative effect was impressive, as *the events themselves* would be. Or it is like reading a newspaper, day by day, about some matter of absorbing interest —say the reports of a divorce, murder, or libel action. If you say *anyone could write it*, you are mistaken there, because, to obtain that smooth effect, of commonplace reality, there must be no sentimental or other heightening, the number of words expended must be proportionate to the importance and the length of the respective phases of the action, and any false move or overstatement would at once stand out and tell against it. If an inferior reporter to Hemingway took up the pen, that fact would at once be detected by a person sensitive to reality.

It is an art, then, from this standpoint, like the cinema, or like those 'modernist' still-life pictures in which, in place of *painting* a match box upon the canvas, a piece of actual match box is stuck on. A recent example of this (I choose it because a good many people will have seen it) is the cover design of the French periodical *Minotaure*, in which Picasso has pasted and tacked various things together, sticking a line drawing of the Minotaur in the middle. Hemingway's is a poster-art, in this sense: or a *cinema in words*. The *steining* in the text of Hemingway is as it were the hand-made part—if we are considering it as 'super-realist' design: a manipulation of the photograph if we are regarding it as a film.

If you say that this is not the way that Dante wrote, that these are not artistically permanent creations—or not permanent in the sense of a verse of Bishop King, or a page of Gulliver, I agree. But it is what we have got: there is actually *bad* and *good* of this kind; and I for my part enjoy what I regard as the good, without worrying any more about it than that.

That a particular phase in the life of humanity is implicit in this art is certain. It is one of the first fruits of the *proletarianization* which, as a result of the amazing revolutions in the technique of industry, we are all undergoing, whether we like it or not. [....]

[Lewis continues with a lengthy quotation from a courtroom account of a mutiny at sea, saying it quite well might be Hemingway. As further evidence, he juxtaposes it with a long quotation from Hemingway's story, 'Indian Camp'. The courtroom account is a slice of 'real life', Lewis comments. 'How close Hemingway is to such material as this can be seen by comparing it with the second passage out of *In Our Time*.']

That, I think, should put you in possession of all that is essential for an understanding of the work of this very notable artist : an understanding I mean; I do not mean that, as a work of art, a book of his should be approached in this critical and anatomizing spirit. That is another matter. Where the 'politics' come in I suppose by this time you will have gathered. This is the voice of the 'folk', of the masses, who are the cannon-fodder, the cattle outside the slaughter-house, serenely chewing the cud—*of those to whom things are done*, in contrast to those who have executive will and intelligence. It is itself innocent of politics—one might almost add alas! That does not affect its quality as art. The expression of the soul of the dumb ox would have a penetrating beauty of its own, if it were uttered with genius—with bovine genius (and in the case of Hemingway that is what has happened) : just as much as would the folk-song of the baboon, or of the 'Praying Mantis'. But where the politics crop up is that if we take this to be the typical art of a civilization—and there is no serious writer who stands higher in Anglo-Saxony today than does Ernest Hemingway—then we are by the same token saying something very definite about that civilization.

NOTES

1 From *Men Without Art*, pp. 17–25, 27–9, 34–5, 36–7, 40–1.
2 Lewis, *Rude Assignment*, p. 203.
3 Carlos Baker, *Ernest Hemingway*. Harmondsworth : Penguin Books, 1972, p. 393.
4 Lewis, 'What Books for Total War?', *Saturday Night* magazine, Toronto, October 10, 1942, p. 16.
5 Gertrude Stein, *The Autobiography of Alice B. Toklas*. London : John Lane The Bodley Head, 1935, p. 296.
6 The 1920 work by Major C. H. Douglas, pioneer of Social Credit, a doctrine with which Pound was for a time associated.
7 William Faulkner, 'Ad Astra', in *Thirteen Stories*. London : Chatto & Windus, 1931, p. 51.
8 Liam O'Flaherty (b. 1897), whose works include *The Informer* (1925).

9   Prosper Mérimée, *Chronique du Règne du Charles IX* (1829), in *Romans et nouvelles de Prosper Mérimée*. Paris: Editions Garnier Frères, 1967, pp. 218–19 of Tome I.

10   Hemingway, *In Our Time* (1925). See Hemingway, *The First 49 Stories*. London: Jonathan Cape, 1968, p. 96.

11   Walter Pater, *Miscellaneous Studies*. London: Macmillan & Co., Ltd., 1910, pp. 13-15.

12   Bruce Bairnsfather, creator of the World War I cartoon soldier, 'Old Bill'.

13   The pioneer study (1929) of a 'normal' American community—Muncie, Indiana—by Robert and Helen Lynd.

14   The National Industrial Recovery Act of 1933, a New Deal law under which President Franklin Roosevelt tried to regulate working conditions in American industry.

15   Originally the 'Pidgin' language of the Western Pacific spoken by fishermen in the sea-slug (*bêche-de-mer*) industry.

11

William Faulkner

(From *Men Without Art*, 1934)

The chapter—subtitled 'The Moralist with the Corn-cob'—from which the following is excerpted[1] was one of the first long essays on Faulkner published in England. Lewis was distantly linked to the South through the sentiments of his American father, Charles Edward Lewis, who fought on the Northern side in the Civil War. 'I am not at all sure that he fought upon the side that was most congenial to his outlook on life', the son wrote.' 'The "love", and "heroism", perhaps, was too much on the other side, for the peace of mind, or even the military purposes, of this confirmed romantic.'[2]

If I said that William Faulkner was composed in equal measure of Sherwood Anderson and of Powys,[3] I should say all that was necessary, from my standpoint. A gigantic 480-page Morality, like *Light in August*, is to me profitless and tiresome : a Calvinist moralist, delecting himself with, and turning to good library-sale's account, scenes of chopping, gashing, hacking, and slitting, is to me 'abomination' if it is not 'bitchery'—to use the words of one of his more typical figures, 'Old Doc Hines'. But his subject-matter, I agree, cannot be helped—no doubt the great rustic heart of America *is* moralist through and through, with a brand of fierce and blood-lustful sadic morality. With me, it is just that *La Terre* of Zola or the *earthy* works of Lawrence or Anderson, is not my favourite reading; just that the ranting sadism of melodrama is out of date and should be kept out of date : that the symbolical villagers of Mr. Powys are so ethically mechanized, into an abstract system as heavily centred in Sex, with the full stature of its serpentine capital-letter, as any Freudian tract, and so they, for me, become dull and empty exercises in Bunyan, which prevent me from reading far: merely that writing of the following order, from *Light in August*.

'Now it was still, quiet, the fecund earth now coolly suspirant,'[4] is as I see it irretrievably second-rate, built out of a wordy poetic padding, and every time it occurs (every half-dozen pages that is) it puts me off (I become 'coolly suspirant' myself, with the best will in the world to salute the qualities I think I perceive elsewhere in William Faulkner): it is simply that I have listened to all the 'Black Laughter' that I ever want to hear in the pages of Mr. Sherwood Anderson, and now, five years afterwards, find myself listening to it again in his disciple. Hemingway I can read with delight; but Faulkner fills me periodically with *White Laughter* and I do not thank him for it, I want to forget I am White for a while.

Having made this confession, and so warned you that I am not the person to come to for resounding appreciations of Faulkner's books, I can proceed. For this moralist is not an insignificant man, and, as one might expect, his books do contain a moral, which, for our purposes, we may assist him to drive home and develop.

I will begin with purely literary criticism. First of all then, Faulkner, unlike Hemingway, is a novelist of the old school—the actual texture of his prose-narrative is not at all 'revolutionary' or unusual. Just occasionally (as in the opening page or two of *Sartoris* and here and there in *Sanctuary* and *Light in August*) a spurious savour of 'newness' is obtained by a pretended incompetence as a narrator or from a confused distraction—a 'lack of concentration' it would popularly be called if it occurred in the narrative of a police-court witness. There is, very occasionally, a clumsy slyness of this sort, of the *faux-naif* variety, but it is quite a minor thing. Just now and then—only for a page or two—he will Joyce for a bit, but merely to the extent of innocently portmanteauing a few words just to show he is on the right side, such as 'shadowdappled' or 'downspeaking': but he has not much luck with this, as he is apt to arrive at such a result as the following: 'The rank *manodor* of his sedentary . . . flesh'—which looks too like *escupidor* to be a happy conjugation. For the most part his books might have been written by a contemporary of Trollope or the early Wells. [. . . .]

There is no reason whatever why a novelist today should not use the most 'straightforward' methods of narrative—the *code napoléon* was good enough for Stendhal, and we might do far worse than model ourselves upon it—I am not at all quoting [. . .] to damn Mr. Faulkner for being 'old-fashioned' : my object is to place him technically. More than half of his text belongs, as far as the *genre* of the writing is concerned, to the 'psychological' method of Conrad (or the translations of the great nineteenth-century Russian authors).

> So he would trick and avoid Brown in order to reach the cabin first. He expected each time to find her waiting. When he would reach the cabin and find it empty, he would think in a kind of impotent rage of the urgency, the lying and the haste, and of her alone and idle in the house all day, with nothing to do save to decide whether to betray him at once or torture him a little longer. By ordinary he would not have minded whether Brown knew about their relations or not. He had nothing in his nature of reticence or of chivalry toward women. It was practical, material. He would have been indifferent if all Jefferson knew he was her lover.[5]

That is his way of telling a story. It is not 'from the inside', nor yet 'from the outside', nor anything new-fangled of that sort. It is just the very respectable method that served for a century, from Stendhal to Conrad, say.

But there is a lot of *poetry* in Faulkner. It is not at all good. And it has an in the end rather comic way of occurring at a point where, apparently, he considers that the *atmosphere* has run out, or is getting thin, by the passage of time become exhausted and requiring renewal, like the water in a zoological-garden tank for specimens of fish. So he pumps in this necessary medium, for anything from half a dozen to two dozen lines, according to the needs of the case. This sort of thing :

> Moonlight seeped into the room impalpably, refracted and sourceless; the night was without any sound. Beyond the window a cornice rose in a succession of shallow steps against the opaline and dimensionless sky.[6]

His characters demand, in order to endure for more than ten pages, apparently, an opaque atmosphere of whip-poor-wills, cicadas, lilac, 'seeping' moonlight, water-oaks and jasmine—and of course the 'dimensionless' sky, from which the moonlight 'seeps'. The wherewithal to supply them with this indispensable medium is as it were stored in a *whip-poor-will tank*, as it might be called :

and he pumps the stuff into his book in generous flushes at the slightest sign of fatigue or deflationary listlessness, as he thinks, upon the part of one of his characters.

To compare him with Ernest Hemingway as an artist would indeed be absurd : but actually he betrays such a deep unconsciousness in that respect as to be a little surprising. In the above passage (about the *impalpable seeping of the moonlight*) you may have remarked a peculiar word, 'sourceless'. If in reading a book of his you came across this word—say upon the first page of *Sanctuary* where it occurs ('a thick growth of cane and brier, of cypress and gum in which broken sunlight lay sourceless')[7] and said to yourself '*sourceless*—what for mercy's sake is that !' you would soon find out. For a dozen pages farther on (where more poetic atmosphere was being pumped in, in due course) you would probably come across it again : and after you had encountered it half a dozen times or so you would see what he meant. [....]

[Lewis then lists examples of Faulkner's repeated use of 'sourceless' and 'myriad' in *Sartoris, Sanctuary, These 13* and *Light in August*.]

'The Spring will soon be here now in Southern Indiana !' exclaims with ecstatic monotony the hero of Hemingway's brilliant skit, *The Torrents of Spring*, as he sniffs the *chinook*.[8] And this type of writing (it was Sherwood Anderson that Hemingway was parodying in *The Torrents of Spring*) is dealt with as it deserves, and once and for all, in that little critical masterpiece. It must be extremely irritating for him (as for any other American possessed of a critical sense, and desiring to see established in America a school of prose-fiction of a technically tough, non-romantic order) to find this more recent, and now immensely advertised version of Andersonism perpetuating the very type of romantic bric-à-brac which *The Torrents of Spring* was composed to discourage. There is no occasion to pursue any further this analysis of the purely artistic quality of the work of Faulkner. His entire output, from that standpoint, is elementary. But it must be remembered that 'the novel' does not stand or fall by its artistic excellence. The work of a certain great Russian novelist, who was a harrassed bread-winner as well as a great dramatist, has demonstrated that. And there is much more to be said for Faulkner than this exposure of his technical equipment might suggest.

149

Faulkner is as full of 'passion'—of sound and fury—as Hemingway is austerely without it. He is as hot and sticky as Hemingway is dry and without undue heat. He works up and up, in a torrent of ill-selected words, to his stormy climaxes. With Hemingway the climaxes are registered by a few discreet touches here and there. The characters in Faulkner's books are as heavily *energized* as the most energetic could wish. And if they are all futilely energized and worked-up to no purpose—all 'signifying nothing'—if each and all of his stories is 'a tale by an idiot'—that does not make his Sartorises, Popeyes, Christmases, the priest in *Mistral* or Temple Drake, any the less an impressive company, in their hysterical way. All are demented : his novels are, strictly speaking, clinics. Destiny weighs heavily upon every figure which has its being in this suffocating atmosphere of whip-poor-wills, magnolias, fire-flies and water-oaks (not to mention the emanations of the *dark* and invariably *viscid* earth). And the particular form that that destiny takes is *race*. Whether it is Christmas or Sartoris, it is a matter of a fatality residing in the blood. They are driven on in a crazy and headlong career by the compulsion of their ancestry. [. . . .]

Violent death, as this indicates, is a matter of such importance in Faulkner's universe, it has such a baleful attraction, for his most ordinary puppets, in expectation or in memory, that it is able, two generations away, to so paralyse the imagination of one of them as to turn him into a dream of death-on-horseback !

The Civil War, and that apparently central problem of the American soul, the Black and White (for it is rather an important issue, all said and done, whether you shall give the negro equality and a century hence have a mulatto America, or on the other hand lynch him as soon as look at him) are the shadows over every life dealt with by Faulkner. The Sartoris family is literally rotten with fatality—there the *doom* becomes deliberately comic :

> It showed on John Sartoris' brow, the dark shadow of fatality and doom, that night when he sat beneath the candles in the dining-room and turned a wineglass in his fingers while he talked to his son. . . .
>
> 'And so,' he said, 'Redlaw'll kill me tomorrow, for I shall be unarmed. I'm tired of killing men. . . . Pass the wine, Bayard.'
>
> And the next day he was dead, whereupon, as though he had but waited for that to release him of the clumsy cluttering of bones and

breath, by losing the frustration of his own flesh he could now stiffen and shape that which sprang from him into the fatal semblance of his dream.[9]

Death is a bagatelle to a Sartoris—and indeed a Sartoris only becomes really effective after demise. As a ghost he is *some* ghost! But it is *de rigueur* that the death itself should be particularly *violent*—that every Sartoris exacts. And in that respect, where all his characters are concerned, Faulkner is a bit of a Sartoris himself. [. . . .]

The war is, in a sense, a complication for a 'doomed' Sartoris, because 'doom' in such a war as that of 1914-1918 becomes as cheap as dirt. One Sartoris vulgarly succumbs, but the other goes home, and commits suicide in an aeroplane as soon as the war is over and normal conditions of safety restored. And yet of course a man beneath a curse, predestined to a violent death, is, in a sense, in his element in a world-war—the element of the lightning-flash and thunder-stone. 'And that's all. That's it. The courage, the recklessness, call it what you will, is the flash, the instant of sublimation; then flick! the old darkness again. That's why. It's too strong for steady diet. And if it were a steady diet, it would not be a flash, a glare.'[10]

A flash, a glare—that is what Faulkner's books are intended to be—a very long flash, and a chronic glare, illuminating a 'doomed', a symbolical landscape—centred in that township of the Old Dominion symbolically named *Jefferson*.

The longest flash and glare of all is *Light in August*—and that, I think, is a flash in the pan. It is full of wearisome repetitions and is long-winded to the last degree : it is hysterical and salvationist more than is necessary, and it is comical where it is not meant to be. It contains, however, a great deal of good observation and passages of considerable power. Christmas, the half-negro, supplies us with all of these. He is a quite empty little figure, like 'Popeye' in *Sanctuary* : but he carried round a big 'doom' with him all right, and he makes it sound. His doom is of course his *blood*—or rather his two bloods, the white and the black. [. . . .]

But I should doubt if Faulkner is the master of any systematic notion of fatality. Evidently he took a great fancy at some time to the conception of a rigid destiny controlling human life, as exemp-

151

lified in the Greek Drama : and it supplies the melodramatic back-
bone of his books. That is all, I think.

There can be nothing harder to define than *melodrama* in distinction to tragedy. But a too great addiction to a notion of 'fate', and
a consequent loosening and slackening of the 'realistic' web of
'chance' or 'accident', will undoubtedly lead a writer more surely
than by any other path—especially if his purposes are sensational,
and mainly directed to excite and to entertain—to what would
probably be described as the *melodramatic*. Faulkner seems to me
to be melodramatic, distinctly. All his skies are inky black. He deals
in horror as in a cherished material. Coincidence, what he would
call 'fate', does not stand on ceremony, or seek to cover itself in any
fussy 'realistic' plausability, with him. When the doomed man, at
long last, is to be run to earth, there is every probability (according
to the law of these *improbable* narratives) that after wandering all
over the world, he will be run to earth at the very door of the cot-
tage in which dwells, quite unknown to him, his old grandmother,
who, however, has never set eyes on him until that day, and who
has no idea whether such a person as he exists or not until she finds
him with the rope round his neck. In short, there is *no* coincidence
that this robust fatalism is not prepared to admit. This certainly
makes novel-writing easier.

Of course, the intellectual morale of a destiny-crank, on the grand
model, is sorely tried in any case. It is enervating for him in that
respect, even as it is for men at large, in its influence upon their
general outlook. The conception of an all-embracing destiny has
its concomitant in an obviousness of association, and imposes at
once a mechanical form upon existence : as it is pre-eminently the
philosophy of the pure determinist.

A man like William Faulkner discovers fatalism, or whatever
you like to call it : it at once gives him something to live for, or
rather gives his characters something to live for—namely a great
deal of undeserved tribulation culminating in *a violent death*. That
simplifies the plot enormously—it is, in fact, the great 'classical'
simplification, banishing expectation. No one who knows Faulkner's
work is in any doubt, in picking up a book of his, as to what will
happen to the principal character; he will unquestionably die a
violent death, there is no occasion to turn to the last page. He is,
in fact, as dead already upon the first page, to all intents and pur-

poses, and bloodily dead, as is the corpse at the opening of a Van Dine[11] crime-novel. And it takes a more powerful and subtle intelligence than Faulkner's to cope with this essentially mechanical situation in such a manner as not to make it appear over-mechanical to the reader—or to prevent it from degenerating into a flabby and artificial structure, with eventually the necessary pawns practically emerging from a trap-door, or being telepathically spirited to the spot desired, blatantly in the nick of time. And where everyone knows what is going to happen the temptation merely to moralize the mechanism into *such* a preordained pattern that the march of events is a purely *ad hoc* progression, highly unreal and unconvincing, is very great. In fact, increasingly, there will be little incentive to do anything else, for such a story-teller. His attitude will tend to become like that of the doomed man himself. Why worry? A supernatural agency is at work. Miracles are the stock in trade of a supernatural agency.—Indeed, once you have admitted the existence of a supernatural agency, the unlikely and fortuitous are more 'natural' than the reverse. Indeed, it only remains a question of what quantity, if any, of non-fatalist, non-miraculous, constituents you shall include.

Since the climax is from the start in full view of *everybody*, including the figure who is destined to suffer it, the tendency must be at least to slacken the tension and conventionalize all that comes *in between*. And in *Light in August*—that last of this fatal series and the best example of its working—that is just what we find. A great deal of prosy melodramatic talk does intervene, in an interminable, sultry, marking time, until the Player shall produce the carving-knife, and balefully point at the root of all the 'abomination and bitchery', namely the sexual organs of the half-caste hero.

The advantages of the destiny-technique, where a highly-trained and intelligent audience is concerned, are obvious, as of course they have been universally accepted as a canon of European art since the time of the Athenian tragedy. If you eliminate the element of surprise (the capital source of a fevered and inartistic excitement) the tragedy can be regarded purely as a spectacle, and, relieved of all the vulgar tittivation and hysteria accompanying suspense, the individual attention of the audience can be given to the quality of the interpretation, the art factor : the actor becomes more important

153

than the plot, subtleties of 'rendition' are not lost, but may be savoured at leisure, a mood of philosophic contemplation may supervene, in place of the dream-like animal unconsciousness accompanying all violent action. The argument in favour of the *pseudo-statement*, or the *absence of belief*, advanced by Messrs. T. S. Eliot and I. A. Richards, is established upon a similar principle.[12]

But the success of this principle, as it issues in works of creative art, must depend upon the specifically *artistic* quality of the executant. And here William Faulkner is very weak. Then it will depend upon the integrity of the taste of the epoch that has called this conception forth. The early and middle Victorian period had plenty of melodrama, upon the Greek 'destiny' model. But it was very inferior stuff. And then it will also depend, for success, upon the intellectual foundations of the system which is responsible for it. And here, as I have said, in Faulkner's case I take it to be a personal fancy, merely, arising out of his experience, certainly (his war-experience, in all probability) but not of sufficient metaphysical solidity to guarantee it against irresponsible abuse. And, apart from the melodramatic 'Player' (who only turns up once, as far as I know), 'fate' seems to be with him a scientific notion, centred in heredity.

If you base your nomenclature upon an ethical vocabulary—call the township where your people have their being Backbite-on-Avon, make its mayor a Mr. Joseph Graft, its judge Judge Geoffrey Gallows, its local detective Ezra Lynx, and so forth, you are following a classical model, and the attention of the reader can be concentrated upon the game you have proposed to him, according to rules that have been universally accepted. The function of the 'critic' in that case becomes a simple one—that is cricket, from his point of view. All is as cut and dried as could be wished, within those disciplines.

Faulkner does not do that, he does not invite such facile comparisons as does Powys. But the town with which most of his books deal is symbolically named 'Jefferson'; his Sartorises all have the name of Bayard, that 'preux' whose chevaleresque attitudes they emulate: his diabolical half-caste is called 'Christmas', his outcast minister is named 'Hightower' suggestive of a high aloofness, and so on. The christening of his *dramatis personae* tends to the quality-name. But on the whole it approximates more to Dickens than to Bunyan. Lucas Burch and Byron Bunch (children of a Dickens-like coincidence), Dr. Peabody, Brother Strother and the Snopeses, are a Dickensian company.

I have said (not in disparagement) that Faulkner is an 'old-fashioned' writer compared with Hemingway, and this accounts for a good deal. He has gone back to the old conception of 'the novel', or he has never emerged from it would, I suppose, be more exact. He is artistically a contemporary of Conrad or Trollope (his High-tower, for instance, is an American Mr. Crawley of Hogglestock). He is a bold and bustling romantic writer, of the 'psychological' school. That is the main thing to grasp about him. It is, in short, except for a mere handful of *shadowdappleds* and *manodors*, as if Joyce had never jingled : except for *one* little shamefaced flourish, it is as if Miss Stein had never stuttered :

'Memory believes before knowing remembers. Believes longer than recollects, longer than knowing even wonders. Knows remembers believes a corridor in a big long garbled cold echoing building', etc.[13] That is the lot—and it is, now I come to look at it, Joyce rather than Stein—the rhythm is the Irish sentiment, not the Jewish lack of sentiment.

Miss Jenny, in Sartoris and elsewhere, with her 'fiddlesticks!', the racy good sense of her comic relief, and the negro chorus gener-ally, are pure Dickens, and there are swarms of oddities, or 'cards' —most of them, in their lives, blatant examples of coincidence, the victims of the minor operations of his pervasive fatality.

All this is to say that he has to be judged according to conven-tional standards of romantic novel-making : the question of his success or ill-success must be subordinated to the framework of a conventional and unreal pattern. Whereas Hemingway, reporter of genius that he is, fails or succeeds largely upon whether you decide he has got the facts *dead-right*, or, on the other hand, has ever so slightly shifted and conventionalized them in the process of re-porting them, Faulkner neglects or ignores that criterion of 'realistic' method. He must be judged according to romantic standards only— as, for that matter, is the case with most novelists. There are few people, who are professional novelists, able to do anything else, if they are to 'make good', than to conform to the more conventional and romantic standards of this rather slovenly, undisciplined art.

155

And of course it remains an open question whether such an art deserves the more exacting approach at all.

Of the books I have read of Faulkner's I like *Sanctuary* best. Its hero, 'Popeye', is sexually impotent, and what is called 'degenerate'. As a child he cuts up live kittens with scissors; he is sent to a reformatory; and in due course, as a man, he becomes the 'killer' of the sort with which we are familiarized by gangster books and films. The automatic strapped under his armpit satisfies the requirements of the sinister vacuum, of 'blood-lust' and vanity, which Nature has installed at the heart of his being, to be his particular destiny. For 'fate' works full-time here as well, and *Sanctuary* is a highly moral tale.

Popeye is, in this case, the instrument of fate, with his automatic and his corn-cob. The book was no doubt suggested to Faulkner by the *Faux-monnayeurs*, of André Gide—that and Judge Lindsey's *Revolt of Modern Youth*.[14] It is, again, pure melodrama, as a gangster and bootlegging novel could scarcely help being. [. . . .]

But the essence of the book—which I think was missed in the reviews I saw—is to be sought for in the pessimism engendered in any American of intelligence by the spectacle of child-corruption conjoined and coeval with the fantastic lawlessness which came in with Prohibition, culminating in the notorious case of the Lindbergh Baby, and which gave Popeye and his kind (the violent little gutter-Caesars of the Underworld) their chance. For it is not an accident that William Faulkner's gangster is one of the most insignificant and useless of men, brought to the top by the growing chaos in the heart of society—for whom human beings are flies to be dismissed from life as lightly as a troublesome insect, for the reason that he is himself a thing of the same order—that is undoubtedly the idea, and a highly moral one, you will agree.

[Here Lewis quotes three pages from *Sanctuary* (267–70) depicting the rowdiness of youths on a train trip—'the random intense purposelessness of children'.]

What you are intended to see in these scenes is undoubtedly the proliferation of a spoilt, a *purposeless*, a common, an irresponsible bourgeois society, awaiting, surely, if ever a society did, its *coup de grâce.* For nothing could be more bleak and redolent of 'chaos come again' than the pages of this violent morality play.

The drunken 'college-girl' egging on the 'killer' to do his trick, namely to kill, on the way to the dance-hall where 'Red' is put on the spot, is typical of the manner of conveying this ugly lesson.— Temple Drake taunts Popeye :

> 'You're scared to !'
> 'I'm giving him his chance,' he said, in his cold soft voice. 'Come on. Make up your mind.' . . .
> She leaned toward him, her hand on his arm. Then she got into the car. 'You won't do it. You're afraid to. He's a better man than you are.'
> He reached across and shut the door. 'Where?' he said. 'Grotto?'
> 'He's a better man than you are !' Temple said shrilly. 'You're not even a man ! He knows it. Who does know it if he don't?' The car was in motion. She began to shriek at him. 'You, a man, a bold bad man, when you can't even——'[15]

This is the 'little-hipped' doll, 'toothed' with mechanical smiles, *in action*—in the great world outside school and the family circle. She is the little sensational robot pupped by the American million-dollar-drugged capitalist system. That is certainly what this particular 'thriller' is intended to convey. And what Temple Drake gets is undoubtedly what has 'been coming to her'! What Temple Drake actually gets is a corncob; and the author's message to his country is beyond question that that is what Temple Drake, and all her kind, deserves. It is a harsh piece of sardonic pedagogy, no doubt, delivered with the hysterical violence we have come to expect from its author. But is it not salutary? Could anyone in their senses look upon this book as 'obscene', in any morally derogatory sense—regard it indeed as anything but a pure work of edification? None but the most stupid—or those who felt themselves involved in its purgative lessons—could do that. William Faulkner is not an artist : he is a satirist with the shears of Atropos more or less : and he is a very considerable moralist—*a moralist with a corn-cob!*

NOTES

1 From *Men Without Art*, pp. 42–3, 44–6, 48–9, 50, 51–2, 54–9, 60, 63–4.
2 Lewis 'The Do-Nothing Mode', *Agenda* Wyndham Lewis Number, p. 221.

3 Apparently the allegorical novelist, T. F. Powys.
4 William Faulkner, *Light in August*. London: Chatto & Windus, 1933, p. 266.
5 Ibid., p. 256.
6 Faulkner, *Sartoris*. London: Chatto & Windus, 1932, p. 160.
7 Faulkner, *Sanctuary*. London: Chatto & Windus, 1931, p. 1.
8 Paraphrase of the refrain often recurring in *The Torrents of Spring*.
9 *Sartoris*, p. 23.
10 *These Thirteen*, p. 109.
11 'S. S. Van Dine' (1888–1939), pen-name for the American art critic W. H. Wright, who wrote detective fiction starring Philo Vance.
12 See pp. 184–200 of the present collection.
13 *Light in August*, p. 111.
14 Judge Ben Lindsey, *The Revolt of Modern Youth* (1925). Lindsey (1869–1943), was a controversial expert on juvenile delinquency.
15 *Sanctuary*, p. 230.

V

Poets

1

Ezra Pound

(From *Time and Western Man*, 1927)

Before publication of the following attack on Ezra Pound,[1] the poet was deeply involved in musical composition as well as his usual maze of literary activities. He also wrote in support of the modern American composer, George Antheil, and published more of his *Cantos* in a Paris-based magazine called *This Quarter*. A co-editor of *This Quarter* was the young American Ernest Walsh, who died in 1925. Lewis refers to him here as 'Wush' and to the magazine as the *Q. Review*. Lewis's assault may have cooled relations for a time between himself and Pound, whose first prominent association with him was in the Vorticist movement of the previous decade and its celebrated review, *Blast*. But their friendship survived the 1927 storm and Lewis often saluted Pound subsequently for unstinting services to other writers. His monumental pictorial portraits of the poet also radiate admiration. 'He breathed Letters, ate Letters, dreamt Letters,' Lewis wrote of Pound many years after *Time and Western Man*. 'A very rare kind of man.'[2] Lewis also joined vigorously in the efforts to have Pound released from his post-World War II confinement. In an apparent reference to the 1927 attack, Pound wrote of Lewis to T. S. Eliot in 1946 : 'He once sd/a faceful. & apart from 3 dead and one aged [word?] . . . ole W is my only critic . . . all of which please tell the old ruffian if you can unearth him.'[3] But where Lewis asserted that Pound was naïve in the company he kept—'the horde of warblers he woos and wows must poison him with their dullness', Lewis wrote in a 1954 caricature[4]—Pound observed : 'Wyndham Lewis always claimed that I never *saw* people because I never noticed how wicked they were, what S.O.B.s they were. I wasn't the least interested in the vices of my friends, but in the intelligence.'[5]

———

Next [. . .] I propose to range, for analysis, an old associate of mine, Ezra Pound. There are some obvious objections to this, chief among them the personal regard in which I hold him. Since the War I have seen little of Pound. Once towards the end of my long period of seclusion and work, hard-pressed, I turned to him for help, and found the same generous and graceful person there that I had always known; for a kinder heart never lurked beneath a portentous exterior than is to be found in Ezra Pound. Again, Pound is not a vulgar humbug even in those purely propagandist activities, where, to my mind, he certainly handles humbug, but quite innoocently, I believe. Pound is—that is my belief—a genuine *naïf*. He is a sort of revolutionary simpleton!

But my present critical formulations must certainly bring me into conflict with many people whom Pound is pledged to support, or whom he is liable to support. For some time it has been patent to me that I could not reconcile the creative principles I have been developing with this sensationalist half-impresario, half-poet; whose mind can be best arrived at, perhaps, by thinking of what would happen if you could mix in exactly equal proportions Bergson-Marinetti-Mr. Hueffer (with a few preraphaelite 'christian names' thrown in), Edward Fitzgerald and Buffalo Bill. At all events, Pound's name and mine have certain associations in people's minds. For the full success of my new enterprise it is necessary to dispel this impression.

I will start by giving the briefest possible account of how, in the past, we came to work together.

The periodical, *Blast* (the first number of which appeared in 1914 just before the outbreak of war, and the second in 1915—the 'war-number'), was, as its name implies, destructive in intention. What it aimed at destroying in England—the 'academic' of the Royal Academy tradition—is now completely defunct. The freedom of expression, principally in the graphic and plastic arts, desired by it, is now attained, and can be indulged in by anybody who has the considerable private means required to be an 'artist'. So its object has been achieved. Though it is only about twelve years since that mass of propaganda was launched, in turning over the pages of *Blast* today it is hard to realize the bulk of the traditional resistance that its bulk was invented to overpower. How cowed these forces are today, or how transformed!

Ezra Pound attached himself to the Blast Group. That group was composed of people all very 'extremist' in their views. In the matter of fine art, as distinct from literature, it was their policy to admit no artist disposed to technical compromise, as they regarded it. What struck them principally about Pound was that his fire-eating propagandist utterances were not accompanied by any very experimental efforts in his particular medium. His poetry, to the mind of the more fanatical of the group, was a series of pastiches of old french or old italian poetry, and could lay no claim to participate in the new burst of art in progress. Its novelty consisted largely in the distance it went *back*, not forward; in archaism, not in new creation. That was how they regarded Pound's literary contributions. But this certain discrepancy between what Pound said—what he supported and held up as an example—and what he did, was striking enough to impress itself on anybody.

My opposition to Marinetti,[6] and the criticism of his 'futurist' doctrines that I launched, Pound took a hand in, though really why I do not know; for my performances and those of my friends were just as opposed to Pound's antiquarian and romantic tendencies, his velvet-jacket and his blustering trouvère airs, as was the futurism of Marinetti. But these inconsequences were matched by many other disorders and absurdities in our publicist experiments—inseparable from things done just for the day, and regarded as of no more consequence than hand-bills, and possibly rockets or squibs. Pound supplied the Chinese Crackers, and a trayful of mild jokes, for our paper; also much ingenious support in the english and american press; and, of course, some nice quiet little poems—at least calculated to vex Signor Marinetti with their fine *passéiste* flavour.

Until quite recently I heard little of my old friend. Then I was informed that the good Ezra was breaking out in a new direction. He was giving up words—possibly frightened, I thought, by the widespread opposition to *words* of any sort—words, idle words, and their manipulators. He was taking to music—a less compromising activity. For in music the sounds *say* nothing. (M. Paul Valéry, like Ezra Pound, would prefer to believe that they *say* nothing in poetry either.[7] But in spite of these musical dogmatists, *still they speak*. Pound shows his appreciation of this by turning to music.)

In the matter of revolutionary excitement there was indeed not much more to be got out of the plastic or graphic arts. Their purely 'revolutionary' value exhausted after the war (which also eclipsed and luckily put an end to Marinetti's bellowings, besides killing off most of the 'futurists'), their play-boys' place was taken by real, Red Revolution; just as Marinetti's post-nietzschean war-doctrine became War, *tout court*; and then Fascismo, which as Futurism in practice is the habit of mind and conditions of war applied to peace.

The Blast situation, on a meaner scale, repeats itself. Pound is there with a few gentle provençal airs, full of a delicate scholarship and 'sense of the Past', the organizer of a musical disturbance. The real business is done by a young musician, Antheil, of a fiery accomplishment and infectious faith in the great future of jazz. (As I don't know the first word in musical composition I can say nothing about Antheil's work, except that what he has played to me I have got considerable pleasure from.) Not only a typical Pound-situation is thus set up, but (as I see it), a typical 'revolutionary' situation of the bad type.

If Antheil is as interesting as I (quite ignorantly) believe him to be, and if he is really aiming at something *new*, the quality of Pound's championship, or his personal motives, would not concern us; though it is a question if his support is at any time more damaging or useful. But that is merely a practical question. It is *disturbance* that Pound requires : that is the form his parasitism takes. He is never happy if he is not sniffing the dust and glitter of *action* kicked up by other, more natively 'active' men. With all his admirable flair for 'genius' (in which he has described himself as 'a specialist'), it leads him into the support of things that are at once absurd and confusing. He is not always so lucky as I believe him to be in his choice of Antheil. It is the *type* of man that Pound is, or partly is, and the *method that* he advocates and practises, that sooner or later has to be repudiated by the artist.

Pound is, I believe, only pretending to be alive for form's sake. His effective work seems finished. The particular stimulation that Pound requires for what he does all comes from without; he is terribly dependent upon people and upon 'atmosphere'; and, with a sensationalist of his type, in the nature of things little development is possible, his inspiration is of a precarious order, attached as it is to what he regards as his rôle, handed him by a shadow to whose authority he is extremely susceptible, a Public he despises, is afraid of, and serves. So he is easily isolated, his native resources nil.

It is said that Nature kills all lyrical poets young. Perhaps Pound believed that he had found a solution for that distressing situation.

He may have become aware of an up-till-then undiscovered alternative for the lyrical poet. Just as Nature (very busy with other things at the moment), hearing a new lyric rising on the air from a quarter which she esteemed should have discontinued its issue of such youthful trifles, had turned with an obviously ugly intention towards the impertinent minstrel, lo! the utterance might change from the too literal howls and tenor-bursts of the tender passion, to a *romance sans paroles*, discreetly contrapuntal. 'Lips, cheeks, eyes and the night goes.' Nature is appeased. 'Let the lyrical poet, the good Ezra, live, since he has become a mere musician,' Nature might decide.

At all events, there is Pound (glad to be in the neighbourhood of a big drum) making music.

What made me finally decide that the time had arrived publicly to repudiate my association with Pound, was the following interview with him, appearing in the *Christian Science Monitor* two summers ago. Remembering his opposition, following me, to Marinetti and his 'futurism' (to that intellectualist *commis* of Big Business— especially the armament line—and his ridiculous gospel), this interview is especially curious :

'It is possible to imagine music being taken out of the chamber, and entering social and industrial life so completely and so splendidly that the whole clamor of a great factory will be rhythmically regulated, and the workers work, not to a deafening din, but to a superb symphony. The factory manager would be a musical conductor on an immense scale, and each artisan would be an instrumentalist. You think perhaps that George Antheil and I are foolish visionaries, etc.' . . .

It was thus that Ezra Pound, American poet and musician, indicated the possibilities of a convergence of the lines of industrial and musical development. Revolutionary as the notion appears at first sight, it is extraordinarily suggestive. So a thousand men not only would be making material things, but in the process would be producing not a mere cacophany of confused noises, but a gigantic symphony in accordance with a score directed by a *chef d'orchestre* altogether surpassing the *chef d'orchestre* of the concert-room. An entire town might, in Pound's view, become the stage from which would arise the regulated harmony of industry.

Marinetti is rehabilitated by Ezra—music, provençal airs and ballads of Villon, as far as he personally is concerned, taking him paradoxically right to the great throbbing, singing heart of the great god, Industry. I should be tempted to think it had taken Ezra a decade to catch up Marinetti, if I were not sure that, from the start, the histrionics of the milanese prefascist were secretly much to his sensation-loving taste. I observe rather that he has not moved from where he was. [....]

Ezra Pound does not share the child-cult at all with the people I have been considering. But this does not mean that he is unorthodox. He is very orthodox. He would be miserable if he thought he was not conforming to anything that claimed the majority of educated people as its adherents, or slaves. The fiats and orders-of-the-day of the latest encyclical of fashion never would find Ezra disrespectful. He has never desired, himself, to interfere in these mysterious dispensations, or to challenge the invariable worthiness of their origin. At the most, as one Sphinx to another, he may have ventured a wink, and a slight cough. Nor would it ever so much as pass through his mind to set the fashion himself. He receives; his is the receptive rôle; he is the *consumer*, as he would say. It is *we* who produce; we are the creators; Ezra battens upon us. And he is the most gentlemanly, discriminating parasite I have ever had, personally, nor would I desire a cleaner or sweeter (as Wush would say), if he ever wishes for a testimonial.

In the great Past there were creators, too; and there are few of them, from Sophocles to Cavalcanti, that Ezra has not pillaged. But I am sorry to say that I believe Ezra's effective life-work is over, as I have already remarked; for there are not many left, and of late he has steadily weakened.

But if any one supposes from these remarks, or if they think I mean, that Ezra Pound is a nobody, he will be mistaken. Yet how he is a 'somebody' is a little difficult to define. Pound is that curious thing, a person without a trace of originality of any sort. It is impossible even to imagine him being any one in particular of all the people he has translated, interpreted, appreciated.

When he writes about living people of his acquaintance, as sometimes he has done, he shows himself possessed of a sort of conventional malice, perhaps, that says about them things that other people would say about them; but he never seems to have *seen* the individual at all. He sees people and things as other people would see

166

them; there is no direct contact between Ezra and an individual person or thing. Ezra is a crowd; a little crowd. People are seen by him only as types. There is the 'museum official', the 'norman cocotte', and so on. *By himself* he would seem to have neither any convictions nor eyes in his head. There is nothing that he intuits well, certainly never originally. Yet when he can get into the skin of somebody else, of power and renown, a Propertius or an Arnaut Daniel, he becomes a lion or a lynx on the spot. This sort of parasitism is with him phenomenal.

Again, when he writes in person, as Pound, his phrases are invariably stagey and false, as well as insignificant. There is the strangest air of insincerity about his least purely personal utterance; the ring of the superbest conviction when he is the mouthpiece of a scald or of a jongleur.

The hosts of this great intellectual parasite, then, are legion; but in meeting Ezra you find yourself in the presence of a person who, if evidently not a source of life himself, has yet none of the unpleasant characteristics we associate with an organism dependent on others for its habitat and soil. He is such a 'big bug' in his class, that he has some of the airs of his masters. If thoroughly conventional, as you would expect of a good servant—his mind moving in grooves that have been made for it by his social milieu—he is not without personality, of a considerable and very charming sort.

My way of accounting for these discrepancies is as follows :

If Ezra Pound as a living individual were less worthy and admirable, I am convinced he would be unable to enter into the renowned and noble creatures whom he has passed his time in entering, so cleanly as he does—so faultlessly in places that you could not tell which is Pound and which is them. They or their genius or something that is in their work to guard it, would detect the imposture, and would certainly prevent him from working through them, in the splendid way that he has, were there any vulgarity or sham in the essential Ezra.

His dedication to his task has been fanatical. In order to slip in and out, as he does, in order to want to do so, so often as he has, and in such a great variety of cases, it was necessary for him—for his proper dedication to these men-gods—to be a kind of intellectual eunuch. That is my idea.

So I like, respect, and, in a sense, reverence Ezra Pound; I have found him a true, disinterested and unspoilt individual. He has not effected this intimate entrance into everything that is noble and enchanting for nothing. He has really walked with Sophocles beside the Aegean; he has *seen* the Florence of Cavalcanti; there is almost nowhere in the Past that he has not visited; he has been a great *time-trotter*, as we could describe this new kind of tourist. And he is not unworthy, in himself, of these many privileges.

But where the Present is concerned it is a different matter. He is extremely untrustworthy where that is concerned. That is the penalty of his function, like that of the eunuch instanced above. When he tries to be up-to-date it is a very uncomfortable business. And because he is conventional, and so accepts counterfeit readily where no standard has been established, he is a danger as far as he exerts any contemporary influence. He should not be taken seriously as a living being at all. Life is not his true concern, his gifts are all turned in the other direction. 'In his chosen or fated field he bows to no one', to use his words. But his field is purely that of *the dead*. As the *nature mortist*, or painter essentially of still-life, deals for preference with life-that-is-still, that has not much life, so Ezra for preference consorts with the dead, whose life is preserved for us in books and pictures. He has never loved anything living as he has loved the dead.

If this account of him is true, it is obvious how unfit he is to deal with living material at all. He has so much the habit of unquestioning obedience and self-effacement, that he cannot at all manage the unruly shape of things that are in-the-making, and which demand of him also some effort of a creative sort—ask him to set them limits, or direct them even. Ezra, in such a situation, is at his wits' end. He squints at them with an affectation of shrewdness, squares his shoulders, shouts something shrill and incoherent, but contributes nothing to the situation.

Before leaving Pound I feel it would be best to illustrate the foregoing observations a little. His best translations ('The Seafarer', for instance) are classics. It is to his more mixed work that I will go for my extracts. First I will draw attention to a point in the less disintegrated of that mixed type of work, where the translation element pre-dominates.

The reader is no doubt familiar with the word 'terse' in its canting sense. 'He was rather *terse* with me', people say. This can be otherwise expressed, 'He was *short* with me.' 'Terse' and 'short' are ways of expressing the laconic manner of a person who is annoyed, and in consequence uses few words, perhaps sarcastically. (Brevity or conciseness is the original meaning of terse.)

Here is an example of a man being 'terse' with another. Two doctors, Dr. Mann and Dr. Samuels, had a dispute as to whether a patient had fractured his collar-bone or not. In reporting their telephone conversation to a magistrate, Dr. Samuels said, 'Dr. Mann replied, "Tosh and nonsense." ' That was an extreme form of the explosive variety of 'terseness', of a conventional, professional type.

Now a kind of mock-bitter, sententious *terseness* characterizes most of Pound's semi-original verse, and even mars some of his translations. And then there is the 'terseness' that enlivens his journalism, which must be distinguished from the other more fundamental 'terseness' to which I am now drawing attention. In his journalism his 'terseness' is of much the same order as Dr. Mann's; it is of a breezy and boisterous order. For example, such violent expressions as 'bunk, junk, spoof, mush, slush, tosh, bosh,' are favourites with him; and he remains convinced that such over-specifically *manly* epithets are universally effective in spite of all proof to the contrary. But it is not that sort of 'terseness' to which I wished to refer.

The other, more fundamental, 'terseness' of Pound is also of a sententious and, by implication, 'manly' order. It seems to me to make his better personal verse (as distinguished from his translations) very monotonous, and gives it all a rather stupid ring. It is not, or course, the nature of metre chosen to which I am referring, but the melodramatic, chopped, 'bitter' tone suggested by the abrupt clipping and stopping to which he is addicted. It is the laconicism of the strong silent man. Were he a novelist, you would undoubtedly find the description 'He broke off' repeatedly used. In his verse he is always 'breaking off'. And he 'breaks off', indeed, as a rule, twice in every line.

> Cave of Nerea,
>   she like a great shell curved,
> And the boat drawn without sound,
> Without odour of ship-work,

169

> Nor bird-cry, nor any noise of wave moving,
> Nor splash of porpoise, nor any noise of wave moving,
> Within her cave, Nerea,
> > she like a great shell curved[8]

That actually seems to belong to the repetitive hypnotic method of Miss Stein and Miss Loos. 'She like a great shell curved,' and the 'any noise of wave moving', both repeated, are in any case swinburnian stage-properties. The whole passage with its abrupt sententious pauses is unpleasantly reminiscent of the second-rate actor accustomed to take heavy and emotional parts. Perhaps in this next quotation it will be seen better what I mean : —

> Now supine in burrow, half over-arched bramble,
> One eye for the sea, through that peek-hole
> Gray light, with Athene.
> Zothar and her elephants, the gold loin-cloth,
> The sistrum, shaken, shaken,
> > the cohort of her dancers.
> And Aletha, by bend of the shore,
> > with her eyes seaward,
> > and in her hands sea-wrack
> Salt-bright . . .[9]

How you are supposed to read this, of course, is with great stops upon—*burrow, bramble, peek-hole, gray light, Athene, Zothar, elephants, loin-cloth, sistrum, shaken, dancers, Aletha, seaward, sea-wrack, salt-bright.* The way the personnel of the poem are arranged, sea-wrack in the hand of one, Aletha 'with her eyes seaward,' the gold loin-cloth of another, etc., makes it all effectively like a spirited salon-picture, gold framed and romantically 'classical'. It is full of 'sentiment', as is the Cave of Nerea; it is all made up of well-worn stage-properties; and it is composed upon a series of histrionic pauses, intended to be thrilling and probably beautiful.

These extracts are from Cantos [XVII and XIX], and made their appearance in the *Q. Review*. Here is a specimen of Pound's more intimate verse (taken from the same place) : —

> And the answer to that is : Wa'al he had the ten thousand.
> And old Spinder, that put up the 1870 gothick memorial,
> He tried to pull me on Marx, and he told me
> About the 'romance of his business' : . . . so I sez :

Waal haow is it you're over here, right off the Champz Elyza?
And how can yew be here? Why don't the fellers at home
Take it all off you? ...
'Oh,' he sez, 'I ain't had to rent any money. ...
'It's a long time since I ain't had tew rent any money.'[10]

All Pound's comic reliefs speak the same tongue; they are all
jocose and conduct their heavy german-american horseplay in the
same personal argot of Pound. They can never have illumined anything but the most half-hearted smile (however kindly) rather at
Pound than at them. Their thick facetiousness is of the rollicking
slap-on-the-back order, suggesting another day and another scene
to ours. If they were better done and less conventional in their
broad unreality they would be welcome, like belated red-nosed
comedians in the midst of a series of turns too strictly designed to
meet the ultra-feminine drawing-room-entertainer taste, as a contrast. But they are not spirited enough to serve even that purpose.
They are a caricature of Pound attempting to deal with real life—
they are Pound at his worst.

If Pound had not a strain of absolutely authentic naïveté in him,
had he possessed the sort of minor sociable qualities that make the
trivial adjustments of the social world an open book to their pos-
sessor, he could not write in this clumsy and stupid way, when
attempting to stage scenes from contemporary life. So though they
represent Pound the artist at his worst, they show us, I believe, the
true Pound, or that part that has not become incorporated in his
best highly traditional poetry. And a simpleton is what we are left
with. That natural and unvarnished, unassimilable, Pound, is the
true child, which so many people in vain essay to be. But some in-
hibition has prevented him from getting that genuine naïf (which
would have made him a poet) into his work. There, unfortunately,
he always attitudinizes, frowns, struts, looks terribly knowing,
'breaks off', shows off, puffs himself out, and so obscures the really
simple, charming creature that he is.

NOTES

1 From *Time and Western Man*, pp. 54–8, 85–90. The latter pages bore the
   chapter heading 'A Man in Love with the Past'.
2 Lewis, *Blasting and Bombardiering*, enlarged 1967 edition. London: Cal-
   der & Boyars, pp. 288-9.

3 Quoted in Lewis, *Letters*, p. 394 n.
4 Lewis, 'Doppelgänger', reprinted in *Unlucky for Pringle*. London: The Vision Press, 1973, p. 210.
5 'Ezra Pound: An Interview', *The Paris Review*, 28, Summer-Fall, 1962, p. 34.
6 The Vorticists loudly opposed F. T. Marinetti's Futuristic glorification of the machine, speed and violence.
7 The French poet (1871–1945) actually published essays on music as well as language and other topics.
8 Ezra Pound, *The Cantos of Ezra Pound*. London: Faber & Faber, 1954, p. 80.
9 Ibid., p. 82.
10 Ibid., p. 88.

2

The Machine Poets

(1933)

In a somewhat curt obituary tribute to W. B. Yeats for Geoffrey Grigson's magazine *New Verse*, Lewis wrote that the Irish poet had afforded him 'a sort of kick : a kind of soft, dreamy kick. I am obliged to him. I am certain he will live. . . . I am *for* this particular ghost.'[1] He seemed much more interested in the poetry of some of his younger, left-wing contemporaries in the Thirties, notably W. H. Auden, Stephen Spender and their circle. In *Blasting and Bombardiering*, his 1937 autobiography, Lewis—while discussing changes in the literary climate of the time—referred to Auden and Christopher Isherwood. 'Is he [Auden] *the new guy who's got into the landscape?* No : but he's got the technique of a new guy. I like what he does. He is all ice and woodenfaced acrobatics. Mr. Isherwood, his *alter ego*, is full of sly Dada fun too. Both pander to the uplifted, both flirt robustly with the underdog, but both come out of Dr. Freud's cabinet. . . . If I have mentioned these Marxian playboys first, it is not out of bias for the rebellious mind. It is because the right-wing never "creates", for some reason, in England.'[2] Controversy about his own volume of verse, *One-Way Song* (1933), drew Lewis into public comment[3] on the circle of poets involved in the *New Signatures* anthology, first published in 1932. In a preface to the anthology, Michael Roberts, poet and critic, had suggested that the industrial age left traditional rustic imagery outmoded for poets, who had to accept that machinery now was a permanent part of the landscape. But Lewis could find no evidence of 'machine-mindedness' in two anthology contributions by C. Day Lewis and William Plomer. Of the anthology as a whole, which also included contributions by W. H. Auden, Stephen Spender, Julian Bell, Richard Eberhart, William Empson, John Lehmann and A. S. J. Tessimond, Lewis wrote that it was machine-oriented in the publicity provided for it by its preface. Otherwise, the contributors were 'as much a bunch of Shropshire Lads as ever Old England put into the field, or as the most bucolic could wish.'[4]

———————

The Graphic Arts are more suitable for this process of reflecting it is my belief where it is *machines* that are the objects in question, than are words. Being, as is often pointed out, more *direct*, and less involved with our specifically human attribute of speech, (being indeed a form of speech themselves, of a far more direct, and universal, order) the arts of painting and design, have a far greater range and a much more immediate contact with the non-human elements in things. [. . . .]

Meanwhile, it may as well be remarked, in literature a propaganda of 'machine-mindedness' is able to realize itself far more in rhythm and word-apposition than in the mere *mention* of rivets, pylons and driving-belts. And Auden is certainly the writer among the *New Signatures* 'cell' best equipped in that direction. For my part, I am and always have been much attracted by that quality (that is what the history of my doings in English art denotes, of course). And there is a great deal more of the 'mechanical' in draughtsmanship than is generally realized. So really—simple as far as my own personal taste is concerned—it is the most truly 'mechanical' or hard [. . .] concrete and most clearly silhouetted of the performers in this particular 'Machine' circus, that I like best—namely Auden, and Mr. Day Lewis, when he is following Auden most closely. There is no divorce, or discrepancy, in this respect, between my verbal predilections and those, in pigment, line, and plastic art.

Let me quote a verse of Mr. Spender's to bring home to you this point.

> I think continually of those who were truly great.
> Who, from the womb, remembered the soul's history
> Through corridors of light where the hours are suns
> Endless and singing. Whose lovely ambition
> Was that their lips, still touched with fire,
> Should tell of the Spirit clothed from head to foot in song.
> And who hoarded from the Spring branches
> The desires falling across their bodies like blossoms.[5]

The tone of these lines is characteristic of Mr. Spender's *Poems*,[6] and it is anything but the tempo of the Machine Age, I think, that is informing these long and languorous rhythms and generalized imagery. For me it is not 'mechanical' enough—though elsewhere Mr. Spender satisfies my appetite for the sharply defined, the Manteguaesque, or Cézannesque, if you like—far better than in the above quotation. [. . . .]

It is really a question of how far the artistic impulse should merge itself in the Machine, although obviously borrowing from machine technique anything that is useful to it. And what I have felt is that the Fascist or Communist politician, naturally obsessed with notions of *power*, and, in a narrow sense, of *progress* (perfectability in the purely machine sense) would be apt, in the end, to lump all art impulses into one indiscriminate system of *power-mindedness*, as it might be called. For it must be remembered that Italian Fascism owed a great deal to the 'power' doctrine of Friedrich Nietzsche : and, paradoxically as that may seem to many people, there is a good deal of Nietzsche in the Bolshevist Dictatorship. And brutal 'power' notions are not the best ferment for success in an art.

Along with [the] 'power', or Energy, notion, goes the notion of Progress. And of course the ideology of Progress is writ large all over the communist propaganda of 'machine-mindedness'. That the communist 'cell' known as *New Signatures*, is aware of this, and uneasy about it—is conscious, in fact of the doctrine of Progress at the heart of its artistic activity and is anxious to keep it in its place —is proved, I think, by the following passage, to be found in the foreword of this collection :

> The writers in this book have learned to accept the fact that progress is illusory, and yet to believe that the game is worth playing; to believe that the alleviation of suffering is good even though it merely makes possible new sensitiveness and therefore new suffering; to believe that their own standards are no more absolute than those of other people, and yet to be prepared to defend and to suffer for their own standards; to think of the world, for scientific purposes, in terms which make it appear deterministic, and yet to know that a human action may be unpredictable from scientific laws, a new creation.[7]

Here you have a repudiation of the notion of 'Progress', and an assertion that nevertheless, just as a *game*, that notion should be

175

adopted—in order, apparently, to devise new forms of suffering. [. . . .]

The *pseudoism* of Mr. I. A. Richards[8] appears to play some part in this theory of *make-believe*, in which mechanical 'progress' is to be play-acted, for some purpose that remains ill-defined.

In conclusion : the so-called 'Machine Poets' appear to me to possess a programme that is confused and over-political, but, happily, to ignore it, when it come to writing their verses (except for a gesture or two, here and there). There are far less insistent echoes of industrial technique and few images of industrial life, than there was in English Painting twenty years ago. So I cannot see that anyone has anything to complain about. It is indeed such very mildly 'industrialized' verse that a person who is agriculturally-minded can with advantage neglect the mere programme and publicity-matter altogether (what is that but a 'blurb'!) and proceed to enjoy the great open spaces, of which there is a great plenty in these verses. As I have said, there are far more Shropshire Lads and Megalopolitan Robots, believe me. At the *worst* they are only occasionally *pseudo*-Robots (upon I. A. Richards principles)—do not therefore be alarmed gentle reader !

NOTES

1   *New Verse*, May, 1939, pp. 45–6.
2   *Blasting and Bombardiering*, pp. 340–1.
3   The excerpts here come from pp. 11–15 of a typescript in the Lewis collection at Cornell University. A version of the typescript apparently was published in *New Britain* magazine, Jan. 3 and 10, 1934.
4   Typescript, p. 3.
5   From Stephen Spender, 'I Think Continually', as printed in *New Signatures: Poems by Several Hands*. Collected by Michael Roberts. London: The Hogarth Press, 1934 reprint.
6   Apparently a reference to Spender's 1933 collection, *Poems*.
7   *New Signatures*, pp. 12–13.
8   See pp. 192–3 of the present book.

VI

Critics

1

Matthew Arnold

(From *The Times Literary Supplement*, 1954)

As a writer constantly at odds with his time, Lewis must have felt a special kinship with Arnold in the role here ascribed to him—that of the 'sincere upside-down man'. Publicity for Lewis's books proudly included a reviewer's statement that *The Art of Being Ruled* 'should stand towards our generation in the same relation that *Culture and Anarchy* did to the generation of the [1870s].' The following excerpt[1] deals with Arnold as poet as well as critic.

Matthew Arnold is the poet of the Victorian age to whom many people today, I among them, are most attracted; but since he is, in the first place, very severe, and then not an obvious favourite, like Tennyson or Shelley, and consequently liable to sell easily, he is apt only rarely to be selected for reprinting.

Byron had 'the pageant of his bleeding heart' as a standing attraction for posterity, and Shelley was a 'bleeding heart', as the Americans style it, also. Arnold, on the other hand, was not one of those Englishmen dazzled by the French Revolution; indeed, looking back upon that event, he sided with Burke. He felt as Burke did: for his middle class is not the *bourgeoisie*, as an American critic suggests. Politically, he was to the right of his eminent father —but only enough so to conform with the dandy. [. . . .]

The natural disparity between the elegant young poet and the burly schoolmaster was not all; Matthew differed from his parent in more ways than in his head-dress. In a letter Dr. Arnold[2] deplores Matthew's moral shortcomings; which would signify the absence in him of a certain type of earnestness. He developed from the outset a gaiety of mind combined with an airy arrogance. A gaiety adhered to with an arrogant firmness would be an uncomfortable attribute in the eyes of a father who was a professional moralist.

Matthew's mind was marvellously independent. He excelled in disagreement. His country as well as his class was the occasion for routine disagreement. At every turn in his writings one comes upon a comment like this :

> Still to be able to think, still to be irresistibly carried, if so it be, by the current of thought to the opposite side of the question . . . I know nothing more striking, and I must add that I know nothing more un-English.[3]

Here is another example : he is writing about criticism. 'Almost the last thing for which one would come to English literature is just that very thing which now Europe most desires—criticism.'[4]

In every country the most valuable men are those in disagreement—whether critical of America, critical of Germany, critical of Russia, critical of Spain, etc. There is nothing more valuable in a nation than a critic—a sincere upside-down man. I perhaps could not make you see what I mean without quotation : and here is a quotation from Arnold's essay on 'The Function of Criticism at the Present Time' :

> Do what he will . . . the critic will still remain exposed to frequent misunderstandings and nowhere so much as in this country. For here people are particularly indisposed even to comprehend that without this free disinterested treatment of things, truth and the highest culture are out of the question. So immersed are they in practical life, so accustomed to take all their notions from this life and its processes, that they are apt to think that truth and culture themselves can be reached by the processes of this life. . . . 'We are all *terrae filii*,' cries their eloquent advocate; 'all Philistines together . . . let us organize and combine a party to pursue truth and new thought, let us call it *the liberal party*, and let us all stick to each other, and back each other up. Let us have no nonsense about independent criticism, and intellectual delicacy, and the few and the many . . . we are all liberals, we are all in pursuit of truth.' In this way the pursuit of truth becomes really a social, practical, pleasurable affair, almost requiring a chairman, a secretary, and advertisements; with . . . in general,

plenty of bustle and very little thought. To act is so easy, as Goethe
says; to think is so hard!⁵

These are the words of an aggressive intellectual denouncing the
un-intellectual world—for obviously the English population is not
the only one which is Philistine. England was, at the moment, perhaps more perfectly Philistine than any other country ever was. But
really what Arnold was talking about was humanity.

Bernard Shaw was a man who could be depended on to disagree.
What I should say is that his only great merit was that. There is no
other resemblance between Matthew Arnold and Bernard Shaw
than that their function was of the same order. Shaw was always a
Philistine. Again, the subject of Arnold's discourse was culture and
the awful absence of culture. But his attitude was that he had found
himself, at birth, in the midst of a terrible illustration of what the
world ought not to be. Victorian England we, at this comfortable
distance, regard as the ideal age for Arnold's theories about Philistia.
So we would be the last people to protest at his disrespect of Eng-
lishness. Had Arnold been born a German, the German middle class
would have been treated by him exactly as he did the English. In
France, Flaubert was the analogue of Arnold. Only Flaubert took
his criticism a step farther. In *Bouvard et Pécuchet* the French
bourgeois becomes Humanity. Flaubert saw that his passionate ir-
ritation went deeper than the man of the French middle class: it
was Mankind that his disgust was directed against. If Matthew
Arnold had been a Frenchman his Philistine would have been Man.
Perhaps his dislike would not then have been quite so intense. For
civil war, in its bitterness, makes national war seem quite a mild
affair.

As a poet Matthew Arnold is in a class apart. As to his rank, no
greater poetry was ever written than the concluding song of Callicles in 'Empedocles on Etna'. One could not, alas, say as much for
the entire poem, though 'Empedocles on Etna' has everywhere lines
of great beauty.

Before going any farther, it is necessary to speak of his life. Except in his young manhood, everything was particularly difficult.
He began by being secretary to Lord Lansdowne; after a few years
the latter obtained for him a post in the Department of Education.
He became an Inspector of Schools. This was a job involving in-

cessant displacement; but he was about to marry and an income was necessary. This appointment was the beginning of a life of drudgery, to cease only two years before his death. As to his poetry, it did not survive the Inspectorship. [. . . .]

Arnold was perfectly aware that, in order to write verse in the grand style, and at the highest level of perfection, he would have needed a kinder life than this. There was no one to save him from his mode of life, though many people must have understood that the deadly routine to which his job condemned him was an excellent way of stifling this great person, who had made so splendid and paradoxical an appearance in the dull life of Victorian England.

Such a masterpiece as 'Empedocles on Etna' should have been needed incessant work, which Arnold was not able to give it. Perhaps he was at no time temperamentally able to sit himself down to the long hours of work which were required by his creative life.

He made no secret [. . .] of the shattering effects of literary composition upon a nature like his own. Yet so lengthy a narrative poem as 'Balder Dead' might seem to contradict his professions of frailty. In 'Balder Dead' he moved with as much confidence in the surréal atmospheres of the stream called Roaring as he did in the balmy regions of Thun, where the mysterious Marguerite had her being. With Asgard, the city of the polar divinities, Arnold had a masterly familiarity, just as he had with Philistia, even more alien to his senses. I am sure that Arnold is a much greater poet than is dreamed of by the posterity that inherits this little publicized, very intelligent giant. The 'Dandy Isaiah', as Meredith calls him, I would place among the prophets above Carlyle, the too sententiously homespun; poor Ruskin was overtaken in mid-career by an irresistible insanity, whereas Arnold's sanity was his central gift; and, as to Tennyson, the greatest prosodic contemporary, Arnold was incapable of his trivialities, though, as shown by 'The Forsaken Merman', in no way inferior when he wished, in romantic beauty.

NOTES

1 From *The Times Literary Supplement*, Aug. 6, 1954, p. xxii. This was a special autumn number of the TLS and L.'s signed article was partly a review of a selection of Arnold's poetry and prose edited by John Bryson.

2 Dr. Thomas Arnold of L.'s old school, Rugby.
3 From Arnold's *Essays in Criticism*. See Matthew Arnold, *Selected Prose*, p. 140.
4 Ibid., pp. 130–1.
5 Ibid., p. 148.

T. S. Eliot and I. A. Richards

(From *Men Without Art*, 1933)

Eliot and Lewis first met in 1915 and verse by Eliot appeared in Lewis's famous magazine *Blast* later that year. The relationship endured despite occasional strains and candid mutual criticism. Of Lewis, Eliot wrote in a posthumous tribute : 'His criticism was impartial. He had been a frank and merciless critic even of his friends, to whom indeed he devoted more attention than to his foes—witness his comments, in *Time and Western Man*, on Joyce and Pound, and elsewhere on myself. . . . We have no critic of the contemporary world at once so fearless, so honest, so intelligent, and possessed of so brilliant a prose style.'[1] Though refreshingly irreverent in print about a figure treated with such awe by others, Lewis showed his respect for Eliot at its most direct in the portrait paintings and drawings he did of the poet. As will become clear from the following pages,[2] part of a chapter headed 'T. S. Eliot : The Pseudo-believer', he consistently emphasized Pound's influence on Eliot's poetry. 'Mr. Eliot was lifted out of his lunar alley-ways and *fin–de-siècle* nocturnes into a massive region of verbal creation in contact with that astonishing didactic intelligence. . . .'[3] In this chapter as elsewhere, Lewis was intent on defending the principle of personality. 'The personality is not, I think, quite the pariah it becomes in the pages of Mr. Eliot : I do not believe in the anonymous, "impersonal", catalytic, for the very good reason that I am sure the personality is in that as much as in the other part of this double-headed oddity, however thoroughly disguised, and is more apt to be a corrupting influence in that arrangement than in the more usual one, where the artist is identified with his beliefs.' If anything, Lewis added, a man should exaggerate his beliefs 'rather than leave a meaningless shell behind him, and go to hide in a volatilized hypostasization of his personal feelings'.[4]

There is no person today who has had more influence upon the art of literature in England and America than Mr. T. S. Eliot. And what is especially remarkable is the fact that this influence has been exerted equally in the field of theory and the field of practice. If he has caused the budding poet to mind his p's and q's and bethink himself with more than usual concern about the intellectual foundations of his verse, he has also been able, in the practice of that art, to provide the beginner with a compelling model. For ten years now countless young verse-makers both here and in America have modelled themselves upon 'Ara Vos Prec', *The Waste Land* or 'Prufrock'. At the same time, under the guidance of his critical essays, they have imbibed a criterion which, as writers, puts (in more senses perhaps than one) the fear of God into them.

This mandarin, certainly, has succeeded in instilling a salutary *fear of speech*—a terror of *the word*, into his youthful followers : they have not thought twice, but a dozen times or more, before committing themselves to paper; and when they have come to do so, have spoken, 'neither loud or long'. They may not always have had much to say but they have said it in the fewest possible words. Indeed the mere act of writing (I have heard some of their confessions) has been undertaken with as much trepidation as the Victorian young man experienced in 'popping the question'. There have been those among them who, after endless painful deliberation, have scribbled a half a dozen lines and then fled away for good and all from composition upon such austere terms.

But at last the spell has been broken. And Mr. Auden has done it (even if it was 'John, son of Warner, who pulled his bell'). It is he who has really given the *coup de grâce* to Mr Eliot's spell. Mr. Auden abounds in speech—words have no sinister terrors for him ! So once more the ink is flowing freely and the paper manufacturers are taking on a few more hands. But it is still a pretty constipated 'academic youth', as they call it in Germany, that is having its fling —if it can be called a 'fling'—beneath this tutelage, still in the shadow of this alarming pedagogic presence—for it will take some time for the emancipatory effect of Mr. Auden's volubility to get things flowing easily again. And it is to do but the barest justice to Mr. Eliot to say that his followers might have had many a worse mentor. Indeed, if poets could be manufactured—in the way that thesis-writing in American universities turns out competent semi-experts upon this subject or that—he should have done so.

But if Mr. Eliot has caused his follower's verses to flow with an excessive caution (for the young) he has not diminished the numbers of verse-writers: indeed, oddly enough, it is quite the reverse. At first sight this must seem very odd indeed; unless it is realized (it is a thing I have not seen noted) how fundamentally democratic are Mr. Eliot's teachings. For instance, in his very interesting study of Dante, he expresses himself as follows:

> When I affirm that more can be learned about how to write poetry from Dante than from any English poet, I do not at all mean that Dante's way is the only right way, or that Dante is thereby *greater* than Shakespeare or, indeed, any other English poet. I put my meaning into other words by saying that Dante can do less *harm* to anyone trying to learn to write verse, than can Shakespeare. . . . If you follow Dante without talent, you will at worst be pedestrian and flat; if you follow Shakespeare or Pope without talent, you will make an utter fool of yourself.[5]

What could be more matey and democratic than that? Such words could not have been written by such a writer as Mr. Joyce, say, or by Mr. Yeats. Thoroughout the critical writing of Mr. Eliot, and it is the same with Mr. Pound, the object cannot be said to be to *diminish* the number of servants of the Muses. *The manufacture of poets and poetry*—and of *critics* of same—*that* can be said to be what, looked at from outside, all this 'critical' activity would seem to have been about. And—although it is a little strange to wish to compass such an end—this does not seem to me to be a bad thing from a certain standpoint. Mere *numbers* is of importance, especially today. Ezra Pound is to my mind, first and last, a technician: so it is this gospel of a sort of literary mechanics that was to be expected of him. He is the knowing craftsman, generously imparting the tricks of his trade. And Mr. Eliot—who as critic and poet may be regarded as the outcome of Ezra on the technical side (he stands in the same relation to the latter as does Hemingway to Miss Stein)—he too teaches a mechanism, a little automatically; for it is evident that the good Ezra hypnotizes him, as well as laying him under a deep obligation.

Ezra Pound is a figure of real importance, and the art of letters in our time owes a great deal to his intelligence. Nothing I say here must be interpreted as a lack of recognition of that fact. But one of the peculiarities of Ezra Pound is that he in the same breath will deliver himself of judgements regarding writers of very great intellectual power—say Mr. Joyce—that are discerning and just : and judgements of writers possessing no interest whatever, for man or god, which are undeniably silly. But how is this? It is extremely difficult to reconcile these two types of utterance of the author of the admirable *Cantos*. He knows a good thing when he sees it, and needless to say he does first-rate things himself. But he does not know a dull thing when he sees it.

Having asked *How is this?* let me provide an answer. There is first Pound's fatal democratic expansiveness. He has a big heart. He would really like to see a world of Dantes, more or less—at least that is the impression that his behaviour conveys. He would teach *anybody* how to be Dante—*technically.* And if some earnest and as he would say 'discipular' personage has shown himself an apt learner of tricks, he loses all self-control, throws discretion to the winds, and at the top of his voice proclaims him a super-Dante on the spot. It is magnificent, but it is not criticism.

Temperamentally, T. S. Eliot is as *close* as Ezra is exuberant. He is as arrogant as Ezra is modest—as sly as Ezra is open. He is democratic *in spite* of himself, as it were. And whereas Ezra is pure mechanism, Eliot's critical system is all about something : where Pound's system was *anybody's* system who cared to give themselves the trouble to be a poet, Eliot, working the same system, ostensibly very democratic, does impose extra-mechanical tests for those proposing to use it.

There is much more purpose, in fine, in Mr. Eliot than in Mr. Pound. There is much more personality. And he has paid a great deal of curious attention to the sanctions required for the expression of the thinking subject in verse or prose. In a sense, in spite of his democratic programme, he has made it difficult, rather than easy, for the student to participate in the creative activities about which he has written so much. Anybody with a tongue in his head, anyone certified born of woman, indeed any son of a bitch, can assume the laurel, as far as Mr. Pound is concerned—he is anything but particular on that head : but for Mr. Eliot it is a matter of some moment to know if he has politics, and *which*; and, still

187

more, what his theology may, or may not be. He is as alive to the problems of 'the background', as Mr. Pound is sublimely indifferent to them. And one feels, even, that had he his critical life to live over again he would scarcely take on Mr. Pound's fanatically technical system : he has even said somewhere (Max Eastman[6] exults over it) that he is not quite sure that criticism is necessary at all! He might never start being a critic at all if he had his time over again! He might leave 'mental inertia' where and as he found it. For : 'If we wish for a population easy to control by suggestion,' I quote his friend Mr. I. A. Richards, 'we shall decide what repertory of suggestions it shall be susceptible to and encourage this tendency except in the few. But if we wish for a high and diffused civilisation, with its attendant risks, we shall combat this form of mental inertia.'[7] Mr. Eliot may have tired of the latter of these alternatives.

Of the two provinces of poetry and literary criticism respectively, in which Mr. T. S. Eliot is equally at home and somewhat *maître de séance*, it is the latter into which, in this essay, I am pursuing him. It is Mr. Eliot the critic who requires, to my mind, some serious scrutiny—not only far more 'scrutiny' than he is ever likely to receive at the hands of his adherent Mr. Leavis, for instance (or from Mr. Leavis's master, Mr. Richards), but far more than he has, in fact, received from any of his casual critics. Mr. Stonier, for example,[8] though on the right tack, has traversed a little too heedlessly this unsubstantial but tricky system, though his chapter on Eliot is very well worth reading. There is one main subject to be studied in connection with anything that can be described as Mr. Eliot's critical system : namely the whole question of *sincerity*, in all its ramifications. That notion, with all the values attaching to an actual doctrine of *Make-Believe*, has gradually become for Mr. Eliot, as for Mr. Richards, the central affair.

The latter has been responsible for giving definition to Mr. Eliot's critical impulses, and bringing into a glaring prominence the essential muddle-headedness of this strange classicist and 'revolutionary' poet—this odd 'cultural' humanist and true believer. [. . . .]

Mr. Eliot stands for the maximum of *depersonalization*, and Mr. Richards for the maximum of *disbelief* or suspension of judgement. But let us hear Mr. Eliot and Mr. Richards. First let us hear Mr. Eliot and make some comments upon his statements, and then do the same with Mr. I. A. Richards.

Mr. T. S. Eliot

'What is to be insisted upon is that the poet must develop or procure the consciousness of the past and that he should continue to develop this consciousness throughout his career. What happens is a continual surrender of himself as he is at the moment to something which is more valuable. The progress of an artist is a continual self-sacrifice, a continual extinction of personality.'[9]

'My meaning is, that the poet has, not a "personality" to express, but a particular medium, which is only a medium and not a personality. . . . Impressions and experiences which are important for the man may take no place in the poetry, and those which become important in the poetry may play quite a negligible part in the man, the personality.'[10]

This is Henry James's 'sense of the past' : it is also Mr. Pound's sense of the past, which is the main and sole feature of Mr. Pound as an artist : and Mr. Eliot has taken that over entire and intact from his master in counterpoint. But Mr. Pound is, in his practice, a *reductio ad absurdum* of this theory of literature, a brilliant and delightful one, but nevertheless absurd. Where Mr. Eliot recommends 'a feeling that the whole of the literature of Europe from Homer and within it the whole of the literature of his own country has a simultaneous existence and composes a simultaneous order,'[11] he is dutifully teaching the doctrine of Ezra Pound, and he has in his own major pieces given effect to that teaching with important variations of his own. But I think that anyone who peruses Mr. Pound's *Cantos* must agree, while admiring extremely the great patches of magnificent translation, really granitic landslides from other times into our tongue, and recognizing the great technical resources displayed, that there is such a tendency to regard a scuffle in fourteenth-century Siena as fundamentally more interesting than a similar scuffle in Wigan or Detroit today, that even the historic *depersonalization* has not been achieved : since the fourteenth-century Sienese would probably regard the twentieth-century *fait-divers* as more curious and interesting than the *fait-divers* at his own front door. And I think we are compelled to conclude that romance *has* entered into this too strictly chronologic amalgam—that the *time-view* is eminently present, and that this is not the 'impersonal' but the 'romantic' temper. For it is easy to say 'the historical sense involves a perception, not only of the pastness of the past, but of its

189

presence.'[12] But that past is, at the best, seeing its proportions, very selective, and its 'presence' is at the best ideal. You cannot purge it of the glamour of strange lands. Strange times, after all, *are* strange lands, neither more nor less. And so this theory of 'the presence of the past' results in a new exoticism (proper to our critical and chronological civilization)—an exoticism of exactly the same order as Baudelaire's exoticism (*'les cocottiers absents de la superbe Afrique,'* etc.): of that of Monsieur Paul Morand,[13] or that of Gauguin, Firbank or Stevenson. And so the *here and now* is diminished too much : and we desert the things that after all we stand a chance of learning something concrete about, for things that we can never know except through a glass darkly and as it were in a romantic dream.

This historical or chronological attitude would have been incomprehensible to the classical mind, as has often been pointed out : and the classical mind (that of the man who lived firmly in the present) gained in coherence and strength. But, it is argued, today we cannot do that. The Hellene of the classical age possessed no libraries, full of the material of history, whereas we do. He knew nothing of the world about him, whereas we do. We are committed, willy nilly, to an interminable historic research : this is taken for granted, though often deplored. 'It is arguable,' writes Mr. Richards, 'that mechanical inventions, with their social effects, and a too sudden diffusion of indigestible ideas, are disturbing throughout the world the whole order of human mentality, that our minds are, as it were, becoming of an inferior shape—thin, brittle and patchy, rather than controllable and coherent. It is possible that the burden of information and consciousness that a growing mind has now to carry may be too much for its natural strength. If it is not too much already, it may soon become so, for the situation is likely to grow worse before it is better.'[14]

The 'burden of information and consciousness' does in fact overbalance the man of today, in many instances. What with the consciousness or the 'sense' of the past, and the labour of gathering 'information' about it, to enable it to become an integral part of the present, those who succumbed to the theory of Mr. Pound or Mr. Eliot should scarcely expect not to lose coherence—they must expect to 'sacrifice' more and more of that 'self' or 'personality', which is merely a living adequately at any given moment, to become an 'impersonal' rendezvous for two-dimensional phantoms, and to look more or less like a bric-à-brac shop, observed from the outside.

Of course I know that such a statement as 'the poet has, not "a personality" to express, but a particular medium, which is only a medium and not a personality,' fits in very well, for instance, with Bertrand Russell's account of the psyche—a rendezvous as it were for a bundle of sticks, not the *sticks* but just the rendezvous—or with the functional picture of the Behaviorist. But those are *not* the affiliations to which Mr. Eliot is most apt to give his official recognition! And of course he never misses an opportunity of showing his disapproval of Bertrand Russell. So that, it would seem, should not be invoked to help us. But what I think may be said is that in a great deal of his literary criticism Mr. Eliot has indeed tended to confuse scientific values with art values. It *might* be a good thing— I do not say it is—for an artist to have a 'personality', and for a scientist not to have a personality : though here of course I am not using a 'personality' in the *Ballyhoo* sense—I do not mean an individualist abortion, bellowing that it wants at all costs to 'express' itself, and feverishly answering the advertisement of the quack who promises to develop such things overnight. I mean only a constancy and consistency in being, as concretely as possible, *one thing*—at peace with itself, if not with the outer world, though that is likely to follow after an interval of struggle—something like what Montaigne meant, in fact, when he wrote of his work :

> L'ouvrage eust été moins mien; et sa fin principale et perfection, c'est d'estre exactement mien. Je corrigerois bien une erreur accidentale . . . mais les imperfections qui sont en moy ordinaires et constantes, ce seroit trahison de les oster.[15]

Mr. Eliot and Mr. Richards, I have said, stand for the maximum of *depersonalization* and of *disbelief* respectively (and to a large extent interchangeably). We have heard Mr. Eliot on the subject of *depersonalization*, and have supplied a fairly thorough commentary upon that. Now I suggest that we hear Mr. Richards upon the subject of *disbelief*.

Mr. I. A. RICHARDS.

In the first place, immensely useful as Mr. Richards has been to Mr. Eliot, and much as the latter has been influenced by him, the outspokenness of his logic has at times a little disturbed the more cautious, muffled and circumlocutory author of 'Mr Prufrock' : and never more so, I imagine, than when, in *Science and Poetry*, he triumphantly produced Mr. Eliot as *the man with absolutely no beliefs whatever* (though of course, expediency aside, such a theoretic *depersonalizer* as Mr. Eliot could scarcely be surprised at such a *dénoûement*, however disturbing he might find it). The words complained of were as follows—the italics are those of the text :

> [...] by effecting a complete severance between his poetry and *all* beliefs, and this without any weakening of the poetry, he (Mr. Eliot) has realized what might otherwise have remained largely a speculative possibility, and has shown the way to the only solution of these difficulties. 'In the destructive element immerse. That is the way.'[16] [....]

But I have still to give a brief account of Mr. Richards's theory of *pseudo-statement* or *pseudo-belief*. 'It is *not* the poet's business to make true statements,' says Mr. Richards. [17] What he makes are rather *pseudo-statements*. Some people—mathematicians for instance—simply cannot read poetry because of this *bogus* quality which governs it—'they find the alleged statements to be *false*,'[18] and that puts them off. 'It will be agreed,' Mr. Richards gravely remarks, 'that their approach to poetry and their expectations from it are mistaken.'[19]

Poetry (or any form of pure art, I suppose) is emotional, not logical : 'the acceptance which a pseudo-statement receives is entirely governed by its effects upon our feelings and attitudes.'[20] Again : 'A pseudo-statement is "true" if it suits and serves' some emotional attitude—which 'on other grounds' is 'desirable'.[21] So the 'truth' of art turns out to be what we *desire*. Anything that we *desire* is *true*. Mr. Richards and Mr. Eliot, these two pseudo-believers, are, in other words, highly subjective thinkers, to say the least of it ! But subjectiveness of mind is *not* a quality that the criterion of Mr. Eliot professes to applaud !

Thus the *pseudo-believer* is the perfect pragmatist. 'A pseudo-statement is a form of words which is justified entirely by its effect in releasing or organizing our impulses and attitudes,' to a useful and desirable end.[22]

'Statements true and false alike do of course constantly touch off attitudes and *action*.'[23] Whether a thing is 'true' or 'false' matters very little, if it stimulates effective action. 'Our daily *practical* existence is largely guided by them.'[24] But this, it appears, 'is one of the great new dangers to which civilization is exposed. Countless *pseudo-statements*—about God, about the universe, about human nature, the relations of mind to mind—pseudo-statements which are pivotal points in the organization of the mind . . . have suddenly become, for sincere, honest and informal minds, impossible to believe. . . . This is the contemporary situation. The remedy . . . is to cut our pseudo-statements free from belief, and yet retain them, in this released state, as the main instruments by which we order our attitudes to one another and to the world.'[25]

There you have it : the agreeable, the life-giving, lies that we tell ourselves must be cut off from all embarrassing logical entanglements, and erected into autonomous systems—the *pseudo-belief* takes the place of *belief*. And that this will be quite all right and perfectly in order is proved by poetry : '*for poetry conclusively shows that even the most important among our attitudes can be aroused and maintained without any belief entering in at all.*'[26] And then comes, in a footnote, the statement already quoted that made Mr. Eliot uncomfortable, namely that he had affected 'a severance between his poetry and all beliefs.' [. . . .]

Since writing the foregoing [. . .] upon 'Mr. Eliot—*pseudoist*', a new book of his has appeared.[27] There is nothing much new in it, except that at last he shows definite signs of a resolve to wriggle out of the Richards dilemma, by hook or by crook. [. . . .]

Of course, Mr. Eliot is still very civil, outwardly, to his honoured colleague : but this is no longer a case of the 'detachment' one has to expect in the ordinary way, as a characteristic attitude on the part of this 'royalist, classicist and catholic' for all those (from that standpoint) decidedly *shady* figures by whom he is surrounded, and by whom he has been so faithfully supported : for instance, his recognition of anomaly, as proved by his uneasy attitude to Mr. Herbert Read (psychoanalyser and dutifully sex-dissector of William Wordsworth—how this scandalized Babbitt![28]—who asked me whether Read was *really* approved by Eliot in this romantic Freudian foray !—Read, as critic less sound than as poet, all too undiscriminating admirer of those great contemporary figures, Erich Maria Remarque, Lion Feuchtwanger, and the sham-Tolstoy, Wassermann).[29] Mr. Eliot, as skipper of the *Criterion*, always has the air of glancing a little sardonically askance at this first mate, as though he had got on board while he wasn't looking, and was not quite a sufficiently orthodox seaman to be entrusted with the navigation of such a ship—as indeed he is not (solely from the purist standpoint —he would be an excellent mate, or for that matter skipper, of some *other* ship—and if you are to be a purist, you must at least take care a little in such matters)—at least *he* is not the man, it is pretty clear, if the *Criterion* is to fly the royal ensign, and steer according to classical canons, to a pseudo-Roman port!—But I have dealt already with that sort of central absurdity in Mr. Eliot's position in the matter of his paper—that strange organ of Tradition : and so long as his colleagues do not blow the gaff, or over-conscientiously drag out all these damaging contradictions into the light of common day, all is well, and Mr. Eliot, sardonic but decorous, goes peacefully his *pseudo* way! Indeed, stretched out in a comfortable deck-chair under his poop-awning (the latest *Crime Club* romance upon his knee), he is perfectly ready that his first mate should head the good ship *Cri* for *any* old port—the most *liberal* in the world, or the *reddest*, for that matter, in the universe—he will put the telescope to his blind eye—perfectly agreeable that navigation should be conducted upon the best relativist principles, with the Einstein chronometer and the Marx sextant, or any other instruments whatever, however heterodox—providing only the boatswain *pipes* at the right time, in the true traditional fashion, and so long as the royal colours continue to float aloft and the crew touch their forelocks and say *sir* when addressing an officer !

But Mr. Eliot's most recent critical book is notable for one thing; and that is a new dismemberment of his much-discussed 'personality'. The present stratifications of public taste, Mr. Eliot tells us, 'are perhaps a sign of social disintegration.'[30] I heartily agree of course—as I do to so much that Mr. Eliot says, paying lip-service to an ideal of Order. And individual 'stratifications'—Mr. Eliot— whether temporal or other—are *likewise* 'a sign of disintegration'! And Mr. Eliot has exhibited a yet further sign in this direction. For now he has disowned the Mr. Eliot of 1923 (driven to this, it is true, by the haunting dilemma of Mr. Richards and *The Waste Land* 'without belief'). 'In the course of time,' he tells us, 'a poet

194

may become merely a reader in respect to his own works.'[31] And Mr. Eliot has become that. He reads *The Waste Land* with astonishment now—in the light of his friend Mr. Richards's account of it! He cannot *contradict* Mr. Richards, for Mr. Richards knows as much about the intentions of the Mr. Eliot who wrote it as he does himself. So 'when Mr. Richards asserts that *The Waste Land* effects "a complete severance between poetry and *all* beliefs" I am no better qualified to say No! than is any other reader.'[32] Mr. 1933 Eliot picks up this much-discussed work, and, with some diffidence, gives his partner, Mr. Richards, the benefit of his opinion as regards what this fellow (bearing his name) of 1923 meant; and he 'admits' that he 'thinks' that his colleague and critical crony *for once*, is *wrong*. But that is a mere opinion, and he merely offers it for what it is worth, which is not much, seeing how little he knows about this poet-fellow (an American I believe!) who was responsible for this cross-word puzzle, of synthetic literary chronology, of spurious verbal algebra. Did the author of *The Waste Land* believe in God? —'How can I say?' drawls Mr. Eliot, testily.—But he confesses that it is difficult for him to believe that *anyone* bearing his name should not believe in God; and, under correction, is of opinion that *some* belief or other must have been present when the lines 'She bathed her feet in soda-water' were written. Mr. I. A. Richards shakes his head dubiously however. He does not detect much orthodox theology, he makes it perfectly plain to his plausible partner, in *The Waste Land*. He is sorry, but there it is! And Mr. T. S. Eliot (1933) does not insist. A mere namesake has no more claim upon him than the next. It is not a question of Mr. Eliot having *forgotten*, he assures us. He has 'merely' *changed*.

What all this means is that, in order to escape from giving a *Yes*, or, as he says, a *No* to his trusty but incorruptible partner, and fellow-pseudoist, Mr. Richards—unable any longer to just say he 'does not *understand*' Mr. Richards, and leave it comfortably at that —he is driven to the expedient of announcing a further piecemealing of his personality (already one would have thought sufficiently cut up between the private self—the believer; the poet—the unbeliever; and the literary critic—not always very flattering to the poet, though of course not without certain evident partiality for him all the same!).

It is rather an extreme device—this disintegration into a multiplicity of chronologic selves. What, however, it does effect is to exempt him from providing an authoritative answer to the no doubt more and more puzzled questions of the crowd of ardent followers of himself and Mr. Richards—on the grounds that he is no longer the *same* Mr. Eliot, but another, so cannot possibly know what *The Waste Land* Tom planned and intended. But it is not at all certain that, even if it had been written this week, he could be pinned down any more : for later on, where he is describing how a poem comes to be written, we are told that 'this disturbance of our quotidian character . . . results in an incantation, *an outburst of words, which we hardly recognize as our own*'.[33] He would 'hesitate to say that this experience at which I have hinted is responsible for the creation of all the most profound poetry written. . . . Some finer minds, indeed, may operate very differently; I cannot think of Shakespeare or Dante as having been dependent upon such capricious releases.'[34] But it is Mr. Eliot's way—the automatic way. Something touches a button, and out it comes. So, if you marched up to him five minutes after he had 'released' some 'outburst of words' in this manner, and exclaimed, 'Ha ha! Got you this time my fine fellow! What did you mean when you wrote *that*—and *that*!' he would be quite capable of replying with the utmost detachment? '*Who* wrote *what*? I am sorry, I am entirely unable to answer you. I have not the least idea! It is not to *me* you must address such questions. Go rather and address yourself to my partner Mr. I. A. Richards! He is not very reliable, but he probably knows more about it than I do.'

Or he might say it was incubated a twelvemonth beforehand, and that so much had happened in the meantime. Or he might retire, with infinite grace, into the shadow of a modesty as remarkable as it was sudden. 'The essence of poetry *if there is any*, belongs to the study of æsthetics and is no concern of the poet or of a critic with my limited qualifications.'[35]

If there is one thing more than another paraded by Mr. Eliot, the literary critic, it is a supposed logical precision of statement, a fastidious carefulness in the use of words. Is it a gross self-delusion, one sometimes wonders, or a mere barefaced bluff, that causes him to level accusations against Matthew Arnold say (whom of course he a good deal resembles) of slipshod terminology, of mental vagueness and lack of consistency—of holding a doctrine that was 'vague and ambiguous'?[36]

For instance : 'Arnold had little gift for consistency or for definition,' he blandly informs us. 'Nor had he the power of connected reasoning at any length : his flights are either short flights or circular flights. Nothing in his prose work, therefore, will stand very close analysis.'[37] Or again : '(Arnold) lacked the mental discipline, the passion for exactness in the use of words and for consistency and continuity of reasoning, which distinguishes the philosopher.'[38]

How fatally this describes Mr. Eliot himself no one, I think, who has followed the exposure of his doctrine in the foregoing pages can fail to perceive. And that his confusions and inconsistencies are, or look like, barefaced confusions and conscious inconsistencies does not make it any better : for I dare say to some extent that was the case with Arnold too—only he had the decency to cover up his tracks a little more carefully than has Mr. Eliot. Or, if you like, he did not draw attention to his logical insecurity and sleight of hand by *plugging* those defective portions of his critical system with a tortuous padding of pretended precision. He at least left the thing alone, once he had done it, as neatly as the matter warranted.

It may of course be true, it is possible that Mr. Eliot really believes that he displays 'a passion for exactness'.[39] Even if, compared with the general critical standards of the day, it may be that his critical writings *do* look, to the casual student-reader, as pretty 'closely-reasoned,' and characterized by 'exactness'. He certainly *wants* them to look like that.

No doubt with his infant-milk, he must have imbibed a great respect for the traditional scientific attributes—(1) impersonality, (2) exactness. And this survives. So perhaps, after all, it is not so much bluff as sheer self-delusion.

But philosophy and criticism stand or fall, in one sense, together. Mr. Eliot underlines this fact. 'You cannot deplore criticism unless you deprecate philosophy.'[40] The day of philosophic systems, however, is passed : no philosopher is allowed to claim any more, today, than what is, in fact, a systematic arrangement of his *personal* idiosyncracies. The idea is this : the *person* possessed of a philosophic bent—whether it be Kant, Hobbes, Spinoza, Spencer—*wishes* that a certain number of things were true, and, very naturally proceeds

—with all the impersonal pomp of the paraphernalia of an absolute 'system'—to bestow upon them the appearance of revelation. Such and such a cosmos appeals to him—say, because of the teaching of Maimonides, and the general, even racial, colour of his mind—and he proceeds to build such a cosmos, from such and such a set of axioms : that is his 'system'.

But why should what is denied to the philosopher be granted to the literary critic—or to the critic-mongering poet? Should not the 'depersonalization' notion we have been considering, for instance, so airily thrown out, be received on the same footing as any other 'system' (only there is this important difference between the two cases, namely that the literary critic is saved a lot of unnecessary trouble with his little 'system'—even, when he is a poet at the same time, it can peep out as a sort of professional 'tip'—*he* does not anyway have to build any self-consistent architecture : he can murmur, with a musing expression, that he *believes* that this that or the other should be thus and thus, and usually add that he has not *worked it out* properly yet, but perhaps may do so soon—though he is very vague about it just at present (in fact, a bit confused!) and (being by way of being a scholar and so very very *cautious*, as all true scholars must be, it is generally conceded) he does not wish to commit himself *at present*, more than just to say that, in his opinion, *it is quite on the cards*, that such and such a thing *may* be proved to be—someday—by somebody far abler than himself (for a spectacular 'modesty' is very important too—it goes with 'caution') *may* be shown to be of such and such an order.

(This caricature of the manner of the scholar, this caricature of the technique of the philosopher, is scarcely an exaggeration of what can be discovered in Mr. Eliot's text.)

Yet 'our individual taste in poetry bears the indelible traces of our individual lives with all their experience pleasurable and painful. We are apt either to shape a theory to cover the poetry that we find most moving, or—what is less excusable—to choose the poetry which illustrates the theory we want to hold. You do not find Matthew Arnold quoting Rochester or Sedley. And it is not merely a matter of individual caprice. Each age demands different things from poetry.'[41]

How very true that is. And yet how it seems to contradict, somehow, Mr. Eliot's critical attitudes elsewhere. But he *will* sometimes

times shrink on you like that, all in a moment! and become a poor lost person, 'not qualified' to pronounce upon anything to do with the subject he has just been discussing at all.—But there I must leave the matter for the present, in the hope that, faithful to the lead given us all by Mr. I. A. Richards, I have made some contribution, at all events, to this intricate question.

NOTES

1 T. S. Eliot, 'Wyndham Lewis', *The Hudson Review*, Summer, 1957, pp. 169–70.
2 From *Men Without Art*, pp. 65–9, 72–6, 85–6, 92, 94–100.
3 *Blasting and Bombardiering*, p. 285.
4 *Men Without Art*, p. 91.
5 Eliot, *Selected Essays*, p. 252.
6 American essayist and poet (1883–1969).
7 I. A. Richards, *Practical Criticism*. London: Kegan Paul, Trench, Trubner & Co. Ltd., 1929, p. 314.
8 G. W. Stonier, *Gog Magog and other Critical Essays*. London: 1933.
9 Eliot, *Selected Essays*, p. 17.
10 Ibid., pp. 19–20.
11 Ibid., p. 14.
12 Ibid.
13 Peripatetic French novelist and diplomat, b. 1888.
14 *Practical Criticism*, p. 320.
15 Montaigne, *Essais*, Tome II. Paris: Editions Garnier Frères, p. 303.
16 Richards, *Science and Poetry*. London: Kegan Paul, Trench, Trubner & Co. Ltd., 1926, pp. 64–5 (n).
17 Ibid., p. 56.
18 Ibid.
19 Ibid.
20 Ibid., p. 58.
21 Ibid., pp. 58–9.
22 Ibid., p. 59.
23 Ibid., pp. 59–60. Italics L.'s.
24 Ibid., p. 60. Italics L.'s.
25 Ibid., pp. 60–1. Italics L.'s.
26 Ibid., p. 61. Italics L.'s.
27 Eliot, *The Use of Poetry and the Use of Criticism*. London: Faber & Faber, 1933. The 1955 printing is used here.
28 Read, who became an Enemy bugbear, was associated with Eliot on the monthly *Criterion*. Irving Babbitt was the anti-romanticist thinker.
29 For unflattering comments by L. about Remarque, author of *All Quiet on the Western Front*, see pp. 214–15 of the present book. Lion Feuchtwanger (b. 1884), author of the best-selling *Jud Süss*, and Jakob Wasserman (1873–1934) were both German novelists.
30 *The Use of Poetry and the Use of Criticism*, p. 153.

31   Ibid., p. 130.
32   Ibid.
33   Ibid., p. 145. Italics L.'s.
34   Ibid., pp. 145–6.
35   Ibid., pp. 149–50. Italics L.'s.
36   Eliot, *Selected Essays*, p. 439.
37   Ibid., p. 431.
38   *The Use of Poetry* . . ., p. 122.
39   Ibid.
40   Ibid., p. 21.
41   Ibid., p. 141.

VII

Writers and Politics

1

Gustave Flaubert

(From *Men Without Art*, 1934)

Of all writers dealing with the problem of the artist's attitude towards politics, Flaubert[1] probably appealed to Lewis most. Lewis admired Flaubert's attacks on the human principle, calling this 'the Satire of nihilism'. He added : 'For Flaubert it was not a few men selected here and there for attack, as especially wicked or peculiarly foolish. It was mankind that was chosen.'[2]

———————

Flaubert was all that he was, not as an artist but as a great civilizing influence, because all these hostile currents of a world in dissolution met in him with a greater bitterness and with a more dramatic impact than in any other European of the nineteenth century, unless it was Dostoevsky. '*Gardons notre coeur et notre esprit,*' he writes to the Princess Mathilde[3] (September 6, 1871)—this was the period of the Paris Commune—

> Veillons sur la flamme, pour que le feu sacré brûle toujours. Plus que jamais, je sens le besoin de vivre dans un monde à part, en haut d'une tour d'ivoire, bien au-dessus de la fange où barbote le commune des hommes.[4]

Two days after that he is writing to George Sand, with reference to the same events :

> Pourquoi êtes-vous si triste? L'humanité n'offre rien de nouveau. Son irrémédiable misère m'a empli d'amertume, dès ma jeunesse. Aussi, maintenant, n'ai-je aucune désillusion. Je crois que la foule, le troupeau, sera toujours haïssable. Il n'y a d'important qu'un petit groupe d'esprits, toujours les mêmes, et qui se repassent le flambeau.[5]

Or in another letter :

> Ne t'occupe de rien que de toi [he advises a friend]. Laissons
> l'Empire marcher, fermons notre porte, montons au plus haut de
> notre tour d'ivoire, sur la dernière marche, la plus près du ciel. Il y
> fait froid quelquefois, n'est-ce, pas? mais qu'importe? On voit les
> étoiles briller clair et l'on n'entend plus les dindons.[6]

'Let the Empire go its own way—let us bolt our door and go up
to the summit of our Ivory Tower.' In that statement and in the
letter to the Princess Mathilde, 'the Ivory Tower' makes its appearance—an important historical landmark. But for that statement of
Flaubert's to be a complete record of his attitude, after 'Empire',
should follow the words 'Republic', 'Commune', and a long cata-
logue of words that stand for all other imaginable forms of government. He did not ever, in fact, quite reach the point at which he became conscious of this desolating inclusiveness, although that he was
spasmodically aware of it there is evidence enough.

In his 'political' letter, as he called it, to George Sand, of September 8, 1871, he expressed himself again as follows—which proves
sufficiently how little he was either a royalist or a republican :

> Les mots république et monarchie la feront rire (à la post-
> érité). . . . Car je défie qu-on me montre une différence essentielle
> entre ces deux termes. Une république moderne et une monarchie
> constitutionelle sont identiques.[7]

A modern republic and a constitutional monarchy are identical
—so much for royalism and republicanism, in the eyes of Flaubert :
and as to Communism, the 'Gothic notion of a Commune' pleased
him just as little. His was a complete political nihilism, or at first
sight it seems to be that. 'Pauvre France,' he cries, 'qui ne se dé-
gagera jamais du moyen âge! qui se traîne encore sur *l'idée gothique
de la commune*, qui n'est autre chose que le municipe
romain !'[8]

Mr. Edmund Wilson, who contributed a series of ingenious articles
called 'Critics of the Middle Class' to the *Herald Tribune*, selected
L'Education Sentimentale of Gustave Flaubert as the great par
excellence anti-bourgeois book of books. (Mr. Wilson is a recent
convert to Communism.) 'The most remarkable of Flaubert's novels
from the point of view of social criticism is *L'Education Sentimen-*

tale.' Flaubert was bracketed in these articles with Karl Marx as the greatest guy of all in the anti-bourgeois racket; with some skill and many omissions he made out a quite good case :

> *L'Education Sentimentale,* though we may rebel against it and become angry at it when we first read it, still sticks in our minds and plants deep there an idea which we can never get rid of—the idea that our middle-class society of business men, manufacturers and people who live on or deal in investments, so far from being redeemed by the culture and idealism which have come out of it, has ended by cheapening and invalidating culture in all its branches—politics, science, and art—and not only these, but the ordinary human relations, love, friendship and loyalty to cause—till the whole civilization has become suspect.[9]

What has been done to art and to pure science under Capitalism has at all times been one of the main sticks with which to beat the latter. So it is important to consider how the organization that seeks to overthrow it is likely to make good its claim to revive culture and rescue it from the cheapening effects of the contamination of the Capitalist mind.

And you have in me a person who is as nearly impartial as it is humanly possible to be—and, further, one who takes it as axiomatic that the present type of Western Democracy cannot and should not survive.

Flaubert having been rudely wrenched out of his French nineteenth century context ('bourgeois' bursting from his lips as if in a political print) by the ingenious Mr. Wilson, let us take up that challenge, and interrogate Flaubert rather more closely than Mr. Wilson had cared to do. But first I wish to put upon a proper footing a little matter that concerns me *personally.* So you will perhaps excuse me if at this point I draw your attention to what the *Zeitgenossen* of Boz archly referred to as Number One.

Here is what I have to say : if Gustave Flaubert is going to be run as a rival to Marx as the enemy of the *bourgeoisie,* I think I should like to advance my own claims as a bourgeois-baiter—they are not mean ones I believe! I know that at some future date I shall have my niche in the Bolshevist pantheon, as a great enemy of the middle-class idea. Keats said : 'I shall be among the English Poets after my death.' I say : 'I shall be among the bolshie prophets.' My 'bourgeois-bohemians' in *Tarr,* and oh my *Apes of God*—will provide 'selected passages' for the school children in the Communist or semi-Communist State, of that I am convinced, to show how repulsive unbridled individualism can be.—But this will not be yet. I refer to these books of mine not out of vain glory by any means, but in order to demonstrate the complete absence of bias with which, in view of the special honours in store for me, I am able to approach these topics.

But (at the risk of spoiling my chances in the matter of the above-mentioned honours) I must point out—or I had better say I must humbly hint—to Mr. Wilson that Flaubert had not in mind, when he was drawing up his damaging pictures of nineteenth-century society, any other society in particular to set up against it. It is one thing to be turned sick by the spectacle of the organized vulgarity of a given social group : but it is quite another thing to accept just any ideology that happens to be opposed to it. [. . . .]

It is certainly true that in a general way Flaubert did possess a very healthy appetite for destruction precisely in those directions where also the Marxist thunder-bolts most commonly fall. To him almost everything and everybody are suspect, except the artist, or what Mr. Shaw has called 'the philosophic man'. (At the mere sight of a politician he would turn aside and violently spit. There are no doubt politicians and politicians. But we are justified in supposing that Flaubert would not have distinguished much between those of the Right and Left. And the horror experienced not only by Flaubert but by all his great contemporaries at the contact of the political animal seems at least to me to indicate a reasonably intelligent instinct.) [. . . .]

The paradox in the Marxist standpoint today is, of course, its fiercely anti-democratic tone. For what can 'democracy' mean (unless it is used in a very special sense), except the Rule of the Many ? And is not the Bolshevist salvationism based upon that principle ? But all the great Frenchmen of the last century, or almost all, in so far as they possessed any political bias, were anti-democrat. And it is not (in view of the above paradox) so strange as it otherwise might seem to find the Communist of today quoting them in support of Marxist doctrine. And that should give all Socialists something to think about.

NOTES

1 These comments on him are taken from *Men Without Art*, pp. 265–8, 271.
2 *Rude Assignment*, p. 47.
3 Princesse Mathilde (1820–1904), cousin of Louis Napoleon and celebrated literary hostess.
4 Gustave Flaubert, *Correspondance* (1869-1872). Paris: Louis Conrad, 1930, pp. 279–80. Italics L.'s.
5 Ibid., pp. 280–1.
6 Ibid.
7 Ibid., pp. 281–2.
8 Ibid., p. 224. Italics L.'s.
9 Cf. Edmund Wilson, *The Triple Thinkers*. London: John Lehmann Ltd., 1952, pp. 80, 82–3. This is an apparently revised version of the newspaper article.

2

Charles Péguy

(From *The Art of Being Ruled*, 1926)

Lewis was a student in Paris at the height of the influence of Péguy and the latter's periodical, *Les Cahiers de la Quinzaine*, a famous vehicle for the Frenchman's mixture of mystical patriotism and peasant Catholicism. Before World War I, he was also familiar with the fiction of another notable French Catholic, Léon Bloy. But his attitude to them both along with their English co-religionist, G. K. Chesterton— 'a ferocious and foaming romantic . . . the dogmatic Toby-jug'[1]—was highly critical. Chesterton, Lewis wrote, represented a liberalism 'complicated with a romantic conversion to roman catholicism, and installed in an obsessing and cartoon-like John Bull physique. . . . The well-fed high spirits of the old liberal England, the strange association of humaneness with religious intolerance, a sanguine grin fiercely painted on the whole make-up, compose a sinister figure such as you would find, perhaps—exploiting its fatness, its shrewdness, its animal violence, its blustering patriotism all at once—in the centre of some nightmare Bank Holiday fair.'[2] In Bloy Lewis abominated the Frenchman's Napoleonic nationalism. 'There is a sort of writing . . . that the French can tolerate which to the English reader is like melted chocolate cream and cotton wool thrust into the mouth at the same time,' Lewis remarked. The truth was, he added, that Bloy's hero was 'a highly successful little Corsican gangster'. And, looking back on the pre-World War I period, Lewis commented : 'Aggressive Frenchmen —Sorel, Barrès, Maurras, Péguy—were, as much as the Prussian professors who usually get all the blame, pepping up the French for the slaughter.'[3] The section below on Péguy forms a chapter of *The Art of Being Ruled* called 'The Hypnotism of the Anti-Intellectual Fashion'.[4]

––––––––––

When Péguy says, 'Je ne suis pas un intellectuel, qui descend et condescend quand il parle au peuple,'[5] you know what he means : the noble sincerity that marked all he said and did is our guarantee. He is not a great personage, a *bourgeois*, condescending when he speaks to the plain man. If it were almost anybody else saying that, it would be necessary to see whether this were not the usual publicist's or demagogue's manœuvre to prejudice the 'people', their lucrative clients, against another leader, whom that seemed the best way of attacking. He would probably be saying : 'He (the rival) is a "high-brow"—he comes to you from *l'école normale*, or Oxford or Harvard. He does not speak your language. His voice is that of the hated aristocrat in reality. Do not listen to him : he will betray you, or at the best condescend to you. Listen to me : I am one of you. I have worked in a mine (or driven a train, or canned meat).'

But Péguy himself was by no means secure. His *Cahiers* were attacked repeatedly on the ground of their *dilettantism* (as can be seen, for instance, in the piece entitled 'Pour moi' : *Oeuvres Complètes*, Vol. I). He was dealing in literature and forgetting the social revolution. He was a normalien, an amuser, a dilettante, and so on. Yet he was of the most irreproachable peasant stock, and by nature ideally aggressive. He was installed in the midst of a mass of quarrels. The hatred he provoked on all sides was the result of his aggressively simple sincerity—that is quite easy to appreciate at this distance. His stiffness and straightness caused endless dislocation in the smooth (that is, the crooked) running of life. So a hub-bub arose wherever he appeared. There was something Rousseau-like in his situation, one in which he had the entire world against him—though of course on a different scale. But I think also that the reasons for it cannot be sought in any particular similarity between Jean-Jacques and himself.

But although by no means immune from criticism on the score of his academic accomplishments and love for letters, Péguy shared his adversaries' (or colleagues', as they of course also were) dislike of the 'intellectual'. In *La chanson du roi Dogobert* he gives an eloquent expression to this :

Eloi. J'ai connu des hommes qui ne te ressemblent pas. Heureusement qu'il y a deux races d'hommes. Et j'ai connu la deuxième race des hommes. J'ai connu des hommes qui ne connaissent pas par des livres. J'ai connu les hommes qui connaissent les réalités.

(Eloi I have known men who do not resemble thee. Happily there are two races of men. And I have known the second race of men. I have known men who did not know things through books. I have known men who knew realities.)[6]

Like another very learned man, Descartes, he recommended and praised the *tabula rasa*. Even Montaigne was on the side of the ignorant. 'O que c'est un doux et mol chevet, et sain, que l'ignorance et l'incuriosité, à reposer une teste bien faicté!'[7] But of course all learned men prefer ignorant people, but scarcely for the flattering reasons that they pretend.

But to know the stream of Vouzie, rather than the bulging, buzzing name Vouzie, was a capital part of Péguy's philosophy, which took its colour, as did that of Sorel, from bergsonism and its vital flux. And perhaps, without knowing it, they were fouling their own nest to order. The orders perhaps came through channels they had not charted, from the very sources against which their revolutionary rage was directed. This question—that of the credentials of 'the intelligence,' of 'the intellectual'—is such an important one that I will devote a few more pages to elucidating it. Such 'intellectuals' as Sorel, Péguy, or Berth,[8] to take no others, were hypnotized to strike at themselves; their clamour against the mind, of which they possessed a fair share, was the result, I think, of an enchantment.

The 'war' of the highbrow and the lowbrow [. . .] is a very important class-war indeed for the world at large. In killing the intellect, or its trained servants, men would certainly be killing the goose that lays the golden eggs : not the eggs of Mammon, which are devoured only at the tables of the millionaire world, but the more universally valuable eggs of intelligent endeavour. It is worth pausing to think whether this war is a very sensible one. Bergson was one of the principal administrative figures in its earlier stages. Poor Péguy was, I am afraid, a hallucinated victim, rather.

NOTES

1 *Time and Western Man*, p. 373.
2 *The Art of Being Ruled*, p. 193.
3 *Rude Assignment*, pp. 31–2. Georges Sorel (1847–1922) was a member of Péguy's circle and an advocate of direct working-class violence. The extreme royalist Charles Maurras (1868–1952) and the novelist Maurice Barrès (1862–1923) were both radical nationalists.
4 From *The Art of Being Ruled*, pp. 379–81.
5 Cf. Charles Péguy, 'Pour Moi', *Oeuvres Complètes*, Vol. I. Paris : Editions de Nouvelle Revue Francaise, 1917, p. 314.

6   Péguy, 'La Chanson du Roi Dagobert', in Ibid., p. 444.
7   Montaigne, *Essais*, Tome II, p. 526.
8   Edouard Berth, follower of Sorel and author of writings which, said Lewis in *Rude Assignment* (pp. 30–1), were 'a long panegyric of action—of the sword at the expense, expressly, of the pen, the tommy-gun contrasted favourably with the typewriter.'

3

The War Writers

(From *The Old Gang and the New Gang*, 1932)

As one of the foremost war painters of 1914–18, an artillery veteran and an intellectual crucially influenced by his front-line experiences, Lewis was well qualified to dissect the reactions of other soldier-writers to World War I. In *Blasting and Bombardiering*, one of the finest 'war books', he transcended the simple theses of writers who blamed the holocaust on inept elders acquiescing in, if not actually plotting, the slaughter of the young. Such theses squared with the 'age-against-youth' antics of post-war political and commercial publicists described in Lewis's *Doom of Youth* and *The Old Gang and the New Gang*.[1] On the battlefields, Lewis pondered the causes of such bloodbaths and finally sought them in 'the intricacies of the power-game, and the usurious economics associated with war-making'.[2] It was this broader perspective he failed to find in Siegfried Sassoon and Erich Maria Remarque or in angry lamentations about 'the great blank of the missing generation'. Nor could he tolerate the war being used as a pretext for the sense of paralysis and decay he considered artificially induced in the Twenties.

———

But this emotional attitude (or rather theatrical, not very serious—mainly self-advertising-by-self-pitying rage) is marvellously exemplified in the recent War Literature of England and of Germany. The 'Lost Generation' and the 'Great Blank' stuff of Age-War Peace politics is nothing compared with the 'Great Blank' hysterically insisted upon by all the Unknown Soldiers who suddenly became very well known a few years ago—who, like Remarque, wrote sentimental accounts of experiences they had had, or had never had—and, by mixing blood and ink, arrived at a decent business proposition—

212

a blood and thunder best-seller—by stealing the thunder of old bombardments, and abusing (all over again) all the Old Generals and all the Old Admirals—and (beyond them) cursing their grandpapas for being such selfish old sycophants.

But the 'Lost Generation' stuff started of course at the beginning of the War—nearly twenty years ago the first shot was fired in this 'Old Gang' crusade. Perhaps it was Mr. Siegfried Sassoon, with his War-poems, who fired it. What that naturally rather detached 'Fox-hunting Man' did was to raise the 'Old-Gang' hunting cry. He was in full Tallyho in his very sentimental battle-doggerel, against the 'Old Generals'—on whose behalf (in league with other Aged Men) the War had been got up by, by whom it was run, and by whom it was turned to profit—that was the idea.

> 'Good morning, good morning!' the General said,
> As we passed him one day as we went up the Line.
> But the lads that he spoke to are most of them dead,
> And we're cursing his staff for incompetent swine.
> 'He's a cheery old sport,' muttered Harry to Jack.
> But he did for them both with his plan of attack![3]

That some scarlet-faced, white-moustachioed, old Anglo-Indian General, eighteen years ago, was to *blame* for the European War, or, secondarily, for not understanding the art of War on the grand —the European—scale—if one reflects that the poor old sheep had spent all his life as a polo-playing 'pukka sahib' doing frontier police-work with a handful of men in some garrison in Hindustan—'that' is so absurd, surely, as to be evident to even the most dull-witted. I have never ceased to wonder how it was that people did not remark it at the time. That Mr. Sassoon had no suspicion that these facile and florid revolutionary outbursts were essentially unreal and mis-leading is possible : he may never have been aware that it was as absurd to turn upon his Corps Commander and put the 'War-guilt Lie' (as the Germans call it) upon him, as to denounce a sergeant-major for all the massacres that befell his battalion. Mr. Sassoon's gallantry, is, I presume, beyond dispute : So the truth is, we must suppose, that when the 'lads' by whom he was surrounded got killed, he vented his romantic displeasure upon the nearest object—the 'Hun' received some of this 'trop-plein' his fine military record suggests—and the Colonels, Corps Commanders and other emblems

213

of imbecile Authority were requisitioned as targets for the rest of his wrath. These poor old Anglo-Indian cattle who were the 'Leaders in the Field', but in no other place on earth (of those other sheepish multitudes), received the full blast of Mr. Sassoon's emotional, mutinous satire, and a fashion (of superficial, 'rebel', and of course 'youthful', discontent) was set.

That these foolish, self-important, elderly 'Brasshats' could command no intelligent sympathy there is little need to say—any more for that matter than it is possible to experience the least sympathy for their civilian successors of the Peace—the political 'Old Gang' of today. It is not that. It is because the role of these quite unimportant people is grossly misrepresented in these lyrical diatribes, and the true complexion of both the War, and the Peace that has followed it, risks to be obscured, that I break silence.

In *Front*, a continental review, the first number of which appeared recently (1930, I think), there was a poem in German, which was a piece of pure Siegfried Sassoonism, with the emphasis on Siegfried. Fifteen years after the date of Mr. Sassoon's satirical lyrics, here was the same thing all over again. Such fashions die hard. Here it is, for your instruction :

DIE ALTEN GENERALEN

> Sehr müd und still mit weissen Haaren
> Auf ihre Pläne und Karten
> Gebeugt, vergessen seit den Jahren
> Des grossen Friedens und allein
> Brüten die alten Generale.
> Durch ihre Träume brüllt der Schrel
> Des Schlachtens. Klirrende Pokale.
> Das Kaiserhoch im Schloss Versailles.
>
> Gesenkte Fahnen und Standarten.
> Die Front grüsst sie zum Tod bereit.
> Sie gehen stolz mit einem smarten
> Gelächter in die Ewigkeit.

Whoever started this fashion, which culminated in *All Quiet on the Western Front*,[4] that particular sentimental attitude (of the crude 'War-Guilt-Lie' order, which has persisted)—that is the important

214

thing. The Peace has not, any more than the War, enlightened the general run of people. [. . . .]

What is it that we must object to more strongly in the work of Remarque? That is not at all difficult to explain.—The animalizing and caricaturing of the human being, subjected to the mental and physical agonies of modern war, that is what is so ugly to start with. This distracted civilized Tom Thumb is turned into a schoolboy 'joke'. But what was the War, after all, but a gigantic practical joke which was played upon mankind? By way of the Bairnsfather-Remarque type of art he is seduced into *joining in the insane laughter.* Living in hysterical hordes—of mud-caked, ravenous, little savages —all these millions of Europeans had their legs pulled—their legs swaddled in mud-coloured puttees—their legs drawn by Bairnsfather —and of course their legs shot off! European science having 'conquered nature'—so that, had Europe possessed the intelligence to will it, a veritable Golden Age could have been enjoyed throughout the world, of the most absolute abundance—behold, that political intelligence, or the plain good-sense necessary to effect that consummation, is found utterly wanting. And instead, all the populations of Europe are thrown back into this colossal (artificial) savagery— savagery, danger, and want. And in order not to become demented, these multitudes, upon whom this gigantic, circean, conjuring trick has been played, are invited to snigger, to chuckle and to grin at their own misery!

The human intellect is delicately organized, and in the face of dementia will be driven to any expedient, no doubt. So the joke of 'If you know of a better 'ole!' order, and all the 'scrounging', bilking and stealing (all the mice-jokes, the magpie-jokes, the cat-and-the-milk jokes) were no doubt necessities, imposed upon men by their desperate case. But ten years after the event a sort of comic Fenimore-Cooperism is suddenly released in the pages of Herr Remarque. The 'Three Musketeers,' the three 'Fritzes' [. . .] with boyscoutish war-whoops and chuckles fling themselves, in the gutted shell of a village, upon unexpected provender and gluttenously raven, in pseudo-criminal glee: and because that is 'historically true'—as unfortunately it is—it is none the less the type of history that should never be written. Or if it 'must' be written, it should not be written without a furious gloss [. . . .]

The pillorying of the simple *foreground* figures in the English

215

War-poet (of the 'Old Generals', of the elderly political leaders, —and in the Sitwells, after Sassoon) of necessity has tended to occult and to mask more and more the prime movers in the *background*. The 'Children and Parents' war-cry, indulged in, in some cases, with an almost cissyish unction; in others with an indulgence of that slightly young-lady-like streak which often has been detected in the Undergraduate Briton by the German observer (as an instance Keyserling)[5]—that has been in the nature of a red-herring (and the 'red' explanations of orthodox Marxism, although much nearer the mark, has been in this connection another red-herring). The deliberate 'Youth-hysterics' of now ageing men, young at the outset of the war, has thrown smoke-screens of emotion around the cold facts.—A fashion is set, a romantic cry is taken up, and indefinitely repeated. Engaged in these clamorous disputes with his ancestors (just as one felt that during the War the majority regarded 'Kaiser Bill' as the ultimate source of all their troubles, and 'Old Fritz' as a 'Hun' after all) the War-novelist of 1927–30 never even began to think of who his real enemy might be ! So this orgy being over now, a different and less emotional account of what was the Great War of 1914–18 should at last drive out the histrionics of the War-poets and War-novelists. But if no one dares, or cares, to write the truth, or if there are really so few people who understand it, it would be far better definitely to taboo that subject in fiction for ever : for a falsification is worse than nothing. And as for the War of the Old Gang and the New Gang, that, once more, has its roots emotionally in the Great War—in 'Flanders Fields', and for that matter is a plant belonging, at bottom, to the same mental climate as the Flanders Poppy.

NOTES

1 This section is excerpted from Lewis, *The Old Gang and the New Gang*. London: Desmond Harmsworth, 1932, pp. 45–8, 54–5, 61–2.
2 *Rude Assignment*, p. 138.
3 A different version of this poem appears in Sassoon's *Collected Poems* and elsewhere.
4 Erich Maria Remarque, *All Quiet on the Western Front* (1929).
5 Prince Hermann von Keyserling (1880–1946), philosopher and traveller. The continental review mentioned earlier in this chapter may have been the German periodical *Die Front*, published by Hans Conrad.

4

The *transition* Writers

(From *The Diabolical Principle* ... , 1931)

Founded in 1927 by Mr. and Mrs. Eugene Jolas, *transition*—'An International Quarterly for Creative Experiment'—quickly became embroiled in battle with Lewis following the latter's attack on Joyce, whose *Work in Progress* it was enthusiastically serializing. First from the Paris magazine came a counter-attack called 'First Aid to the Enemy', by Jolas and his editorial associates Robert Sage and Elliot Paul, a fellow-American.[1] Jolas interpreted *The Diabolical Principle*, on its first appearance in *The Enemy* No. 3,[2] as Lewis's answer to 'First Aid'. Replying to the Lewis blast, Jolas branded it 'the wordy document of a pseudo-revolutionary'[3] and defended *transition*'s championing of the French poet, de Lautréamont, against the Enemy's assault, which follows. Lewis's attack on Paul's 'new nihilism' is dismissed as hysterical though Jolas concedes favouring a new romanticism. 'We want complete liberty from all narrowly circumscribed forms of expression,' Jolas wrote.[4] He accused 'the London sage' of a braggadoccio which 'is a kind of hysterical substitute for creation. . . . And so we leave the self-styled "Diogones of the Day" in his "tub", where he may continue to scratch the back of his Bismarckian complex and strut his little philosophical stuff to the delight of his innocent heart!'[5] Thus Lewis had become the chief antagonist of the expatriate Anglo-Saxon writers encamped in Paris—a group contemptuously termed by Lewis 'an excrescence upon english literature, as it is a growth upon the workaday body of France.'[6]

[The *transition* radicals] are, for me, false revolutionaries. They wish for a *transition* into a New Philistinism (smeared over with a debased intellectualist varnish) and accompanied with a quite needless material violence, and not a *transition* of a more truly revolutionary order, into an order of things radically different from the 'capitalist state',[7] For it is precisely a capitalist state of mind of which the Russia of today is often with some reason accused. The *violences* of expression I spoke of disparagingly are violences that are deliberately sought and which are artifically entertained and exploited, as *violences*, for violence sake. They always are given an as it were physical connotation. It is almost as though, when a persian or chinese artist dislocated the arm or leg of some figure in a composition, for the purposes of his design, a critic had applauded this device on the ground that it symbolized the artist's desire to put upon the rack half the population of Persia or of China, as a punishment for being such terrible *bourgeois*. Whereas in fact the artist might not relish his countrymen being such deeply-ingrained *bourgeois*, but, once he started painting, in order to paint well he would have to banish his political sensations altogether, or so I believe. [. . . .]

The doctrinaires that I am thinking of are then, for me, on the side of the 'romantic'—sensual average—majority, and must sooner or later, as the night follows the day, betray the artist whom they use to that majority, for they are as philistine as it. It is not their politics, but this fact, to which I primarily object. And it is owing to this philistine affinity of the professional false-revolutionary (however much disguised beneath a *fard* of intellectualist fashion) that I am the critic of those other Philistines.[8] [. . . .]

It is not a political interest at all that drives me to this critical activity. I advance the strange claim (as my private *Bill of Rights*) to act and to think non-politically in everything, in complete detachment from all the intolerant watchwords and formulas by which we are beset. I am an artist and my *mind*, at least, is entirely free : also that is a freedom that I hold from no man and have every intention of retaining. I shall act as a conventional 'radical' at six this evening if that seems to me appropriate to the situation, and at ten a.m. tomorrow I shall display royalist tendencies if I am provoked by too much stupidity or righteous pomp from some other quarter.

Yet if an art has for its function to represent manners and people, I do not see how it can avoid systematizing its sensibility to the extent of showing some figures much as Molière, for instance, did, as absurd or detestable. But the *bourgeois*, or the *bourgeois-gen-*

tilhomme, in the work of Molière, is not an advertisement for 'bourgeois' civilization exactly. So today such a creation would be serving a political end, since the 'bourgeois' is the favourite comic Aunt-Sally of the communist.

But here is the point that is essential to my argument. Molière would have done you a *bolshevik* with as much relish as a *bourgeois*, for his *Précieuses* were equally *ridiculous*.

Plomer is probably the best novelist in South Africa today.[9] D. H. Lawrence in England and Sherwood Anderson in America are among the very best writers produced by those countries recently : and as to Paris, it is necessary to say that almost all that is good, in formal tendency, or in actual achievement, as either painting or writing (and there is not much) is to be found here and there between the covers of *transition*? You may not accept this as true, but it is what I believe and it is upon that basis that I am arguing. In the anglo-saxon world, that is to say, all the best artists are engaged in some form or other of political revolutionary propaganda as much as was Tolstoy in Russia in the last century. Almost the only conspicuous exceptions to this rule are to be found among artists of pronounced theological bias.

In anglo-saxon countries today then a first-rate or very talented artist or man of letters or philosopher is invariably (with the exception of the theologian) a destructive political revolutionary idealist. In their several ways these persons are as fervent propagandists as was Tolstoy. So it seems to me we get back, in one degree or another, with all of them, to the problem of Tolstoy—of the artist who is at the same time a fanatical politician.

Is it possible to launch and develop this criticism without being accused of bias of an opposite sort—in a word, of being a 'reactionary', of the nature of Thomas Carlyle? My answer is that it is impossible. But that does not make the accusation necessarily true. You may object to Tolstoy, as an artist, on the ground of his politics, without that charge being levelled at you : but it is not possible to make the same criticism of a contemporary without it being said that you are a politician (of opposite sign) as much as the people you arraign.

Yet surely to root politics out of art is a highly necessary undertaking : for the freedom of art, like that of science, depends entirely upon its objectivity and non-practical, non-partisan passion. And surely you should be able to employ the same arguments for a living artist that everyone has always been allowed to employ for one that is dead! [. . . .]

Next as to their willingness to be classed as 'romantics' : about that, fortunately, too, there is no question. 'In plain and direct words . . . *we believe in a new romanticism*.[10] They suggest that this statement would not have taken such a 'plain' and 'direct' form but for my criticism. But everywhere the fact it defines is so explicit that, even without this special effort at 'directness', it would have been 'unescapable'.

Romanticism is a word that covers a great quantity of things differing among themselves very widely indeed. Spengler, with his 'faustian' philosophy of catastrophic fatalism : Chesterton, the poet of the 'beer-drinking Briton can never be beat' frame-of-mind : Edgar Allan Poe, Doughty of *Arabia Deserta*, Hoffmann;[11] Nietzsche and Longfellow, Browning and Mr. Theodore Hook,[12] are, severally, examples of *romanticism*. But it is possible to narrow down the 'New Romanticism' in question here. First of all, therefore, a definition of the sort of 'romanticism' that is at stake is required.

In the first place it is not new; it is a return to the feverish 'diabolism' that flourished in the middle of the last century in France, and which reached England in the 'nineties,' with Oscar Wilde and Beardsley as its principal exponents. Huysman's exploitation of the mediæval nightmare and his *Messe Noire* interests; Nietzsche's turgid satanism and the diabolism of Baudelaire and Byron : the 'Drunken Boat' of Rimbaud, and the rhetoric of Lautréamont, are its basis. All that is new, therefore, is that a band of communizing journalists, living in Paris, have chosen to found a political school for middle-class anglo-saxon and french students, mainly art-students, and *fils de papas*, upon the diabolic text of the famous authors mentioned above.

This romanticism is in fact that of the Communes and the minor revolutions which followed in the wake of the great Eighteenth-century eruption in France—that epoch to which the revolutionary aristocrats, Byron and Shelley, and, later on, Swinburne, belonged, in England, and which produced, in the french mind in violent reaction against the traditional academic restraints, a wild flowering of literature that threw up a number of poets of the greatest power. If you add to this the 'illumination' of german mystics, of the order of Weishaupt,[13] throwing in the theory of Einstein as a congenial late-comer, you obtain what is 'super-reality.' It is merely a flowery cocktail, but it has a grand name. What is most remarkable about it so far is that, swallowed whole, it leaves things just as they were before : it does not enable anyone to write anything except criticism of a not very original order. [. . . .]

> While the Dostoevsky, or the Christian, spirit, if you like, has been given over to a few recluses to guard for more propitious ages, its *converse* is beginning to find expression, and a literature completely dehumanized and functioning in a sphere which knows neither morals nor compassion, is coming out into the open. . . . There can be no more doubt as to its existence and scope. It goes way beyond the Russian Nihilism of Turgenev's time.[14]

That is the new Nihilism and that is also the New Romanticism. It is the New Paul's creed.

But the above Pauline pronouncement is historically inaccurate. (I shall revert to this inaccuracy later on, when I take up other points of his article.) *The Possessed* of Dostoevsky describes exactly the same sort of 'nihilists' as Paul is concerned to advertise. The strictly 'inhuman' or rather anti-human vindictiveness that makes possible the massacres of the various contemporary Revolutions, is a 'nihilism' : it has to its credit a holocaust. But substantially it is the same as the demented doctrine of universal destruction which Dostoevsky despairingly observed, and put on record with such clairvoyance. By calling the 'inhumanity' of today, or of the 'October Revolution,' a *super*-nihilism you do not change or intensify its character : but you do describe its latter-day *scale*—for it has now become universally effective and has multiplied its power many times. Civil War in this is like its sweet-flavoured sister, Nationalist War : in *scale* it can indeed claim to go 'way beyond' all former efforts of the same sort. So this paralysis of our civilized or human instincts, which now has crept over the whole of humanity, instead of over only the Russians, is *extensively* a super-nihilism. The anaesthesia and mechanization involved in the nihilistic orthodoxy is represented by its adherents as a liberation. [. . . .]

The *Lay of Maldoror*[15] and *Zarathustra* have this much affinity, that they are both byronic declamatory and romantic prose-poems. Both their authors are 'satanists.' But Lautréamont is very far even

221

from an Ossian. He is, as a matter of fact, a kind of happy mixture of the Marquis de Sade and Friedrich Nietzsche, but without remarkable talent. His 'lays' are full of the juiciest machinery of inverted dope-diabolics : wild animals drag naked snow-white virgins across moonlit mountains, tearing their tender flesh upon the jagged rocks and leaving a trail of blood. [. . . .]

The 'satanic' flavour prevailing throughout his *Lays* is fully presented for your inspection. It is the order of satanic romanticism popularized by Huysmans in *Là-Bas*. Had Victor Hugo become enamoured of the philosophy of the Marquis de Sade and gone to work in the same gothic spirit (shown perhaps more fully in his remarkable drawings than in his writing) you would have got something of the sort. It is a very tiresome and monotonous bellow. [. . . .]

That this simple-hearted satanism, transparent as the vindictive day-dreaming of a rather vulgar child, in its infallible inversions, but presented with the leering pomposity of an eager stylist, smiling behind his pasteboard mask of conventional 'hideousness', boasting as he goes of his *effects*, of the sensational reactions he is competent to produce in his listeners—that this bric-à-brac should be seriously presented as the exemplar of the best or newest seems impossible. That it should be [. . .] published to catch *l'homme moyen sensuel*, on account of its blood-dripping fangs associated with the milk-white bodies of virgins, is as natural and harmless as that *Fanny Hill* should never be quite out of print, or that the *History of a Flea* or even the 'bourgeois' pornography of Paul de Kock's *Ten Pairs of Drawers* should remain scandalous best-sellers. But there, you would suppose, the joke would end—once the gull's money was safely transferred from his bank to that of the sagacious literary reprint-publisher (to whom of course the best of luck). But that is not the case. Another and a still higher destiny has been reserved for Isidore. [. . . .]

Isidore-Maldoror is 'the poet in whom the modern spirit of *conscious revolt* . . . has found its greatest flourescence.'[16] You must *consciously*, deliberately, embrace the revolutionary principle, if you wish to be 'a poet'—in that you have no choice, oh anglo-saxon *publicum*! In real life Isidore was a famous agitator and revolutionary under the Third Empire. What is most 'striking' about his work in his pre-occupation with so-called 'evil' functions of life. And, as we have seen, it is characterized by a spirit of demented hatred of other men, and an obsessional attachment to apocalyptic images of horror and destruction.

This is what America (and no doubt even more so England) needs! exclaims Jolas. So far, says Jolas, american poets have merely expressed feebly an echo of 'pseudo-revolt', caught from the stimulating events that have occurred on this side of the Atlantic. Here is their chance! Why not give 'evil' a trial? he pleads. Why not take Lautréamont as a model? Just once! Just for fun—one vacation, or one week-end.

But what more does the *New Masses*[17] ask of its readers? What is the difference, spiritually, between these two ventures, except that one is labelled 'communist' quite frankly and the other coming at it from the art-angle, calls itself art-for-art's sake [...] though obviously it is art-for-revolution's sake in fact, and not at all for art's. I, as a doctrinaire of art-independent-of-life, very naturally resent these obsessing politics. That, once more, is what this dispute is about. It is not about politics.

The tenour of the philosophy of *transition* is then a romantic nihilism, and the springs of its action are to be sought not in any specific doctrine of art, but, as its name suggests, in the political chaos of this time, and in a particular attitude towards that chaos.[18]
[....]

The certain philistinism in Tolstoy (and in a much ranker form the same must apply to the less interesting mind of Shaw) caused him to mistake his problem and to moralize his excellent and humane observation to such a degree that he was led into the most fantastic thesis upon the subject of art. He became a sort of a russian Bunyan, and art for him eventually appeared under the form of an endowment in the service of ethics, a purely utilitarian activity and nothing more. It is against this conception of art (only in a form neither humane nor noble but injected with all the jealous passion of a gospel of *hatred* instead of a gospel of *love*) that I am writing.

The *politicization* of art is a human catastrophe of the same order as the politicization of science. The lip-service offered to the man of science is associated with his achievements as an inventor of venomous gases or ironclads, or because of the immense economic value of his technical genius. If he had never invented anything but economically useless and physically inoffensive things he would never have been heard of, naturally. Art cannot compare with science on those grounds. But it is not politically negligible. It is to prevent the organization of art as a political instrument, either on behalf of a benevolent idealism such as Tolstoy's or one subserving the 'diabolical' interests of a Paul, that I am engaged in my present critical task.

Further, it is necessary to insist (over and over again, since there are so few to do it) that the, in the popular sense, 'moral' interests of Tolstoy—great credit as they do him as a citizen and I do not mean to laugh at that—are not so far removed as is supposed from the 'diabolical' enthusiasms of Lautréamont, for example. Such men as the latter are in fact inverted moralists, as was well seen in the case of Nietzsche. The 'wicked', the 'naughty', 'perverted', 'maso-chistic', the sentimentalism or snobbery of the 'bad', is the other side of an obsession about some wooden 'virtue' of the german protestant mind. From that there is no escape. The 'daring' Ballet or the 'daring' book would no longer be 'daring' if there were nothing there to be 'daring' about. It would just be an interesting creation of art or a dull one, and there would be no incentive to insist, out of proportion to its place in normal life, upon this or that, if there were not an absurd Censor standing ready to advertise it with anathema, or a persecutory puritan upon the spot to exclaim and point.

The *politicization* of art, then, in modern Europe, usually takes one of two forms. Either, in its milder and more benevolent form it results in Tolstoy's puritanic bias; or otherwise it issues in *diabol-ism*—when it becomes automatically Nietzsche's 'Anti-Christ', or Lautréamont's hymns of hate against mankind, or Baudelaire's *Fleurs du Mal*. 'Messe Noire' must always be the mystical counter-part of a too fanatically conceived White Mass.

Why the notion of *the diabolical principle* affords such a useful insight into the meaning of what we have been discussing is because it at once reveals the motif of romantic, satanic *revolt*. A Commune directed at the rule and order established not by men but by a god is involved. It is, in short, a mystical revolution that is proposed, against a spiritual Power, to match the other revolutions of a more prosaic type against Capitalism or Kingship. Definitely as a twin of armed political revolt it presents itself : it seems to assert 'It is no use being a *revolutionary* in every other way—it is idle to be in the van with the feminist, on the barricade with the communist, in the Black ranks against the White, and so forth—if you are not also a revolutionary in the spiritual sphere. You must not forget Heaven however much you fix your insurgent eye upon the Bastille!' That is what the Diabolical Principle means upon the lips of Paul, or what 'giving Evil Functions a chance' is intended to convey.

NOTES

1   *transition*, December, 1927, pp. 160–76.
2   The present excerpts come from *The Diabolical Principle* . . ., pp. 33–4, 35, 37–40, 41–3, 45–6, 50–1, 55–6, 62–3, 122–5.
3   Eugene Jolas, 'The Innocuous Enemy', *transition*, June, 1929, p. 208.
4   Ibid., p. 210.
5   Ibid., p. 212.
6   Lewis, 'The Paris Address', *The Enemy* No. 2, September, 1927, p. xxii.
7   Cf. Elliot Paul, 'The New Nihilism', *transition*, May, 1927.
8   Jolas angrily termed this 'claptrap' in his 1929 reply.
9   South African-born William Plomer (1903–73) was a novelist as well as a poet.
10 Cf. *transition*, June, 1929, p. 210.
11 E. T. W. Hoffmann (1776–1822), German Romantic writer, composer and caricaturist.
12 Theodore Hook (1788–1841) was a High Tory journalist and author of racy novels.
13 Adam Weishaupt (1748–1830), founder of the Order of Illuminés.
14 'The New Nihilism', p. 164.
15 *transition*, October, 1927, published a translation by John Rodker of Canto I of *Les Chants de Maldoror*, by Comte de Lautréamont, or Isadore Ducasse (1846–1870). At one point (p. 53) in a series of long quotations from the *Lays*, L. wrote 'For the next passage we must wrap our winter coats about us, and shiver, to be warmly sympathetic with the bleak scene, like a sort of inverted christmas-card, with the maledictions of the season and a peep of the *Messe Noire*, genre 1840, into which we are to be plunged.'
16 Jolas, 'Enter the Imagination', *transition*, October, 1927, p. 159. L.'s italics.
17 American left-wing magazine of the period.
18 In his 1929 article, Jolas defended *transition's* advocacy of Lautréamont 'because I feel that, like Blake and Young, he revealed to us a state of mind that has recently been neglected in Anglo-Saxon literature' (p. 208).

5

André Malraux

(From *The Writer and the Absolute*, 1952)

The following[1] is by no means Lewis's only attack on Malraux. In *The Demon of Progress in the Arts* (1954), Lewis assailed what he considered to be Malraux's excessive politicization of the arts. 'He casts "art" for the role of destroyer of bourgeois values,' Lewis complained.[2] The fact was that 'a plate of Cézanne's apples could not even stimulate a man's hunger'.[3] But Lewis credited Malraux's *The Voices of Silence* with incisively analysing the contemporary art scene and discerning a diabolical, destructive principle working through primitivism, infantilism and similar fashions. 'He applauds the coming back into currency of the diabolic. . . . Where Malraux and I differ is that I am not one of those who climb upon the bandwagon of the Fiend. But I applaud Malraux's advertisement of the true position.'[4]

In André Malraux we have another extraordinary case, even more so than that of Jean-Paul Sartre, of a political flirt. His was a far more *violent* flirtation, as everything about him is more violent. Malraux never became a member of the Communist party—and now he is publicity chief in the entourage of the French Franco, General Charles de Gaulle. He did everything that can be done *short of* becoming a party member. He took part in the Communist revolution at Canton: he was with the Russian air force in the Spanish Civil War; he went to party rallies in Moscow. Why did he not regularize this long-standing relationship? I know the answer in Sartre's case: but as regards Malraux I do not think I know it. I can only suppose he is one of those men-of-action who is really only an actor.

Although Malraux is not an existentialist, he is more *existent* and

226

concrete than most. 'Il n'y a de realité que dans l'action', Sartre insists : Marlaux's life has been all action, the penalty of which—from the writer's standpoint—is that the vitality in his books is only borrowed from his life, and less dense than it otherwise would be. Yet Malraux studied and wrote of 'the Asburd' before Camus, or Fondane, or Sartre : the influence of his mind has been very considerable. My purpose in writing about him here, however, is mostly to fill out the Sartre picture.

When Sartre aspires to be violent he goes to the brain (as in *La Nausée*) : he uses madness as Thomas Mann uses disease. His dramatic power is very small : an example of this is *Huis-Clos*, which has the familiar air, from the first page, of a Palais Royal farce, written with great spirit. The stock figures and stock dialogue of the *Garcon d'Etage* and the *Locataire* reek (delightfully) of the French theatres which cater for those who wish to give themselves up to laughter. Comedy it remains to the end, where another writer would have made it Grand Guignolesque. *Les Mouches* though philosophically interesting, is as unpurgative as a play by Mr. Shaw. The most dramatic thing in it is where the murderer of Agamemnon, seeing Orestes with drawn sword, receives him kindly, saying among other things 'I am glad it is too late (to call for help). I want you to assassinate me' : which of course Orestes does. Sartre outdoes the classical fatality in the flatness of his dénouement.[5]

Having read most of Sartre's books, I find him a gentle philosophic spirit (which is what I like most about him—I am paying him a compliment)—with a great salacious appetite for life, like many Frenchmen. He is not a bad man, of that I am sure. In his best-known novel, *L'Age de Raison*, the hero Mathieu steals 3,000 francs from a woman performer in his favourite night-spot : Mathieu's favourite pupil is thievish—books is what he mainly steals; this young man's sister, Ivich, is a lesbian, who squeezes her thighs together and has an orgasm while sitting in cafés; the de facto hero of the book, Daniel Sereno, is a very active homosexual indeed, who among other drolleries, has an amusing fight with a scrubby little *tapette* in whose room he is passing the night : and so on. In order to play a major rôle in a novel of Sartre's you have to be able to do some parlour trick of this sort (though homicide is barred). Sartre must not be blamed for this. He writes faithfully about what he knows. If a hospital-nurse wrote a book, there would be something the matter with all her characters : one would have ulcers, another would be incontinent, a third would suffer from epileptic seizures.

When Malraux aspires to be violent it is a different matter. Homicide is *not* barred with him. In fact, homicidal propensities are an indispensable qualification for starring in one of his novels. I have here a paper-covered volume, from the cover of which one is vamped by a very interesting dark brooding young man. Its author is M. Claude Mauriac (son of François Mauriac) : but he is *not* the dark-eyed young man. That is André Malraux *jeune*, in the days when he was starting his career of political filibustering and Byronism up-to-date. The title of this study is *Malraux ou Le Mal du Héros*. It seethes with romanticism, like so much French writing. Malraux is of course the 'Hero'. The personalities of M. Mauriac (*fils*) and Malraux, in contact as we find them in this book, provide a demonstration interesting to the critic; for the critic cannot fail to remark that Mauriac's is the sort of mind for whom Malraux's books were destined. We may observe his books in action, as it were, within the mind of an admirer, who may be regarded as a reagent. I look upon this book as a critical 'find'.

With regard to the Hero's 'mal', one of the principal forms it takes is a blood-obsession—he is 'haunted by blood'. But Mauriac has not selected this particular hero to write about without having as we shall presently see a certain taste for it himself. Action appears to him to be the highest good. And M. Mauriac is in no doubt as to the *kind* of action which is the most worthy of our admiration. 'Perhaps even,' he writes, 'the intelligence does not reach its final perfection except in action, and pre-eminently in what is its ultimate form, namely combat.'[6] The fighting-man is the flower of mankind : the human intelligence only reaches its perfection when it plunges its sword into a human body, or blows it up with a bomb. If no war is going on at the moment, and an *exceptionally* intelligent man is waiting (rather wearily) for peace to stop, he can always pick a quarrel with a stranger in the street, and try to bash his face in.—M. Mauriac does not like people who do not share these views. He growls : 'There is no literature more abject than that which speaks ill of war.'[7]

Murder is not quite the same thing as spitting your man in a charge, or blowing him up with a landmine, or dropping a bomb

228

on his head : however, let me quote M. Claude Mauriac, where he is considering his hero's penchant for assassination.

> [Malraux's] . . . obsession with murder assumes the form alternately of temptation and remorse. Do the heroes of his books wish to liberate themselves by a subterfuge from the memory of one of their murders : or do they in fact see in crime—already committed or in prospect—an indispensable experience?[8]

All these writers suffer from the disadvantage of never having killed anybody, says one of (Malraux's) heroes, in speaking of the Russian novelists. He expounds as follows :

> If the characters in their books suffer after having killed somebody, it is because the world has hardly changed at all for them. I say *hardly*. Had it happened in life, instead of a book, the world would have been transformed for them completely, all its perspectives altered : it would have become not the world of a man who 'had committed a crime', but that of a man who had *killed*.[9]

(I shall comment as I go along; in the above passage Dostoevsky is doubtless the Russian author most obviously involved : *Crime and Punishment*, the book that would first come to mind. The first thing to remark is that Dostoevsky was very actively a Christian, and none of Malraux's heroes are that. Secondly, to suppose that Dostoevsky was incapable of imagining the state of mind of a non-Christian murderer is to under-estimate the insight and imaginative faculty of a great creative genius. But that is not all. The implication of course is that Malraux himself has murdered one or more people. This seems to thrill M. Mauriac (though it by no means follows that Malraux *is* a murderer) : he even believes, if I have not misunderstood him, that the murder done by Tchen (in *La Condition Humaine*) is in fact one done by Malraux—his favourite one. Probably his *first* (when he lost his virginity as a man-who-had-not-killed)! This is our point of departure—for M. Mauriac's book begins with the passages I am quoting : that André Malraux was a murderer. A real man—an *homme tout entier*, as Sarte would put it.

I may be mistaken, but I should say that very few of the writers I know have cut a man's throat or plunged a dagger into his heart. Even Hemingway has probably murdered no one. Except for the murdering that a great many of us have to our credit as soldiers, I very much doubt if Hemingway can claim to have taken life—a humiliating thought, which puts him in the same category as Dostoevsky, Tolstoy, Gogol and Tchekov).

I continue my quotation—M. Mauriac is still speaking of *La Condition Humaine*, which he describes, correctly, as one of Malraux's best books. His best, I should say.

Tchen, asking Gisors if he had already killed, and receiving a negative reply, suddenly had the feeling 'that there was something lacking in Gisors.'

> Gisors asked :
> 'The first woman you slept with. . . . What did you feel afterwards? . . . .
> 'Pride.'
> 'At being a man?'
> 'At not being a woman,' Tchen replied. . . .
> 'And you were right to have mentioned women. Perhaps one has a great contempt for the person one kills. But one despises him less than one does the others. . . .'
> 'You mean than those who do not kill?'
> 'Than those who do not kill—than virgins (*les puceaux*).'[10]

(Practically all the readers of this book of Malraux's must have been in this sense virgins, or *des puceaux*. What would their sensations be, I wonder? From the great success accorded to it, shame must have been experienced, I suppose. Its readers were intended to feel small, and they did feel small—if writers they must have experienced something of the feeling of the sexually impotent. Being French (with vanity as a national vice—*vide* Stendhal) they must have promised themselves at the first opportunity, with a reasonable assurance of impunity that is, to correct this oversight, due to a cissy upbringing).

M. Mauriac tends to suggest, however, though he does not say so outright, that Malraux only committed *one* murder.

> It is always *the same murder* that these exucutioners of Malraux's commit, as if a precise recollection, a constant and immutable reference, forbade the novelist to change in the smallest particular narratives of which the intangible contents were once and for all fixed.[11]
> ' "Hong asked me once," said Klein, "what my feelings had been in executing Kominsky. . . . I replied that all the time I was think-

ing I ought to have used a revolver. . . . With a revolver I should have finished him off without touching him. . . ." '[12]

(The idea in this last passage is that when he was committing his one and only murder he used a knife and that he found contact with his victim's body disagreeable.)

Leaving murder, we arrive, under the guidance of M. Mauriac, at sadism.

> To humiliate is one of the principal pleasures of the erotic heroes of Malraux. . . . This madness—dry, meticulous, reasonable even in its ever more imperious unreason—this gloomy fury has a name, which is *sadism*.[13]

M. Mauriac quotes all through the book from Col. Lawrence who greatly influenced Malraux it would seem, and with whom he had, according to this writer, many points of resemblance : except of course that Malraux was not his own hero. He had Garine, Perken and so forth to stand for him. Chapter II of *Le Mal du Héros* opens with a discussion of these parallel destinies; and then an incident in *The Seven Pillars of Wisdom* is placed in evidence. It is Lawrence's account of the execution which he carried out, the victim being an Arab called Ahmed, a member of his escort who in a dispute with another Arab had killed him.

Lawrence pushed Ahmed into a damp and sombre gully : standing at the entrance he gave him a few moments of respite, which the condemned man spent upon the ground weeping. Then, having made him stand up, he fired into his chest :

> He fell bellowing into the grass : the blood spurted out in bursts, running over his clothes : the convulsions of his body flung him almost up to my feet. I fired again, but trembling so much that he was only hit in the hand. He continued to cry out, but with less and less force, now lying upon his back, his feet towards me. I leant forward to give him the coup de grâce, beneath the jaw, in the fat of the neck. The body gave a shudder and I called the Ageyls. . . .[14]

Two sub-titles accompany this page (in *The Seven Pillars*) A MURDER (this refers to the Arab's act) : ANOTHER MURDER (namely the execution).

A lot of dialectic accompanies this ecstatic taking of life in Malraux's stories, however. The second line of the first page of *La Condition Humaine* contains the word 'angoisse'—anguish ('L'angoisse lui tordait l'estomac'). This is one of the words some people get tired of reading in his books : it occurs very often. Tchen is discovered about to murder a man lying inside a mosquito net. I speak of this event most humbly as a mere *puceau* : but would a tough Chinese have *quite* so many sensations (of a European kind) while going about this little bit of revolutionary business? Would he experience 'une atmosphère de folie', etc?

In the 'twenties, in describing not only himself but those who shared his temperament and outlook, Malraux wrote : 'pensée nihiliste, destructrice, foncièrement négative'.[15] According to a critic, M. Gaëtan Picon, he built for himself in contemporary literature a place beside Chateaubriand, Byron, d'Annunzio, Barrès, Montherlant. This unsympathetic critic speaks of the romanticism which entered into his revolutionary *parti pris* (and this is what the Communists found embarrassing too) : of the 'goût du spectacle, de l'apothéose, de l'apocalypse'.[16] Then 'le néant' was haunting the pages of Malraux long before it took up its quarters as the major concept of Sartre's system. And did he [Mauriac] not write : 'In imposing his personality upon the external world man finds the only outlet which remains open to him, his one and only chance of escaping—imperfectly—from Nothingness (au néant)'?[17]

Here you see in this *escape through action* theory none other than J.-P. Sartre's conception of Freedom. How this *action* theory of 'imposing your personality upon the world' may very easily develop into a quite substantial *power-complex* may be judged by pondering these further words of Malraux's. 'To lead, to be he who decides, to coerce. That is to live!'[18] Those ways of feeling are contagious, who can doubt? How many people were there in Western Europe between the wars nursing feverish power-complexes, besides the Duces and the Führers? Malraux's account of his own power-impulses represented them as *an escape from Nothingness*—on the part of a 'nihilistic' and 'negative' thinker—would not some such formula have accommodated Hitler very well? The filling of a void with shouting crowds, and tramping feet, by a man who was convulsively wrenching himself out of Nothingness?

What was—and is—this Nothingness, which began filling Europe at the beginning of the 'twenties like an evil fog? Which plunged all kinds of people into acts of violence—which were in a sense acts of *escape*? Which caused men frantically to snatch at power? All men are able to examine this intangible, dark and chilling emanation, and answer that question for themselves.

At the time of the publication of Malraux's *La Lutte avec L'Ange,* a certain M. Mounin, what Sartre would call a Communist watchdog, described it I gather as a 'backsliding'. But here are his words.

'All that Malraux, we had thought, had got out of his system—anguish regarding man's destiny, [absurdity of the world] the obsession of death—erupts into his work once more, without other opposition than that of fragile emotions, of brief *"evidences fulgurantes"* such as we get with Sartre.'[19] Another Communist, Pierre Hervé, speaks of his 'degradation of man' : which is the same criticism that Henri Lefebvre [. . .] brought against Sartre.[20] In all cases these Communist critics approach the writings in question from a basis of hard debunking good sense. It is a pity these people seem to have almost a monopoly in France of that firmness—where so much is jelly. Why Sartre wrote his *Existentialism is a Humanism* was to counter such criticism as this. So I think I have been able to establish how close is the relationship between Malraux and Sartre, but that both come out of the same Night and Void as the Western European politics of the past quarter of a century. [. . . .]

I should point out that these writers—Sartre, Malraux, Camus and others of this group—are unusually gifted, remarkable both for their creative ability and philosophical ability. I should be very sorry if it were thought that I was treating them with insufficient respect, or throwing doubt upon their genius. It is their *Weltanschauung* which I deplore. [. . . .]

NOTES

1 From *The Writer and the Absolute,* pp. 88–95, which appeared under the chapter heading 'Malraux and *Escape Through Action'.*
2 Lewis, *The Demon of Progress in the Arts,* p. 75.
3 Ibid., p. 81.
4 Ibid., p. 87.
5 Jean-Paul Sartre, 'Les Mouches' in *Huis Clos suivi de Les Mouches.* Paris: Gallimard (Le Livre de Pôche), 1947, p. 158 (Act II, Scene IV).
6 Claude Mauriac, *Malraux ou le Mal du Héros.* Paris: Editions Bernard Grasset, 1946, pp. 12–13.
7 Ibid., p. 14.
8 Ibid., p. 53.
9 André Malraux, *Les Conquérants.* Paris: Bernard Grasset, 1928, pp. 97–8. L.'s italics.

10 Malraux, *La Condition Humaine*. Paris: Gallimard, 1946 reprint, p. 73.
11 *Mal du Héros*, p. 56.
12 *Les Conquérants*, p 184. Quoted here by Mauriac, p. 56.
13 *Mal du Héros*, pp. 69, 70.
14 Cf. T. E. Lawrence, *The Seven Pillars of Wisdom*. London: Jonathan Cape, 1940, p. 187. The two sub-titles referred to in the paragraph after this quotation are on pp. 186–7 and in the 1940 edition read 'Murder is Done' and 'Another Murder'. L.'s version of these and of Lawrence's paragraph were translations back into English from a French translation of *The Seven Pillars* since, as he explained in a footnote about the English version, 'a copy . . . is not immediately available.' (p. 93).
15 Quoted in *Mal du Héros*, p. 193.
16 Ibid., p. 183.
17 Ibid., p. 199.
18 Quoted Ibid.
19 Georges Mounin, a Marxist writer, is quoted in Ibid., p. 250.
20 Cf. Henri Lefebvre, *L'Existentialisme*. Paris: 1946.

6

Camus and Sartre

(From *The Writer and the Absolute*, 1952)

On his return to Europe in 1945 from his six-year stay in North America, Lewis was quick to take note of the controversies stirred up by the existentialists and their associates in Paris. 'Much more life is to be found in Paris than here,' he wrote in a 1947 letter from London. 'There always was. . . . Even as it is the world of Sartre and Camus is a very sick one indeed.'[1]

I began with a quotation from an article by Albert Camus.[2] He is the author of *La Peste*, of *L'Etranger*, and other books, was active in *la résistance*, and has been an editor of *Combat*. His books are probably the best that are being written in France today, of the new writers. To what he says we are therefore bound to listen attentively. His objections to political absolutism—to the man who refuses to discuss anything with you, whose theories are fiats—are shared by every civilized man. 'We suffocate among people who think they are absolutely right.'[3] What pleasure it gives one to read those words—gives us who suffocate. [. . . .]

In Camus we have a writer of great distinction who declares himself as *not of any party* : or at least desirous of being that. Yet there is nothing in the world so difficult today as not belonging to a party. It is easier to grow hair on your head if you are bald, or to add a foot to your height if uncomfortably short, than not to belong to a party. Remain outside of a party, and you flout and affront all the beautiful (and extremely touchy) groups who would like you to succumb to their attractions. [. . . .]

The French astound one by their vitality—whereas the English tend, if not to sag, to fall silent beneath the crushing burden of debt, their kidneys stunned with watery cataracts of beer. Whatever the cause, the literary scene in London resembles a Butlin Camp in an off-month, or a mews in a once prosperous quarter taken over by small-time spivs and hard-up swells (both sexes, from *Debrett*). Had it occurred to me to make use of the London literary scene instead of Sartre's Paris, patriotism would immediately have stepped in and dissuaded me. [. . . .]

The kind of independence of mind which it is essential for the writer to possess cannot be secured in such a society as is depicted by Sartre—and to which the case of Sartre himself bears vivid and exquisite witness. As one watches him feverishly attempting to arrange himself to the best advantage—in accord with the conditions of the post-war forties in France—upon the political scene, which is identical with the literary scene : as far Left as possible without being *extrémiste* : accepting many Communist attitudes but railing at the Communists : peddling an individualism of sorts in the collectivist camp : in a word, attempting to secure all the advantages of an all-out Left position without sacrificing his independence—watching him, one feels what a pity it is that a writer of great talent should have to deflect so much energy into this stupid game. It is even worse when one come to his novels, for there his talent is unmistakable, they are of great interest. Luckily the damage is not as pervasive as it might be. Still, this admirable observer often falsifies a situation to satisfy some political requirement. [. . . .]

Sartre has written, as I suppose my readers will be aware, novels, plays, stories, and philosophy. His philosophy is one of the French offshoots of German 'Existenz Philosophie'. Martin Heidegger, the most prominent German exponent of this school of thought, is the thinker closest to Sartre, who is merely a gallic variant of Heidegger. If Sartre has borrowed his metaphysics, existentialism owes to him its main international advertisement. Since 1939 any German thinker needs a chaperone or escort to circulate in the outside world, or even someone who will *impersonate* him. Sartre performed this office for the most recent great German pessimist.

We may wonder how a man of Sartre's temperament found his way into the bleak labyrinth of *Sein und Zeit*—or at least how he came to take up his quarters there permanently. There is no spiritual congruity between the creator of Daniel Sereno (*Monsier Lalique*) the de facto hero of his novel *L'Age de Raison*—between this master

236

of farce, devotee of the absurd—an amused analyst of life's lazy surface (ignoring its fiery centre), picking his way with delight through all its unexciting paradoxes—and a philosopher who is the sub-zero climax of German pessimism, whose theme-word is not 'existence', but 'anguish'.

This anomaly may be accounted for in the same way as the others which are discussed in this chapter and those that follow. He seems to possess a talent for getting into compartments where he does not belong and then experiencing much difficuty in getting out again— or in feeling that he ought to be something that he is not. So he neglects the excellent material which is by nature his, because of these romantic aberrations. Among the heretics—that is to say those writers who are neither Catholic nor Communist—he stands, with Albert Camus and André Malraux, for what is most alive in con-temporary France. Sartre is much the most genial and human of these three. As a novelist he has none of the dry, concentrated force of the novels of Camus, of *La Peste*, of *L'Etranger* : nor the power of that extraordinary play, *Le Malentendu*. Both Camus and he have compiled metaphysical treatises, the principles of which they have developed in their creative writings. But their metaphysical notions resemble each other much more than do the novels and plays that allegedly issue from them. Then the philosophy of the Absurd, as we find it in Camus, is reminiscent of the theories of the Absurd which haunt the pages of Malraux. Sartre's answer to those who assert that his and Camus' philosophy are one and the same is that this is not at all the case : and Camus says the same thing. Camus is more French, says Sartre, than himself, his is the classical Mediter-ranean pessimism : whereas—presumably he means—*his* (Sartre's) pessimism is of the modern German nihilistic type.—For the rest, Sartre's activity as editor of a fat existentialist monthly (who says there is no paper in France?) as *chef d'école*, lecturer, playwright, etc. etc., is a wonderful testimonial to the intellectual vitality of a bankrupt society.

Now I can return to this new 'pressure' of which I have spoken : 'the pressure of history'.[4] In reply to an inquiry as to what that might signify, some quite elaborate explanation would be forth-coming. What is in fact involved is something as unmysterious as the following. Had you happened to find yourself in the Black Hole of

Calcutta, or in the camp at Auschwitz when the gas-ovens were working; were you a member of a Hindu working-class family in Lahore in the summer of 1947, a few hours after the announcement of the decision of the British boundary commission, and discovered yourself unexpectedly in Pakistan—even more so were you a poor Moslem in Amritzar about the same time : or had you been a private in a Russian regiment defending Stalingrad—you would be experiencing a great deal of 'historic pressure'. I do not believe that Sartre could dispute the validity of my illustrations.—Again, had you been a French writer in Paris at the time of the German occupation— were you an active 'resister'—you would undoubtedly have experienced the pressure of History, in the form of the Gestapo. I may have overlooked something, but this I believe conveys the idea. History, pushing up against what History is for—Man.

Sartre in this article asserts that we must not 'abdicate before what the unspeakable Zaslavski refers to in *Pravda* as the "Historical processus" '.[5] Yet it seems to me that Sartre *does*, after all, abdicate precisely to the 'historical process', in a way that Camus does not. It is far from my wish to find fault with Sartre : but in this particular respect I will again compare his attitude with that of his Algerian contemporary, whose fortitude one cannot but admire. The latter does not, like Sartre, waste time pretending to be something that he is not.

Like those who assert that 'war brings out the best in people' (it is a saying of which I am not very fond) Sartre tells us that 'L'homme tout entier' (man, *all* of him, or total man—a first cousin of 'L'homme tout nu', another objectionable abstraction) is only visible during bombardments or massacres, at the moment of a *coup d'état*, or in the torture chamber. [. . . .]

Now Camus, as you will see from what I have quoted of his, has quite different reactions from these. Far from welcoming 'the tragic' as 'heroic' material for the literary artist, he is against those things in men which produce it. Incidentally he produces great tragedy that way, as a literary artist, which Sartre does not. He does not wish to see men living in terror—in the midst of massacres, bombardments, tortures, and *pressure*. We find him reacting as violently against these conditions, as Jean-Paul Sartre with a fatalistic gusto exploits them.—But let us patiently follow Sartre upon this path, and allow him to convince us if he can of the beauties of *cyclone literature*.

'Circumstances', he asserts, 'have plunged us back into our time.'[6] Whereas the novelist of before-the-wars removed himself outside (or above) the contemporaneous, so that his characters might retain their due proportions, and that—thus advantageously placed for all-over observations—judgements might be arrived at (and Sartre in *L'Age de Raison* was of those who thus abstract themselves), this same helicopterizing author would be kicked back into his time in short order.

What happens to the author 'plunged back into his time' in this unceremonious fashion? How can he focus this period of his if he is *inside* it—swallowed by it as Jonah was by the whale ?—Well, the following is Sartre's account of how the author converts this necessity into a glorious virtue.

If we are going to handle such a time as the present, we must, as novelists, abandon the Newtonian system, as it were, and pass over into the General Theory of Relativity. (This is not a very original step, even for a novelist to take). In this way 'we people our books with half-lucid, half-dim intelligences.'

In pursuance of this theory of historical immersion Sartre moved into the cinematographic method (known as *simultanéité*) of *Le Sursis*. The obvious inconvenience in writing 'au sein de l'histoire', covered with blood and sweat and tears—of treating of an epoch which is 'incomprehensible' because you have your face jammed up against it—the difficulty and inconveniences of this theory and of all of its class may be explained as follows.—You are in a fire at a theatre, say : caught in a stampede you find yourself at the bottom of a pile of struggling bodies. That is the kind of situation that Sartre postulates in his expression 'au sein de l'histoire' : were it yours and were you able to express yourself, you could certainly give to this 'évènement' a 'brutale fraicheur' all right—its 'opacité menaçante', as likewise its 'imprévisibilité'. The hot and passionate immediacy of the crudeness of living would be there : and all its *blindness* too.

Of this blindness Sartre makes a great deal : of the beauty of not understanding what is happening to one. Not only helplessness, but non-comprehension, is somehow an asset. At this point another and quite distinct issue becomes visible. It is that issue which possesses most relevance for my present argument. Before turning to it, however, I will attend to the purely aesthetic objections to Sartre's theory.

His 'cyclone aesthetic', as we may call it, offends of course against the classic rules of restraint and intelligibility : but it is not for that reason that it fails to recommend itself to me. My criticism would be this : what this fragmentary peepshow may gain in sensational intensity, it loses in the more comprehensive satisfactions which intensity rules out (or perhaps intensity is not the word but a technique of the naïve close-up). Though it may feed—perhaps over-feed —the senses, it starves the intellect. Then since there is no person of vigorous mind who does not possess the will to understand, nor does anyone care to be left permanently in the dark, this method must always leave a disagreeable sensation, as also will its kaleido-scopic chaos. Any art which condemns its public to the stunned confusion experienced at the climax of a 'great historical event' can hardly satisfy for long.

Even apart from all question of shock, or the character to be expected of 'crisis literature', there are the unalterable objections to any impressionist technique, the piece of pioneer impressionism— which is a landmark in literary history—to be found in *La Char-treuse de Parme*, is the classic illustration.[7] It showed people that all that need be done is to cut a little bit out of a material : the entire bolt of cloth is not indispensable. So you get a minute fraction of a great total event—namely the Battle of Waterloo.—For myself the massive totality, Napoleon in his hat pointed laterally, Wellington in hat pointed fore and aft, Blucher stuffily Prussian— these with all their respective hordes slowly clashing, weaving and reclashing, alone would satisfy me.—Impressionism is too doctrinally the art of the individual.

Having disposed of the purely aesthetic problem, I will now return to the blindness—the 'non-comprehension'—of Sartre's victim of History. This type of writer is supposed, you recall, to be confined to the heart of a cyclone, and to know no more than a new-born earth-worm would know in that situation. He does not know what a cyclone is—he does not even know it is a *cyclone*.

He apparently does not *want* to know what causes cyclones, or

240

to consider how best to guard against their accidence. All he wants to do is to experience their awful *pressure*—and to express his profound pessimism at the thought of this meaningless adventure between two Nothings. It is an attitude that might recall the Puritan, for whom life could not be disagreeable and wild enough to suit his taste. What makes it so exquisite for Sartre is that it is purposeless.

'An author who two centuries hence decided to write a historical novel about the war of 1940'—*he* would know a great deal more about it than we do, Sartre affirms.[8] Therefore he would not have to act as if he were practically flattened out beneath 'the pressure of history'.—But this is strange. I should have thought myself that I know more about it than will anyone two hundred years hence. And I should have said, too, that we knew a good deal now about the causes of wars in general. Of course we feel their *pressure*. Indeed, they leave us ruined, loaded with debt, on each occasion with far less freedom than before. But there is nothing mysterious or, as Sartre calls it, 'enigmatic' about them. It is a pretentious affectation, I think, to call them that.

If in a war I had my leg blown off by a bomb I should know perfectly well how that bomb had come to be made. Its historic pedigree I should have no difficulty whatever in drawing up. I cannot believe that Sartre is more innocent than I am.

Sartre is too much a man of policy; an opportunist where Camus is not. It is, however, today in France difficult for a writer not to adopt, for political reasons, all kinds of unnatural attitudes. In Sartre's creative work these pressures are not, as I have said, present to the same degree. But whenever some false position has to be taken up, in a novel, to satisfy opinion, a dead patch is there in his writing—wooden and studied as the photo-group of a newly-wedded pair.

When I was analysing the hero in Hemingway's novels, in an essay which had for title 'The "Dumb Ox" ', I described the characters in his books, I remember, as being invariably the kind of people *to whom things are done*, who are the passive (and rather puzzled) guinea-pig type—as remote as it is possible to be, for instance, from Nietzsche's 'super' type. The young soldier, in what has been called, not inappropriately, 'the greatest love-story in modern literature', would have none of his melting Pagliaccio-like

241

pathos were it not for this. But he is of course—as he *must* be—cattle and not butcher.

This is not a shortcoming in a work of art : it defines it merely. It says that the work in question is classifiable as lyrical. As we know, the *jeune premier* must not be unusually endowed with anything but looks. *Bel canto* is allergic to superman. Then Hemingway has been a chronicler, of exceptional genius, of folk-emotions. It is quite a different matter when a writer adopts the outlook of a bi-valve *for himself.* To draw attention to *that* is not complimentary : he is after all not a pathetic figure in a book. The writer is in life (whether you say he is without intermission making himself out of Nothing, or, contrariwise, that his past and future lies outstretched like a temporal landscape across which he crawls). There —in life—one has to acquire a knowledge of the functioning of the social machine. If, for instance, the writer throw a metaphysical mist over the otherwise easily identifiable operation of power-politics, or cultivate the attitudes of primitive man towards the violence of the elements, and apply it to the more violent phenomena of social life, he is highly artificial.

Social action would be altogether paralysed, that is what I mean, were everyone to adopt the attitude that they were feeling their way about in their time like lost children, describing all that occurred as 'inexplicable', or 'enigmatic'. To which of course it is necessary to add that there have been many other catastrophes in our world prior to world wars *one* and *two.* It is a result of this reasoning that, although the pacifism of Camus seems to me too narrow a position, I prefer it to Sartre's glorification of the 'heroic'.

Existentialism is of course involved to some extent in the subject-matter of this chapter. Existentialism has been called 'the philosophy of crisis.' Therefore, whatever was its origin, it is regarded, in its effects, and especially because of its phenomenal success, to be closely related to the tragic situation in which men suddenly find themselves everywhere. This resolves itself into a question of how 'crisis' should be met : or, to put it in another way, what is the best philosophy for crisis. I think I ought to add, since I have mentioned Hemingway—who with Faulkner has now for some time exercised a considerable influence upon young Frenchmen—that the hero of *L'Etranger*, Albert Camus' admirably written (though not otherwise I am afraid very admirable) novel, is a moron. A moron is not the same thing as a 'dumb ox' : but they are of the same family. [. . . .]

But let me turn again to this small energetic figure [Sartre]. 'If,' we hear him saying, 'the two terms of the possible decision are in fact (1) the bourgeoisie, and (2) the Communist party, then *the choice is impossible* ! . . . we are at once against the Communist party and against the bourgeoisie. That means clearly enough that we write *against everybody*.'[10]

There is another choice that is likewise impossible. 'The present historical perspective being *war*, we are summoned to choose between (1) the Anglo-Saxon bloc, and (2) the Sovietic bloc. We refuse to help either the one or the other in their preparations for this war : so we have fallen out of history—we speak as in a desert.'[11]

I do not know if I have succeeded in evoking the image of a man so consumed with this agonizing problem of where to take up his stand (and how to shuffle a little away from the Left without losing the benefits of his leftishness), that he exhibits, makes a parade of, his anxiety in the paper he edits. Since he is symbolic, and something of these difficulties beset all of us, in one degree or another—though few can have succeeded in getting themselves in so involved a situation—we must not too self-obliviously smile.

'Sometimes the view is advanced that our books reflect the hesitations of the *petty bourgeoisie*, which cannot make up its mind whether to come down on the side of the proletariat or of capitalism. It is false—*c'est faux* !' he cries. 'Our choice is made !'[12]

Sartre is beside himself as to whether he is a patch of putrefaction upon the ignoble cadaver of the *bourgeoisie*, or (as he claims) purveyor of 'liberté' to the working class. The poor fellow cries : '*It is false* ! I *have* made my choice.' But he knows that the implacable 'watchdogs' of the materialist dialectic will not take for an answer however passionate an affirmation. They stand upon their terms. 'To this they reply', he wearily continues, 'that the choice thus made is abstract and inefficacious, that it is merely an intellectual game unless one at the same time lends one's adherence to a revolutionary party.' So we come back, as always, to the same infinitely vexatious predicament. 'I agree—I know it is only an intellectual game,' is his angry retort. 'But is it my fault that the Communist party is no longer revolutionary?'[13] *He* is the great 'revolutionary', you see, and the Communists are a lot of bourgeois !

Here as his words prove he even is prepared to admit that to claim to be a revolutionary assisting the proletariat to liquidate the 'oppressor' is nonsense, so long as he remains politically in splendid isolation. He could not for long maintain the contrary: for confronting as he does the 'bourgeoisie' with Marx's 'proletariat' is an essentially Marxian proceeding—the extermination of the former, in a dialectical paroxysm by the latter, being de rigueur. But the Communist organisation is alone capable of effecting this: so *why not join the Communist party*? There is no escaping from this logic: and the 'Communist watchdogs' as he knows will never allow him to escape.

All readers of this *writer's complaint* cannot but join in our refrain: why not join the Communist party—Otherwise for heaven's sake stop continually talking about the 'proletariat', the 'bourgeoisie', the 'petit bourgeoisie', and the other Marxist concepts—concepts to which you have no right. The farther one goes in this reading, the more one feels that Sartre must loathe these monotonous vocables, which are responsible for so much idiotic anguish. [. . . .]

For him Gaullism, catholicism, and communism in France are rackets—are hoaxes, mystifications. Very well. Suppose he had adopted the jargon and the myths of Gaullism, but, for some inscrutable reason, conducted a violent offensive against General Charles de Gaulle. That would, I think, have seemed very illogical. Or had he installed a prie-dieu and called his room his *cell*: peppered his writings with quotations from Aquinas, at High Mass in the view of everybody had accesses of ecastatic weeping—but violently attacked the priesthood, charging that they were keeping him from God, objected to confession and denounced the liturgy as a hoax (also jeered at the Vatican and sneered at the Pope) people would undoubtedly have regarded him as inconsistent.

I do not see that his public hostility to the Communist party differs in any respect from the above hypothetical cases. He believes all that the Communists believe: but he did not wish to convert this *collage* into a marriage. With him and communism it is an affair of Mathieu and Marcelle. He makes excuses: it would feel quite uncomfortable to be associated with such a *bourgeois* as M. Thorez![14]—But to look at it for the occasion from the standpoint of the Communists—would he have the Communists erect barricades in the streets of Paris, bring on a show-down, and thereby precipitate a third world-war—at a moment when Russia is in no position as yet, to wage it?

In the Thirties Sartre drifted fashionably into the *front populaire* watershed, was the French equivalent of a fellow-traveller. Was that pink aftermath of the revolution in Russia a 'hoax'—a mystification? He engaged in a path in those days which leads either to communism, or to nothing. It was 'le Néant' that he chose.

NOTES

1   *Letters*, p. 411. Excerpts here come from *The Writer and the Absolute*, pp. 66, 67, 77, 78, 79–81, 82–7, 116–18, 119–20.

2   On p. 60 of *The Writer and the Absolute*, L. quoted Camus as saying that 'our period marks the end of ideologies, that is of absolute Utopias which destroy themselves in History, by the price they ultimately exact.'

3   Albert Camus, *Actuelles: Chroniques 1944–1948*. Paris: Gallimard, 1950, p. 144.

4   The phrase occurs on p. 1629 of Sartre's magazine, *Les Temps Modernes*, June, 1947, and in a reprint from it, *Qu'est-ce que la littérature*, appearing in Sartre's *Situations II*. Paris: Gallimard, 1948.

5   *Situations II*, p. 251. David Zaslavski was a faithful disseminator of the Stalin line in literary matters.

6   Ibid., p. 253.

7   L. adds in a footnote: 'It is the battle scene of course to which reference is made.'

8   *Situations II*, p. 254

9   L. adds in a footnote: 'It is in M. Mersault, Albert Camus' little clerk, that this "crisis literature" reaches its ultimate expression.'

10 Ibid., p. 288. L.'s italics.

11 Ibid., p. 289. L.'s italics.

12 Ibid., p. 287. L.'s italics and exclamation marks.

13 Ibid.

14 Maurice Thorez, the leader of the French Communist party.

7

George Orwell

(From *The Writer and the Absolute*, 1952)

Lewis was aware of Orwell's activities at least a decade before the comments on that writer reprinted here[1] finally emerged. In 1941 Lewis asked the publisher of his novel *The Vulgar Streak*—a book about a proletarian con-man's attempted rise to middle-class prosperity —to send Orwell a copy. But, although Lewis and Orwell had something in common after the latter's disenchantment with Moscow Communism, the two remained sharply at odds. This was partly the result of Orwell's 'London Letter' published in a 1946 issue of *Partisan Review*, New York, which depicted Lewis as having become a Communist, or at least a strong sympathizer, and writing a book in praise of Stalin to balance his previous books on Hitler. Lewis branded this 'utter nonsense' and accused Orwell of being obsessed with politically labelling writers and unable to imagine any other literary motive than those connected with revolutionary politics.[2] But, as Julian Symons has suggested, Lewis and Orwell were by no means as different as they seemed. During the Thirties, they were the heretics most fiercely resented by the Orthodox Left. Symons wrote : 'They became, as the decade went on, more and more like some terrible *memento mori*. . . . They were pilloried because they presented such uncomfortable interpretations of the same image of reality that acted as model for the Popular Front orthodoxy.'[3]

My subject, George Orwell, is of the English war and post-war writers, not alone the one most worthy of attention, but he is the only one. It is however not this fact which decided me to select him for analysis. He is very much more than the only good writer of a decade or more. Then, to further the analytical aims of this book, his work offers an invaluable material. Orwell is almost purely a political writer, a political novelist, and a political essayist. Not so richly gifted a man as Jean-Paul Sartre, he is a victim of the same weakness : a weakness which, in the last few years of his life, Orwell overcame. On his death-bed, the gaunt shell of his former self, he was a free man : but Sartre will always remain the slave of a convention.

What in the XIXth Century was described as an *esprit libre* was someone who had emancipated himself from the tyranny of obsolete ideas. Many of the thinkers instrumental in freeing the men of the XIXth Century from limiting conventions and ways of thinking, fastened new conventions on them; *new*, it is true, even 'revolutionary', but actually less desirable than those they had discarded. And a XXth Century *esprit libre* would be a man who had liberated himself from the dead hand of the *new*.

No one must expect to find in Orwell, when turning to him for the first time, an interest in writing for its own sake. There is no trace anywhere of a desire to express himself with the literary competence of, for instance, *Sea and Sardinia* by D. H. Lawrence, or the stylistic resourcefulness of Conrad, though he greatly admired both these writers. Nor is there any of the expository clarity of Wells, on whom he modelled himself. Orwell's *Burmese Days* is a very rough-and-ready piece of work beside *A Passage to India*. Types interest him more than individuals; the plot is everything, the individual nothing. This is not because of a preference for classical procedure, however : it is because character only held a feeble interest for him. Then since he was not at that time a very experienced writer, this leads in *Burmese Days*, to the six or seven figures of the Kyauktada Club being little more than coarsely painted cardboard dolls : they are a two-dimensional lot; all speak and act relentlessly 'in character'. The hero has his birthmark to identify him, he is a nigger-loving sahib with 'bolshie' ideas. But no heart beats in him, and no reader's pulse is ever going to quicken, or heart to warm, at his misadventures.

Orwell's shortcomings as a writer of fiction may be seen most clearly, perhaps, in his best book, 1984. This remarkable piece of work is a prophetic Wellsian nightmare of events in the future. Again we have not persons but dummies. Miss 1984—but the eternal feminine as well—meets Mr. X, a rebelliously inclined robot. They 'click'. It is not a boy and girl business altogether.

Unfortunately Orwell was at the time of writing about forty-five, so his last hero, though not so old as that, is nearing forty. There is, it is true, a further reason why he is obliged to be on the elderly side : it is his function to remember the good old days, when you could go to bed at night without the secret police snooping from their telesnooper on the wall of your flat, or betray a healthy sexual interest without incurring all kinds of penalties.

A little terror, but no compassion for the principal performers can be felt because they are merely convenient abstractions. If the scenario and the machinery are Wellsian, so are the personae. They are conventional properties, secondary to the menacing blueprint of a horrible world of only thirty years hence.

Of course, the leading actors could not possess personalities of such reality as to compete with the scenery and apparatus of the book, which is the big thing, or clog its expository function. At all events, such colour as they have is that drab conventional tint with which his earlier novels will have familiarized us.

Outside of essays and articles, Orwell had no real existence until he had written *Animal Farm*. The only two books of his which are worthy of any serious consideration are *Animal Farm* and *1984*. [. . . .]

I am sure that what may be of enduring interest concerning Orwell is what I shall be indicating here; the story of a man who rescued himself from a convention, and finished his literary life in a burst of clairvoyance.

Biographically the essence of George Orwell was, perhaps, that he was not George Orwell, but Eric Blair. To understand why when Eric Blair began to write he selected as a *nom de plume* the name George Orwell is to have advanced a considerable distance towards an understanding of this writer. For Blair, after all, is a quite pleasing name. It has not the sleepily orotund appearance of Orwell certainly. It is a Scottish name, though personally I should not have been aware of this had I not set myself the task of expounding Orwell. He did not like his Scottish name : he speaks rather snootily and slightingly of the Scotch throughout his written work. Orwell was the name of a pleasant stream near the place in southern England where his family, on their return from India, lived. And Orwell preferred to appear before the public as Mr. Orwell rather than Mr. Blair, as a south English gentleman rather than as a Scottish gentleman. If you will imagine, for a moment, Sir Walter Scott for purposes of writing calling himself Walter Cherwell, or Thomas Carlyle turning himself into Thomas Titmarsh, or David Hume becoming Henry Hobbes then you will see how significant a biographical fact it is for a man called Blair to become Orwell, not to mention George. So much more English than Eric, being, in fact, the name of the patron saint.

Orwell was, as he expresses it in *The Road to Wigan Pier*, a member of the impoverished middle-class. [. . . .]

[He] was so impregnated with Victorian class-snobbery, which was artificially preserved in India up to the last minute of the British Raj, that he could not say simply 'middle-class'; he had to think up the ridiculous 'lower-upper-middle class' [. . . .] All this was too bad, for Orwell's was an honest mind, and he had had a virulent type of snobbery injected into him, but was not really cut out to be a snob. The socially glamorous surroundings of Eton would be as irritating as they were irrelevant. [. . . .]

It could, and I daresay that it will, be argued that his preoccupation with the under-dog was the result of having had too much to do with young over-dogs in his schooldays. There may be something in that: but we must look elsewhere, I think, for the primary incentive. The painful emphasis, resulting in something amounting to eccentricity in his variegated slumming, is traceable perhaps in part to Eton. Exposing himself to the parasitic visitations of bugs is not so easily explained. Like Stevenson he was a romantic Scot. It is interesting that in the last few years of his life he went to live in the western islands of Scotland: although the climate is about as bad as could be found for his disease, which was tuberculosis, he insisted on returning there. In any case his romanticism was of the rough kind we associate with the Scotch and his social conscience was of a dour pigheaded type. It apparently was H. G. Wells, the *New Statesman* and *News Chronicle*, and the Left Book Club, which awakened the dormant social conscience.

He went to fight against fascism in Spain as an I.L.P. man : for he was one of the few 'left-wingers' who took left-wingery sufficiently seriously to risk his life. The Independent Labour Party is by far the most genuine Socialist party that England has known. And Orwell was always genuine, whatever else he might or might not be.

Before that, equally dramatically, he flung himself into the gutters and stinking cellars of Paris. Later in the Thirties we find him an inmate of the filthiest lodging-house that even the Lancashire black country could produce, only leaving it when he found a chamber-pot under the breakfast table in the kitchen. He had stomached black-beetles in the tripe, and not blenched when the landlady, spitting into small pieces of newspaper, flung them into the corner of the eating-room. Verily, this man was determined to identify himself with the 'lowest of the low'. He wore his bug-bites with a grim smile. They were the equivalent of the hotel labels (Ritz-Carlton, Astoria-Grand) which we sometimes see upon the luggage of ardent travellers. [. . . .]

But it is here that we come to the problem of his socialism. *Slumming* was in fact the form that it took in the first instance. From the giddy heights of Eton, and the modest eminence upon which every sahib stood in India, or Burma, in the days of the British Raj, he flung himself with enthusiasm into the menial labyrinths of a great Paris hotel, into the bug-infested garrets where live the poorest of the poor, above the level—but just above— where the underworld of vagrants and beggars begins. It was a Stevensonian bourgeois romanticism. It was not the world of *Creatures that Once were Men* of Gorki. The authentic hell of the Russian novelists, where you are not amongst men, but a new species, is a very different matter.

When Orwell threw up his job as a military policeman in Burma, probably he was, to start with, obliged to accept help from his family. But during a breathing space of a couple of years, some job surely could have been found for him.

Like his hero, Gordon Comstock, he preferred the gutter. Gordon Comstock smiling to himself on the bed is the figure, I think, in this case to remember. It is the middle-class theatrically, sulkily abasing itself.

There was a rather curious factor involved in his seeking out of the lowest of the low, which must now be mentioned. While still at Eton he succumbed to the fashionable pink rash. But it took a serious turn: he asked himself what *was* the working-class about which he was supposed to be so concerned. He realized at once that he knew as little about it as he did of the Head-Hunters of Borneo.

This, oddly enough, worried him : and what he *did* know he did not like.

Socialism he interpreted as meaning the brotherhood of man, and in a quite literal way a declaration of love for the working-class; so when he became a Socialist there was a perfectly terrific difficulty which had to be overcome. [. . . .]

[Lewis then quotes a long passage, on a theme of 'the lower classes smell', from *The Road to Wigan Pier*. Its last section follows.]

Even 'lower-class' people whom you knew to be quite clean—servants, for instance—were faintly unappetizing. The smell of their sweat, the very texture of their skins, were mysteriously different from yours.

Everyone who has grown up pronouncing his aitches and in a house with a bathroom and one servant is likely to have grown up with these feelings; hence the chasmic, impassable quality of class-distinctions in the West.[4]

Myself, I started life in a house with a bathroom, with a nurse, two servants, and a cook; therefore I had four stinkers under the roof with me in place of Mr. Orwell's one. This may have inured me to the terrible stench of females of the labouring class. But I believe that that is irrelevant; Anglo-India is the answer to the riddle of how a man can entertain such eccentric sensations as we have just seen described above. This *stink* business was obviously a first-class complex. Nothing, one feels, could quite root it out. He admits that it was in fact no *physical* problem, no affair of the nostrils, for let us hear him again.

When I was not much past twenty I was attached for a short time to a British regiment. Of course I admired and liked the private soldiers as any youth of twenty would admire and like hefty, cheery youths five years older than himself with the medals of the Great War on their chests. And yet, after all, they faintly repelled me; they were 'common people' and I did not care to be too close to them. In the hot mornings when the company marched down the road, myself in the rear with one of the junior subalterns, the steam of those hundred sweating bodies in front made my stomach turn. And this, you observe, was pure prejudice. For a soldier is probably as inoffensive, physically, as it is possible for a male white person to be. He is generally young, he is nearly always healthy from fresh air and exercise, and a rigorous discipline compels him to be clean. But

I could not see it like that. All I knew was that it was *lower-class* sweat that I was smelling, and the thought of it made me sick.[5]

What a confession! Orwell's 'niceness' is, to put it mildly, unusual. If this sickly fastidiousness had gone a step farther it would have meant that the mere sight of a navvy would have caused him to faint, and he would have been unable to hold a commission in the army because there are, in the army, so many of the lower orders; nor could he have remained in the same railway carriage with a person of the lower orders. But what is even more significant for our analysis is that he shows, in the above passages, that he was by no means cured of his malady, in spite of his, by that time, long frequentations with persons of the most modest social standing. And this book, *The Road to Wigan Pier*, was quite a landmark in the history of the Left Book Club. That at first sight is very astonishing; but then one reminds oneself that the readers of the Left Book Club were scarcely ever members of the working-class. Many were hardly less snobbish than was Orwell himself. [. . . .]

Orwell might be described as the Honest Snob. He is genuinely desirous of curing himself of his snobbery, but he goes about it snobbishly. And so we find him throughout his earlier literary life, in fact up to the outbreak of World War II, engaged in the idiotic quest of this mysterious dimension labelled 'working-class'. Incidentally we may note that, careful as he is to divide the middle-class into all sorts of fancy compartments, the frontiers of the working-class are for him the beginnings of an *outcast* region. For him there are no fine distinctions in this submerged humanity. Literally he does not discriminate between the workman earning a substantial wage and the vagrant living from 'spike to spike'. He has such a snobbish horror of the words 'working-class', that he lumps everything together that is without and below the Middle-pale. Thus, when he wishes to crack the nut of the working-class *Stink*, he plunges right down blindly to the resorts of out-of-work hotel personnel and others living on the fringes of absolute destitution. [. . . .]

In December 1936 Orwell went to Catalonia, originally intending to write articles supporting the anti-Franco Government. However, he found Barcelona in the hands of the revolutionary parties. All the city was painted red and black, or just red.

No well-dressed man or woman, no bourgeois, was in sight : only the hordes of the revolutionary working-class. This was of course very thrilling. It was a dream come true : the dream of the boy at Eton of a blood-red Revolution, and his excitement may be easily imagined, for he was still a boy, though thirty-three.

'I had accepted the *News Chronicle, New Statesman* version of the war as the defence of civilization against a maniacal outbreak by an army of Colonial Blimps in the pay of Hitler.'[6] [. . . .] This extreme straighforwardness of Orwell's is what endears him to us more than anything else about him. Without disguise he presents himself to us as a simple reader of the *New Statesman* and the *News Chronicle*, under Kingsley Martin and Gerald Barry, papers of a violent sentimental 'pink', in the forefront of the press incitement to war or civil war in the interests of the popular front. (And popular front, we must remember, meant acceptance and support of the policies of Communist Russia.) Consequently as an excitable reader of the *New Statesman* and the *News Chronicle* he enlisted in the Militia and got very badly shot in the neck, the wound affecting his vocal chords. In writing of this enlistment he speaks as follows. 'I recognized it immediately as a state of affairs worth fighting for.'[7] It was of course a *sensational* decision, not an act of reason. His boyish sporting instinct 'recognized immediately' that it would be great fun to be a 'Militiaman'.

His Spanish experiences had, I am quite sure, a decisive and most sobering effect upon Orwell. It is extraordinary, but he really *did* go to the Spanish Civil War for no very serious reason. He admits, without the slightest difficulty, that before he went to Spain he was a victim of press misrepresentation and press incitement, and when he reached Spain a victim of 'atmosphere'. ('In that atmosphere it seemed the only conceivable thing to do.')[8]

Although Orwell drifted into the P.O.U.M.,[9] and although to start with he took no interest whatever in the political differences between the parties, he unquestionably ended up with *one* party prejudice. He left Spain an active enemy of the Communists. He describes their policy as rightist, indeed so far to the right as to make Franco a bit of a Lefty. He was not yet, of course, the man who wrote *1984*. In spite of the extraordinary amount of enlightenment he had received his attitudes were still those of a *New Statesman* reader, though an uncommonly disgruntled one.

These two books, the *Wigan Pier* book and the *Catalonia* book, were Orwell's first essay in straight political writing. Their perusal should have enlightened anyone concerned with the organization of the Popular Front in England that this new recruit might prove extremely dangerous. In the sequel, he did in fact prove a far more effective debunker of insincere leftish claptrap than any detached critic could hope to be, simply because of his left-wing status, and his record in Catalonia as a man wounded fighting on the side of the *Frente Popular*.

[*Burmese Days*] is juvenilely 'enlightened', all the stale anti-imperialism of liberal England dished up in its most conventional form. Of books of this type, with an exotic colonial background and written with the object of presenting the white interlopers in a detestable light, *Burmese Days* may be compared with a book called *Samara* by Norman Lewis.[10] Mr. Lewis's book was published very recently; it is as well written as Orwell's was badly written, it is full of fine observation and acute understanding of the situation involved in Berber North Africa. It provides us with a horrific glimpse into the bestialities of White Rule. I make this comparison partly in the hope that it will cause people to read *Samara*, but for the rest to indicate a book with similar backgrounds which is everything that Orwell's is not. [. . . .]

Orwell's last published book before the war, *Coming Up for Air*, is I think his worst. The principal figures in all his narrative books are insignificant, unattractive creatures, and usually colourless. But George Bowling, whose acquaintance we make here, possesses colour, but of so distasteful a kind as to make the reading of the book a peculiarly exasperating labour. Mr. Bowling was an insurance tout of the most aggressive type, and the vulgarity he exudes is, one feels, regarded by Orwell in some way as a virtue. The two authors who contributed most to the production of this book are Wells and Chesterton. 'Wells was the author who made the biggest impression on me,' this dreadful hero tell us,[11] and it was evidently Orwell's idea (for he, like Mr. Bowling, had been greatly influenced by Wells) to fashion his hero after a Wellsesque pattern. But as he accompanies us from the first page to the last, since he is the 'I' that tells the story, confiding to us incessantly 'I know I'm fat' and such like things, even the most patient critic is in constant revolt. [. . . .]

Up to now it must often have seemed as though I were delivering an attack upon Orwell, I am afraid. But his published work before

1939 does not provide many openings for politeness. On the other hand, we are approaching a time when he emerges as a writer of great interest. As he moves through the 'thirties, becoming a 'hero and saint' in the Spanish War, with *Wigan Pier* taking his place as a serious 'left-winger', he persists in his plan to gain a reputation as a writer of narrative fiction. The quality, or no-quality, of these attempts was part of the picture, as well as the political colour to be found dispersed in them. As his reputation as a militant fighter in the ranks of the Popular Front, grew, his literary reputation naturally did not grow with it, because neither Mr. Comstock nor Mr. Bowling is the kind of thing that gains one a literary reputation. Meanwhile a firmer outlook somewhere in the background of his mind is taking shape, though this new understanding still lies almost submerged in the sentimental slush. He perceives that there is a 'hook in the bait' of socialism. But it is rather just the eye that registers the hook as an external fact. He as yet draws very few conclusions.

When the war came he was of course immediately in his element. He had been trained as a soldier, more or less. Moreover, he had been a militiaman in Spain and he must have recognized well enough that his main asset derived from his reputation as a man of action, from his possession of the aura of the militant. For the last thing that the host of excitable 'lefties', who travelled to Spain to get in a cheap thrill or two, thought of doing was to enlist as militiamen and risk a bullet in the neck. [. . . .]

[Lewis now quotes from Orwell's World War II diaries, which he finds indicative of a 'martial ebullience' and 'Blimpish heroics'—compounding his bitter experiences with the Communists in Spain.]

As he had entered Spain profoundly uninterested in party, so he left it still detached from any party 'dogma'. He showed no sign at that time, I mean, of favouring Trotsky: but his remarks about Stalin grew less and less respectful. In his 1940–1 *Notebooks*, for instance, we find him writing: 'One could not have a better example of the moral and emotional shallowness of our time, than the fact that we are now all more or less pro-Stalin. This disqusting murderer is temporarily on our side, and so the purges etc. are suddenly forgotten.'[12]

Such remarks register a tremendous change between the year

1936 when he left England for Spain and the year 1940—when the pro-Russian orgies began in England.

But this revolution in his mind would have the result of making him not only a sceptic where the Great Russian Experiment was concerned, it would also tend to make him critical of socialism in England. For of course the majority of Intellectuals at that time were fellow-travellers, and consequently the low opinion he had of Stalinism would extend to them. Not that he ever became *openly* critical: he knew better than that. But such feelings must have existed underneath. He must have realized by this time that his success as a writer, and as a personality, depended upon his adherence to the conventional Left Wing attitudes of his friends.

At this point I perhaps should turn to the question as to whether Orwell was really a typical Left Wing figure at all. One might regard him as a sort of Colonel Blimp gone wrong; a Kipling (Mr. Muggeridge compares him with Kipling) who ran a bit amok, spat on the Union Jack as an imperialist emblem, embraced the first dark-skinned person he met and took a running kick at the posterior of the first pukka sahib to cross his path. One might regard his early anti-imperialism as a boyish enthusiasm, and his socialism as an attitude adopted to keep step with everybody else. And indeed a good deal of his socialism was skin-deep. The man who set out to discover the working-class in his *Wigan Pier* book was no very profound Socialist.

There are a great number of facts which incline one to think that his left-wingery never ceased to be skin-deep. Had Orwell been of German nationality who can doubt that he would have been an S.S. man. Had France been his homeland it would have been in the ranks of General de Gaulle that we should have found him. In any country where there were as many militant Right Wing organizations as there were Left Wing it should be the militant Right that he would choose. But in deeply and indelibly Liberalist England, there is literally nothing militant except on the Left. Let us take Stephen Spender now: had Germany been the place of *his* birth, he would unquestionably have been a most aggressive *emigré*. When we regard the matter from this angle we can see why Orwell looks such an odd fish politically. A natural Patriot, he has to act seditiously; a born policeman he is obliged to protest that police-work is brutal; a natural Rightist, he has to play the part of a

Left-winger. The patriotism of the ordinary club-man order of his 1940–1 *Notebook*, the joyous acceptance of war as a good purgative, 'la bonne guerre', is that of the extreme Right rather than the extreme Left. The small part that economics played in his political outlook is also significant. His left-wingery probably was a species of sport, as obviously as his plunge into the underworld of tramps was the act of a sportsman, not that of a missionary. His experiences as a militiaman in Spain were an outcome, again, of the soldierly sporting-spirit. Consequently, to sum this up, his convulsive movement of opinion away from his early *New Statesman*-reading days to the state of mind that led him eventually to write *Animal Farm,* was not a movement from a depth over into another depth, but rather a sharp splash out of one shallows into another shallows, though the second of these plainly possessed more depth than the first.

I shall presently have something to say, of course, about Orwell's two important books, *Animal Farm* and *1984*. But I now would like to do some quoting from his collected essays. These are *Critical Essays*, and *Shooting an Elephant*. At the time of writing, this is all that is available in book form. His essays will ultimately take their place beside his last two novels, and with them make a slender but valuable body of work, representing a writer who stood out among his contemporaries as one belonging to the main movement of European thought, or rather of Western thought.

That Orwell was perfectly aware of the shortcomings of the English, owing to their insular situation, in the field of political literature is unquestionable; and indeed in his essay on Koestler *(Critical Essay)* there is a passage specifically stating that 'there exists in England almost no literature of disillusionment about the Soviet Union';[13] and he points out how it is always foreigners who write the books of real political enlightenment. [. . . .]

There is no question at all that Orwell learned a great deal from Koestler. The latter's *Darkness at Noon* helped him to write *1984.* The part of this essay where he is discussing the backgrounds of revolutionary degeneracy responsible for Rubashov's confession are especially interesting as showing how deeply he studied this book, which was a direct outcome of the Russian purges. [. . . .]

The drama of *1984* is the same drama as *Darkness at Noon.*

O'Brien is breaking down the bourgeois prejudices of the robot-hero, who clings to the typical belief in objective truth of the bourgeois world.

As we go along in this essay Orwell appears to be largely agreeing with Koestler's analysis. The Russian Revolution is for him just as disappointing an affair as it is for Koestler. But when it comes to saying that *all* Revolutions are certain to be equally unsatisfactory, and, after a blood-bath to develop into a disgusting tyranny, oh then Orwell ceases to march in step with his Hungarian contemporary. For he *will* still have his socialism, still wear his party badge. Nothing may turn out well, but anything may turn out *slightly* better than it was before. [. . . .]

Orwell wishes as you see, to save socialism; for he cannot imagine himself abandoning that, and surviving in the atmosphere of present-day England. Koestler has no difficulty in convincing him that *all* revolutions, or almost all, are liable to be just as bad as the Russian Revolution. All revolutions are total revolutions, just as all wars are total wars: and it is this total quality (peculiar to our century, owing to the terrifying power of the industrial techniques which confer upon a little group of men a god-like dominion over the surface of the earth which is their realm)—it is this total power which makes the future look so hopelessly black. But after all, Orwell is an English left-winger. Whatever he may say, and he says it very well, about the limitations of the English political writer when compared with the continental, he fails when it comes to the point, to go as far as his continental contemporary. He will not agree that it is social revolution itself which, because of our XXth Century technical powers coupled with our inability to advance intellectually, must be condemned, just as in our day war must be condemned. Of course there will be more wars: but the intellectual the true *clerc*, must denounce war. Orwell is to be convicted of merely personal, career considerations, in refusing to take this final step.

There is only one argument available to save him from condemnation. His objections to Koestler's 'hedonism' are probably genuine. The greatest happiness of the greatest number, indeed happiness at all would not be apt to interest him. Like his hero Comstock he really possessed a capacity to enjoy the disgustingly uncomfortable and the soddenly unhappy. And this relish for the disagreeable

258

would make him look upon what he agreed was a bloody tyranny rather differently from Koestler. But even this argument is unable to banish the belief that, in the last analysis, he was actuated by personal considerations.

Again, he describes Koestler as being driven back by the special nature of Stalin dictatorship, into a position 'not far removed from pessimistic Conservatism'.[14] For Orwell, if you are not a Socialist you have to be some other kind of party-man. So Koestler becomes a *Conservative*.

But what I am saying throughout this essay is *not* that socialism is wrong, but that every party is wrong for a philosopher or for an artist. To make myself quite clear Orwell asserts, and I agree, that personal liberty for the intellectual or really for anybody else, depends upon possessing the right to say that two and two make four. To be in a position to say that one must have no political affiliations. One must inhabit the same strictly objective universe where the true man of science conducts his investigation.

My argument is that Orwell should have taken up a position of absolute detachment, upon having his eyes so thoroughly opened as to enable him to write *Animal Farm*. It is his failure to do that which places him, to some extent, in the same class as Sartre.

At last, in 1945, Orwell's literary ambition was realized. He wrote a good book, *Animal Farm*.

As this is not literary criticism, I need not say very much as to the literary quality either of *Animal Farm* or *1984*. Treating of a society of animals, the theme brings to mind the classical master-pieces, which might, one would say, have inspired him to stylistic emulation. But this is not the case. The language is business-like and adequate but that is all. It is, however, a considerable feat of political lampooning. It is direct and dry, often witty. His 'All animals are equal but some are more equal than others'[15] is a splendidly witty climax to the law-giving of the Pigs. And this little book, this sardonic parable, was a turning-point in the reaction. He showed the same courage in writing this as he had displayed as a 'fighter for Freedom' in Spain (which subsequently he found was not Freedom after all, but slavery). With *Animal Farm* he led the wavering lefties out of the pink mists of Left Land into the clear daylight. Few, it is true, can or will follow him very far.

259

But *Animal Farm*, by reason of its success, made it respectable to think clearly or to write without humbug, if a young man was so disposed. It was in a sense an iron curtain that came down on the period of literary fellow-travelling, the work of an ex-fellow-traveller.

But for himself, as I have just stressed, he remained with one foot on the *Road to Wigan Pier*: the other foot in that region which had been finally opened to him by those foreigners of whom we have read his unqualified praise. To the Europeans of course must be added Burnham,[16] and all the Trotskyite intelligentsia of the United States.

1984 is Wellsian in form, Wellsian in the style of its writing, Wellsian in the colourlessness and anonymity of the personae. I have discussed already, in passing, the reason for the insignificance of the humans who supply the drama in *1984*. There is, in fact, very little drama, in consequence of the extremely unelectrical quality of the human material. O'Brien, one of the two principal figures, is an uninteresting business man. If all the other humans in Orwell's novels had not been of so uniformly devitalized and colourless a type, one would have assumed that in *1984* the human element had been keyed down to show off the inhuman inquisitorial machinery to best advantage.

The manner in which Orwell has utilized the knowledge he acquired of the Communist attitude to objective truth is admirable. [. . . .]

The book as a whole is a first-rate political document. There is only one thing I am obliged to point out. The old London lying all around this floodlit bureaucratic centre, this almost balletesque survival, full of the 'Proles' which are Orwell's speciality, does not (perhaps oddly) make the scene more real. It is unlikely, in a régime such as Orwell describes, that the millions of ordinary people will be left unmolested, treated indeed as though they were not there. The appetite for power involves the maximum interference with other human beings.

But the hero's Orwellian enthusiasm for the 'Proles' ('Proles' meaning 'proletariat') imports a silliness into this book which is rather a pity. It is a silliness of the author of *The Road to Wigan Pier*; and that is not the author who was writing *1984*.

This natural life surrounding the artificial lunacy of the votaries

of 'Big Brother' is the real, unspoilt life of the people : that is the
idea. It is the hero's belief that out of these vigorous, sane multitudes will come salvation. [. . . .]

The Orwell picture is of a long-out-dated socialism. His two
humanities contrasted in *1984*, of, on the one hand, a virgin virile
world of workers, bursting with potential leadership, on the other,
a ruling class on the Stalinist party-pattern, is really socialism in
one of its XIXth Century forms (probably medieval and guildish
confronting the stream-lined, ruthless, efficiency-socialism of today).

I for one would have considered *1984* a better book had the
'Prole' business been left out, and a more realistic treatment of the
probable condition of the mass of the population been employed.

So, finally, I do not regard Orwell as *un malin* like Sartre, but
a parallel with Sartre's case certainly exists. It seemed necessary
to Orwell, in the interests of his reputation, not to withdraw from
his conventionally leftish position. How conscious he was in following this line I do not know. But it is (and this is my argument) a
false position, as with Sartre; and so, too, numbers of other writers
obliged to toe a party-line of *some* sort.

In these politics-ridden times writers experience irresistible pressures, this way or that. Yet this pressure in a still free community
can be almost as destructive as the writing-to-order in Communist
Russia. Every writer should keep himself free from party, clear of
any group-pull : at least this is *my* view of truth. My truth is
objective truth, in other words. In England the entire intellectual
atmosphere is impregnated with liberalism, or rather what liberalism transforms itself into so as to become more-and-still-more liberal. With us the pressure to achieve conformity is very great.
Whether in the matter of costume, or hair-cut, or intellectual
fashion.

Orwell possessed a very vigorous mind, he went much farther on
the road to an ultimate political realism than any of his companions
or immediate English contemporaries. But you have seen him
noting the great advantage the political writer of European origin
has over the Englishman. Orwell, I feel, *did* almost wrench himself
free. But the whole of history is one of misdirected energy, and
when, at the end, he transcended his earlier self, it was still to retain
a bit of the old sentiment, to show his heart was still in the right

place, in spite of the cruel and horrible things he had said about 'The Great Russian Socialist Experiment'.

NOTES

1 From *The Writer and the Absolute*, pp. 153–4, 155–6, 159, 160–1, 162–3, 164–5, 167, 169–70, 172, 173, 178, 180, 182–4, 185, 186, 187–90, 190–1, 192–3.
2 See *Rude Assignment*, pp. 78–9.
3 Julian Symons, *The Thirties*. London: Cresset Press, 1960, pp. 140–1.
4 George Orwell, *The Road to Wigan Pier*. London: Victor Gollancz Ltd., 1937, p. 160.
5 Ibid., p. 175.
6 Orwell, *Homage to Catalonia*. London: Secker & Warburg, 1954 reprint, p. 48.
7 Ibid., p. 3.
8 Ibid., p. 2.
9 A semi-Trotskyite Spanish organization—Partido Obrero de Unificación Marxista.
10 Published 1949.
11 Orwell, *Coming Up for Air*. London: Secker & Warburg, 1971 reprint, p. 124.
12 Reprinted in Sonia Orwell and Ian Angus, eds., *The Collected Essays, Journalism and Letters of George Orwell*. Vol. II. Harmondsworth: Penguin Books, p. 461.
13 *The Collected Essays. . .*, Vol. III, p. 272.
14 Ibid.
15 Orwell, *Animal Farm*. London: Secker & Warburg, 1965 reprint, p. 105.
16 James Burnham (b. 1905), American political philosopher who was a Trotskyite in the Thirties but broke completely with Marxism in 1940.

8

'Detachment' and the Writer

(From ' "Detachment" and the Fictionist', 1934)

The excerpt[1] comes from an article in which Lewis discussed, among other things, the difficulty facing any fiction writer trying to stand above the political mêlée of the Thirties. He considered detachment necessary and 'it is even desirable . . . if for no other reason than that, as a partisan, you will be exceedingly ineffective without it'.

―――――――

That the handling of the material of art or of science—of *fact*, in other words—does 'detach' a man from his personality (composed as the latter is of race, class, period and the rest) is obvious; and the more he abandons himself to this objective material the better the artist, or man of science, he is, that goes without saying. Bias is *not*, clearly, the ideal. But it is after all something to do with the business; for a god would not be particularly interested in 'discovery' at all; there would be nothing to discover; there would be no incentive to all this mechanical application; if you were not mortal, if you were not in the dark, you would not be so spurred. As a *game* it must be regarded, no more, all that we do—a rather maniacal one, passionately engaged in; not a game, or a *sport*, in the traditional English sense at all. The Japanese artist who described himself as an old man mad about drawing, was making use of the *mot juste* all right when he said *mad*. We are, in fact, like the schoolchild of Newton, picking up pebbles upon the boundless ocean of Truth, or however it was he put it.

So in dramatic writing, and a great deal of fiction is that, sides have to be taken; but do not be ashamed of that. Whichever cause you adopt—the red cause of Moscow and materialism, or the

263

Fascist cause of nationalist idealism, or whatever other cause it may be—it is a game purely and simply (nothing that would be recognized as 'a game' certainly by the cricketer or fox-hunter, but yet not anything able to change reality by a pin's point—something very contingent, indeed, even at its utmost expansion). The only important thing is to be on the side to which you belong, if you understand me. There is no right side or wrong side. That is nonsense. *Sub specie aeternitatis* both sides are equally right. But what *is* unalterable is that there is a right and a wrong side *for you*. There is such a thing as being offside! (to make use of a term from the playing-field for things that the sportsman would regard as in a different category altogether to sport—for things that unquestionably are *not* cricket).

But as a fiction writer, and in handling the contemporary scene, and dramatizing it in your novels, you cannot afford to treat contemporary society as though it were *dead*—as you would waves, rocks and clouds. Essentially, of course, it is that; but not *for you*. In order to get the maximum of drama out of it you must 'in the destructive element immerse'; allow it to bring into play your personality—you must encourage it to force that into its proper camp (however much your personality may vociferate, as it is forcibly conducted thither, that it is as *impersonal* as possible, and a good deal more)! You must separate yourself from all the people who would force you into the camp to which you do *not* belong—as a matter of social discipline. You must not be afraid to say, 'In this, I am a partisan!' It would be very silly and girlish of you to object to that.

Further, you will find that the more you use your personality in this deliberate fashion, the less notice you will take of it—the less it will interfere with you. It is the people who try to disguise their personalities (like a certain well-known poet, I need not name him here), with whom the personality becomes a morbid parasite of great power, a skeleton in the cupboard and, in short, an old man of the sea—like petticoat-government by a technically inferior better-half! There is really absolutely nothing to fear on that score. Do not be intimidated, whatever you do, into never uttering a Yes or a No by the propaganda of the *nuance*—the prevarication—the half-light—the *pseudo*-statement and the *pseudo*-truth—those barren lands of fashionable literary criticism.

Enter into the spirit of the game—such, under correction, is what

I recommend; enter fully into the spirit of the side-taking and it will become *a game* for you (in the sense indicated above)—a game in which there is only one rule: namely, that you *must* place yourself on the side to which you belong—and *not* romantically masquerade as a black if you are a white (as D. H. Lawrence did). You will find you will achieve more true 'detachment' that way than by playing at Mr. Fair-Play, and doing as much harm as you can to the people to whom you do belong—as the Anglo-Saxon has been doing for so long, in his cold frenzies of suicidal liberalism, and burning sympathy for every race except his own.

If it is, as has been said, the sign that you are by nature a philosopher, if you are inclined to doubt the reality of the world, it is equally the sign that you are an artist if you recognize that the struggles you engage in are a game, in which *vous jouez votre personalité*. You play at being yourself—and so you *are* yourself; it is quite unnecessary to play at being anybody else to be completely the artist. If you cannot be 'detached' with *yourself*, there is nothing you can be detached with! And if you are so endowed as to wish to turn from the human scene to the less subjective material of nature, you will not find that playing Number One, or the First Person Singular, has cramped your style in a mode where that character is not wanted.

NOTES

1 ' "Detachment" and the Fictionist', *The English Review*, December, 1934, pp. 570–3. For other facets of L.'s ideas on art as a game, see *Wyndham Lewis on Art*, pp 570–3, and *Men Without Art*, pp. 290–1.

Index